UNTOLD VALOR

*Hidden History of the Air War In
Europe in World War II*

To the reading
students of Sharon
Montgomery.
Knowledge is power!
[signature]
3 /9/2005
Eagle Rock Junior High !

Rob Morris

To order additional copies of this book, contact:
Xlibris Corporation
1-888-795-4274
www.Xlibris.com
Orders@Xlibris.com
26820

CONTENTS

Dedicated to All the Men in These Pages
And especially,
Herb Alf,
Leonard Herman
Gus Mencow,
Maurice Rockett
and
Lyle Shafer.

Author Acknowledgments

T he author wishes to acknowledge the assistance of over fifty Air Corps veterans who contributed in so many ways to this book. Many are quoted, but some did important background work suggesting contacts and chapter ideas. Veterans contributing to this project include: Herb Alf, Leo Bach, Deward Bare, DeWayne Bennett, Bob Bland, Ken Blyth, Bruce Bockstanz, Cyril Braund, Paul Canin, Bob Capen, Gene Carson, John Carson, Charles Cassidy, John Chaffin, Ed Charles, Frank Coleman, Harry Connely, Bob Cozens, Dan Culler, Bob Fickley, Herman Fieber, Bob Fischer, Jim Geary, Harry Gobrecht, Werner Goering, Ed Herman, Leonard Herman, Ed Herzig, Bob Hilliard, Shirl Hoffman, Jerome Jacobson, Charles Johnson, William Kaplan, Lee Kessler, Jack Kidd, Norris King, Aaron Kupstow, Owen Larson, Don Lewis, Bob Long, Will Lundy, Sam Mastrogiacomo, Gus Mencow, Robert Morgan, Grif Mumford, Frank Murphy, Earl Don Peterson, Jack Rencher, Maurice Rockett, Robert Rosenthal, Fred Schoch, Joe Sellers, Lyle Shafer, Marshall Shore, and Joe Turpen.

In addition, the author wishes to thank the following family members of Air Corps airmen for their help in telling the stories: Sylvia Alf, Kitty Braund, Buck Burton, Mike Darter, Robert Fickley, David Fieber, Jim Fischer, Edward Herman, Linda Morgan, Damon Rarey, Diane Schoch Russell, and Patti and Jim Turpen.

Survivors of the Displaced Persons Camp at St. Otillien also contributed. These include Moshe Ipp and Yetta Marchuck.

Several historians also shared their expertise on various areas of the air war. Mr. Ian Hawkins made numerous suggestions, read chapters, and was kind enough to write the book's introduction. Vet Ed Charles doubled as the official historian of the 95th Bomb Group and helped considerably. Mike Darter shared his information on the search for MIAs. Colin Heaton offered suggestions and encouragement. Harry Gobrecht helped immeasurably on the chapters dealing with the 303rd Bomb Group. Helga Radau of Germany offered her knowledge of the POW camps. Marshall Shore shared his writings about the 390th Bomb Group. Raymond Toliver shared information about POW interrogation.

I am honored that William S. Phillips, a world-renowned aviation artist, agreed to let me use his painting "When Prayers Are Answered", showing Gus Mencow and the rest of the crew of Betty Boop/Pistol Packin' Mama returning from a mission, as the cover art for this book.

Many thanks to my parents for their encouragement throughout the project.

Finally, I thank my wife Geri and three children, Nicole, Matt and Brianna, for allowing me the time to travel and write, because it meant time away from them.

Author Preface

The men of the Army Air Corps in the European Theater suffered more casualties than the Navy and Marine Corps combined in World War II. Early on, the chance of surviving the obligatory twenty-five missions without death, injury or imprisonment was one in three. The success of daylight bombing was very much in doubt. Yet it was these young men—boys really—who proved that mere human beings could push themselves to do superhuman feats of strength and courage.

Many never came home. Those who did were forever changed by the experience. They knew they had done something special, and they forged bonds with their comrades that have lasted to this day. Now, the passage of years is taking the last of these men from us.

I guess that's what prompted me to write this book. I've been interested in World War II aerial combat since age nine or ten, and one day I realized that there were a lot of stories that were going to disappear like morning fog unless somebody wrote them down. I couldn't write them all, but I could go out and find a few. That would be my way of thanking those who risked everything for their country sixty years ago.

But what to write? I read numerous accounts of the air war over the years, and it seemed like there was no shortage of excellent, eyewitness accounts of aerial combat. I didn't want to cover what had already been done, and done so well, by those who had actually been there. I decided to branch out and find stories that had not been told, or had been told but were not part of the mainstream historical record on the air war. I began to look for stories that touched on universal themes of human existence, things like faith, courage, love, devotion, and perseverance. Guided by men who shared my interest, I found individuals all over the United States who had stories about aspects of the air war that I had never heard about before. I talked to Jewish aviators who ended up as POWs in German camps. I found out what happened to the many individuals who ended up interned in Switzerland or Sweden. I researched the stories of the men who died training to defend their country but never made it to combat. I searched the back corners of the historical closet for stories that added to the historiography of the air war, rather than repeated what already existed.

Most of my work was done first-hand and in the first person. Individuals were contacted and interviewed extensively. Much additional research, using both primary and secondary sources, was done to verify and fill in the 'broader picture' of the participant's story. That is why I have decided to go with footnotes. Anyone who wishes to verify or learn more about a particular topic has only to read the footnotes to open up a broader range of knowledge on the chapter.

This book is very much a collaborative effort. It is as much the work of the men whose stories fill its pages as it is mine. To them goes the honor. To me, the satisfaction of bringing this collection of fascinating stories to the historical record.

Rob Morris
Ammon, Idaho
August 2004

Introduction

By Ian Hawkins

The six-year conflict halfway through the last momentous century will undoubtedly be written about, analyzed and debated long into the future. Controversial episodes will be discussed and conclusions reached as new research is revealed. And if any war can be fully justified the Second World War proved the case. It was truly a desperate fight for survival, a struggle of good against evil, freedom of speech and democratic government against totalitarian regimes.

The outcome of the global struggle was in doubt up to its final months in 1945 due to spectacular advances in space technology by Nazi Germany, at least ten years ahead of the Allied nations. But the tremendous industrial capacity of the Allied nations, especially the mile-long production lines of the United States, ultimately proved decisive.

Among vivid memories of that terrible war, which took the lives of two close relatives—both killed in action within eight months of each other—nothing was as reassuring or as inspiring to me in the final three years as the truly spectacular sights and sounds over Suffolk, England of the rapidly-expanded Royal Air Force and American Air Force's heavy bombers going to war over Occupied Europe. To see the stunning spectacle of over one thousand four-engined B-17 Flying Fortresses and B-

24 Liberator bombers in precise formation, all heading east in a clear blue morning sky five miles high, appearing like so many small silver crosses, was unforgettable for a whole generation of East Anglians.

In April, 1983, distinguished RAF Bomber Command Pathfinder veteran, Group Captain Hamish Mahaddie, DSO, DFC, AFC, RAF, (Ret'd), concluded an outstanding speech at a veterans' annual reunion in London's Grosvenor House Hotel, by quoting a fitting tribute to the men of RAF Bomber Command, of which 55,000 were killed in action. The tribute was written by Noel Coward, the famous actor and playright who lived in wartime London. On occasion, the night bombers were routed to fly over London by their Commander, Air Marshall Arthur "Bomber" Harris, to assure Londoners, who had suffered and endured Hitler's 'Blitz" of 1940-41, that retribution was at hand.

Lie in the Dark and Listen
By Noel Coward

Lie in the dark and listen,
    It's clear tonight so they're flying high.
Hundreds of them, thousands perhaps,
    Riding the icy, moonlit sky.
Men, machinery, bombs, maps,
    Altimeters, and guns and charts,
Coffee, sandwiches, fleece-lined boots,
    Bones and muscles and minds and hearts.
English saplings, with English roots,
    Deep in the earth they've left below.
Lie in the dark, let them go.
    Lie in the dark and listen . . .

Lie in the dark and listen,
    They're going over in waves and waves.
High above villages, hills and streams
    Country churches, little graves,
And little citizens' worried dreams.
    Very soon they'll have reached the sea,
And far below will lie the bays,
    And coves and sands where they used to be
Taken for summer holidays.
    Lie in the dark and let them go,
Lie in the dark and listen . . .

Lie in the dark and listen,
    You city magnates, you steel contractors,
Factory workers, politicians,
    Soft, hysterical little actors.
Ballet dancers, 'reserved' musicians,
    Safe in your warm, civilian beds.
Count your profits and count your sheep,
    Life is passing above your heads.
Just turn over and try to sleep.
    Lie in the dark and let them go,
Theirs is a world you'll never, ever know
    There's one debt you'll for ever, ever owe.
Lie in the dark and listen . . .

That moving tribute is equally appropriate for the young Americans of the US 8th and 15th Army Air Forces. Between 17 August, 1942 and 8th May, 1945 nearly 4,300 B-17s and B-24s of the Eighth Air Force failed to return to their airfields in East Anglia. The cost in aircraft alone is staggering, but the cost in lives in incalculable—nearly 17,650 bomber aircrew made the ultimate sacrifice for our freedom.

It is an honor and a privilege to be associated with the Allied airmen who, during the Second World War, gave so much.

Rob Morris has compiled a fascinating collection of first-hand accounts by veterans of the Mighty Eighth and the Fifteenth Air Forces over a period of five years of research and coast-to-coast travel. The finished product is a major contribution to the history of the Second World War.

—Ian Hawkins

Ian Hawkins is a military historian who lives in Suffolk, England. His works include *Munster: Before and After*, *B-17s Over Berlin: Personal Stories of the 95th Bomb Group (H)*, and the recently-published *Destroyer: An Anthology of First-Hand Accounts of the War at Sea 1939-1945*, published in England by Conway Maritime Press and in the United States by The Naval Institute Press.

Prologue

The Death of an Airman

I met Fred Schoch in Spokane, Washington in the summer of 2001. He was introduced to me by 390th Bomb Group veteran Marshall Shore, whom I was visiting. Before Fred's arrival, Marshall prepared me. "Fred looks like hell," he says sadly. Fred is dying of brain cancer. He's already lost his right eye and his face is disfigured. The cancer is swelling inside his head, much more noticeably in the past few weeks. Marshall guesses Fred has two, maybe three months to live. Fred wants to share some of his experiences with me, since I am a historian.

When Fred comes over, he does, indeed, look pretty bad. He wears an eye patch, like a pirate, and his face is grotesquely swollen in places. Though he is thin, the rest of him looks good. He wears his blue Eighth Air Force windbreaker, and under that, a yellow 34th Bomb Group polo shirt with a B-17 on it. He has a bomb group ball cap with assorted military pins, including his pilot's wings, pinned all over it. He carries a briefcase, which he carefully unloads, arranging the pieces of his life neatly and lovingly on a coffee table. Fred talks like a man who knows he doesn't have a lot of time left. There is an urgency about him. He talks fast.

Fred was a B-17 copilot and flew late in the war with the 34th Bomb Group. He flew thirty-five missions and then rotated home with his crew.

We discuss the items he has laid out on the coffee table. He still has the B-17 emblem from the center of the control yoke of his B-17, 'Asphodel'. After his last mission, "the crew chief said to take whatever I wanted, but not to take the whole plane," Fred chuckles.[1] He also has a piece of heavy black jagged metal about an inch square. "I dug this out of my parachute under my seat after one tough mission," he says. It is easy to see how such evil stuff could have ripped men and machines to pieces.

Fred still has his escape compass, though the face is cracked. It is about the size of a fingertip. He has two silk escape maps of Europe, and many papers and documents relating to his tour. He also has photos of himself, his crew, and his airplane. The photos show Fred as young, handsome, smiling. I look at the photos and try to imagine the young man inside this old, sick body in front of me.

Fred presents a well-organized tapestry of his experience as a young man in England. Based at Mendlesham Station #156, the 34th was just off the main road between Ipswich and Norwich. The runway ended right next to the motor road. His plane, B-17G #43-39179, was named 'Asphodel'. It took the crew weeks to finish painting the woman on the side, since the plane was in near-constant use by many crews.

Though the crew flew later in the war, Fred takes exception to the fact that there were few good Luftwaffe pilots left. "Don't you believe it!" he says emphatically, pulling out a book on German jet fighters. "We saw lots of fighters. We didn't get shot down, because we were lucky and we flew nice, tight formations, but we saw many Me109s, some FW190s, and the new German aircraft, including the double-engine jet fighter, the Me262. We also saw the Me163 Comet, which was essentially a rocket that took off from a wheeled undercarriage. It dropped the undercarriage, flew from zero to forty thousand feet in seconds with four minutes of volatile fuel, and then became a guided glider that zipped through formations before a very hard landing on skids. It didn't have any landing gear. A lot of pilots broke their backs landing those things. It was a dead-stick landing."

"The jets attacked in groups of three. The prop fighters fought in larger groups. They usually came from the front, directed by a German B-17 flying off our formation."

"By 1943, I was one of the old guys at twenty-three. I didn't get to Europe till 1945, or maybe late 1944. One mission I remember was to Schweinamunde, March 12, 1945. We hit an oil refinery and a test facility where Werner von Braun was developing and building rockets. My last mission was March 20, 1945, to Hamburg. By April, I was finished up and was discharged."

Fred returned to Spokane, where he couldn't find a job. Finally, he became a civilian aircraft dispatcher. He stayed in the Air Force Reserve and flew re-supply missions in Alaska during the Korean War, piloting the C-47 'Goony Bird'.

Fred landed his lifelong job at Exchange Lumber and Manufacturing of Spokane, retiring in the nineteen-eighties. He also retired from the Air Force Reserve as a Lieutenant Colonel.

Fred is rightly proud of his accomplishments in the war. And he is happy that of the thirty-six men who went over to England together to fly B-17s for the 34th, all of them came home again.

I thank him for coming over, we shake hands and Fred carefully repacks his old leather briefcase. Marshall helps his friend put on his windbreaker and Fred heads out the door.

When I get back home after the trip, I write Fred a letter thanking him for meeting with me. I discuss my plans for the book and how I hope to include his story in it.

A couple months later, Marshall e-mails me that Fred has died.

In the spring of 2002, I get an email from Fred's daughter, Diane Russell, who lives in the Seattle area. Diane writes that her dad was interested in the book I was writing and talked about it with her. She asks me if I can come up to Spokane to help the family settle Fred's estate. I'm not sure how much help I can be in determining the value of Fred's large collection of books, papers and uniforms, but I drive up that June to help.

Fred and his wife have a very small apartment on Upriver Drive in Spokane. When I get there, the place is packed with boxes. More boxes fill the garage. Diane and her husband Dick greet me

and we start to look through Fred's stuff. A curator from a flight
museum in coming over that day, as well, to look over the collection
and see what he can get for the museum. Diane generously gives
me a number of items of Fred's—his old baseball cap with the
pins, the flak he dug out of his parachute, his escape compass,
some posters and books.

The museum curator shows up. Fred's possessions are laid out
on every available flat surface—medals, paperwork, uniforms,
knickknacks. Much of it is not war-related. Diane shakes her head
and laughs lovingly as she shows me a baseball that Fred bought
some years ago. It is supposedly signed by Babe Ruth, but is a very
poor forgery. "He collected everything," she says. "He bought things
he probably never even unwrapped." Now it is her responsibility
to oversee the dismantling of the collection of a lifelong pack rat. I
sense it is at once heartbreaking and overwhelming.

The museum curator arrives. He goes through Fred's stuff and
finds everything of value from the estate for the museum. He
reminds me of a vulture, and he practically salivates at some of the
rare and impressive items Fred has saved over the years. Diane has
let the curator and me come a day before the estate sale, when the
doors of the small apartment will open to whoever has the money
to pick through the possessions of one man's life. She figures settling
the estate will take months. It is a difficult thing for her to do,
especially since she lives on the other side of the state. Looking at
Fred Schoch's life laid out on tabletops and furniture and on the
carpet, seems almost a trespass into the soul of the man himself,
and is laced with tangible sadness.

The story of Fred Schoch serves as a fitting prologue for this
book on the untold history of the air war over Europe. The story
epitomizes and echoes the stories of many of the men who flew the
heavy bombers over Europe in World War II in any number of
ways.

First, though his story is an ordinary one as far as bomb crew
tales go, the exploits of the dedicated airmen who flew missions
over Europe are anything but ordinary. These men served with
incredible skill, dedication and courage in the bloodiest war in

history. The Air Corps suffered the highest casualty rate of any branch of service in World War II. Though Fred flew his combat tour late in the war, thereby missing the raging life or death aerial struggles such as Schweinfurt, Munster and Kiel, he and all the men in this book are heroes, and heroes of a kind Hollywood can never replicate. They went up into the deadly skies over Europe day after day, for twenty-five, thirty, thirty-five missions, knowing full well that each mission could be their last.

Second, like many heavy bomber veterans, Fred Schoch kept many tangible memories of his war, made possible by the strange type of warfare waged by combat airmen. The combat airman got up each morning from his own bed, ate a hot breakfast, flew for many hours over enemy territory surrounded by the threat of imminent death, then flew home for dinner, perhaps a night in London, and then sleep between his own sheets. Unlike most warriors, he had his own footlocker. He kept things, and he sent them home after his tour was up. Fred saved every scrap of information that dealt with his experiences as a young airman in Europe in the Eighth Air Force. He kept his diary, his flight records, his identification cards, bits and pieces of the life he knew as a young man. He kept the piece of flak that he'd dug out of the underside of his copilot's seat after a mission. He kept his wings, his medals, his photos. Over the years, he added to the things he brought back, building a massive collection of books about the air war, about warplanes, and about war heroes. His interest in the subject never faltered. When old age forced him and his wife to move from a house to a small retirement apartment, he had piles of boxes everywhere. His years in England as a bomber pilot had defined him, and he wanted to hold on to them in every way he possibly could.

Third, like many of his Air Corps peers, Fred beat the odds and survived the fighter—and flak-filled skies over Europe only to succumb, like we all must, to the unavoidable passage of time. Every day in the U.S., over one thousand World War II veterans pass away. These men leave us now at such a rapid rate that there is a shortage of qualified VFW buglers to play Taps at their funerals.

These are the men we often see alone in the supermarket, or occasionally shake our fist at as they drive ten miles an hour below the speed limit. We see them sitting for hours in McDonald's nursing a cup of coffee. Many more, we never see, because they are shut up in nursing homes and the only way to see them is to make the effort to go to them. They walk slowly and in a society where youth and energy is everything, they are old and it is easy for us to look right through them. The youngest of the airmen who flew over Europe would have been eighteen in 1945. Today, that would make him nearly eighty years old. Most are in their mid-eighties. The upper echelon officers from early in the war are pushing ninety.

As these men leave on their final missions, their stories, treasured for over sixty years, take wing with them. Many airmen die without having told families about their war experiences, either because they are still troubled by them or because the family has never asked. All the boxes full of mission lists, dog-eared photographs, medals, scraps of ephemera, so painstakingly stored and moved for nearly sixty years, are suddenly just so much stuff to be disposed of. Some of the more valuable items may end up for sale on the Internet, put up by family members or by shrewd estate sale shoppers. Some items may make their way into thrift shops like The Salvation Army or Goodwill. Most however, are simply thrown away.

Soon, it will be as if these men, and their accomplishments, never existed at all.

The fact that Fred's story is not substantially different from that of any other man who flew in the air over Europe does not make it any less incredible or heroic. What Fred and thousands of other young men and boys did was beyond most of our wildest imaginings. They never forgot their war years because they know what they did. They beat Adolph Hitler. They saved the world.

They did it as kids. Today, many young people still live at home with their parents at age twenty-five. Then, a twenty-five-year old air crewman was "the old man". Pilots, navigators, bombardiers, gunners, tended to be around twenty. Some didn't even shave. They were given the responsibility for a massive piece of equipment, laden with heavy explosives, and told to go bomb targets thousands of miles away and come home again, all the while fighting off enemy fighters and hoping the flak missed. They watched their friends die and wondered if they were next. It was an intense piece of living.

No wonder few ever forgot it or let it go. Many who did let it go during their busy careers now find it coming back in the long hours of retirement. They hope to talk about it, to remember it. Some families honor that, some don't. So they talk to each other. They go to reunions and relive the war years. But in the end, all that will remain are the boxes, boxes like Fred Schoch's.

Some of the stories in this book are about major events and individuals. Most are about events and individuals that have been misrepresented or overlooked by history books since World War II. It is my intention in writing it to shed light on lesser known, but none the less vital, aspects of the Air Corps story in Europe. Though filled with combat, it is primarily a book about people and how each reacted to circumstances presented to him by the worst war in the history of the world. It also examines how each man's experiences changed him as a human being, how each was molded and in turn, went on to mold others and the world he found upon his return after the war ended.

The story of Fred Schoch is the story of every man in this book. It is the story of a regular fellow who did extraordinary things while very young. While managing to cheat death, he also forged bonds and memories that endured his whole life. His combat tour was the epic event of his life. He saved and savored those memories both in his heart and in the many boxes of things he saved for over fifty-five years. And when the time came, he flew his final mission, and left behind the best legacy he was able, including a few hours with a young historian in Spokane, Washington, in June of 2001.

With the passing of these men, we lose the best part of ourselves. Within ten years, nearly all the men who grace the pages of this book will be gone. Since I began writing, I have been saddened by the loss of four: Fred was only the first. Lee Kessler, the subject of the chapter entitled 'The Hand' died in the fall of 2003, only two months after I visited him. Herb Alf, the subject of 'Herb Alf's Journey', died in early 2004. And Robert Morgan, former pilot of the Memphis Belle, died a few months later.

What makes the story of Fred Schoch so exceptional, in the end, is the fact that it is not exceptional to the men of the Army Air Corps. His heroism and answer to the call of duty in the worst war in the history of mankind was no more- or less-than that of the several hundred thousand other men who flew the heavy bombers over Europe. This book, then, is a small monument to the many men who flew, fought, died, or lived, in this pivotal time in human history. Let us never forget them. Let us seek them out and talk with them. Let us preserve their stories. Let us celebrate them while they are still here to know we appreciate their sacrifice.

Notes

[1]   All quotations of Fred Schoch and Marshall Shore are from an author visit on June24, 2001 in Spokane, Washington.

Chapter One

A Place Called St. Ottilien

I t began with a young Air Corps private attending a concert on a news assignment. It ended with a changed U.S. policy towards Displaced Persons in postwar Germany. In the words of the young man who would fight for these changes, it was a concert unlike any other. It was "a liberation concert at which most of the liberated people were too weak to stand. A liberation concert at which most of the people still could not believe they were free"[1]. The American, Private Bob Hilliard, sat before a makeshift stage on a cool spring evening in May 1945. As editor of the Army Air Corps' "2nd Wing Eagle", he had shown up hoping simply to get a good story for the newspaper.

The concert was put on by and performed for concentration camp survivors at the Hospital of St. Ottilien, Bavaria, Germany, only thirty miles from Dachau and Munich. St. Ottilien had been a Benedictine monastery before the war. During the war, the Nazis had used the monastery as a military hospital. When the U.S. Army liberated the Dachau death camp in May of 1945, an American Chaplain and Reform Rabbi by the name of Abraham Klausner, assigned to the 116th Evacuation Hospital Unit, took charge of the plight of some of Dachau's survivors. Embarrassed because he had nothing to offer these people except the little mezzuzot ordinarily distributed by chaplains to Jewish soldiers, Klausner was also deeply disturbed to see that the Jews in Dachau were still dressed in their concentration camp uniforms and still forced to live behind barbed wire.

Captain Otto B. Raymond, one of the first American officers in the area, commandeered several buildings of the Benedictine monastery in the village of St. Ottilien that was being used as a German hospital. Dr. Zalman Grinberg, a survivor of the Kovno ghetto and Dachau, had led 420 survivors to the area and set up a hospital at the St. Ottilien monastery. St. Ottilien became a DP (Displaced Persons) hospital for both Jewish and non-Jewish survivors of the Holocaust.[2]

The concert Hilliard attended was at once a celebration of the living and a lament for the dead. The performers—and most of the audience—were no more than "stick figures, emaciated, pale, skeletal, expressionless, dressed in the striped uniforms of the concentration camps".[3]

In stark contrast to the haunting shadows of the liberated Jews, just outside the survivor's quarters allotted to the Jews, Bob saw dozens of men in German military uniforms walking about on the German side of the hospital grounds, leaning on the arms of white-clad nurses.

It seemed to Bob, looking from the victims to victimizers, that the winners had become the losers and the losers winners. It was a scene he would see repeated over and over during his service in post-war Germany.

The musicians played Bizet and Grieg, and composers whose music had been forbidden for years. After the music ended, the crowd remained silent and unmoving. Bob tried to hide his tears. A man in the front row climbed to the stage. It was Dr. Zalman Grinberg, the man Captain Raymond had placed in charge of the Displaced Persons Camp at St. Ottilien. He was thin, erect, of medium height, perhaps in his late thirties or early 40s.

"We act as delegates of millions of victims," Dr. Grinberg told the audience, "to tell all mankind . . . how cruel people may become, what brutal hellishness is concealed within a human being, and what a triumphant record of crime and murder has been achieved by the nation of Hegel and Kant, Schiller, and Goethe, Beethoven and Shopenhauer." Grinberg traced his life from the time its peacefulness was shattered in Kovno, Lithania on June 21, 1941. He talked of how Kovno's entire Jewish population was resettled in a ghetto in August. He recounted the SS's roundup of all remaining children in the ghetto in March of 1944, the ghetto's end, and transfer of its inhabitants to Dachau and other concentration camps where sixty to eighty percent of Kovno's population died. He spoke of the painful journey to liberation and the flight that carried him and the others to St. Ottilien. Dr. Grinberg ended his speech with these words: "We are free now, but we do not know how, or with what, to begin our free yet unfortunate lives. It seems to us that at the present mankind does not yet understand what we have gone through and experienced during this period. And it seems to us that we shall not be understood in the future. We unlearned to laugh; we cannot cry anymore; we do not understand our freedom: probably because we are still among our dead comrades! Let us rise and stand in silence to commemorate our dead!"[4]

Hilliard, deeply moved, knew what he had to do. He felt in his heart he had an obligation to help the survivors at St. Ottilien any way he could. Little did he know, sitting in front of the makeshift stage at St. Ottilien, that before he was done, he and a few close friends would forever change the lives not just of the survivors at St. Ottilien, but those of thousands of displaced persons throughout Germany.

By forcing the American government to change its policies about displaced persons, Bob Hilliard, Ed Herman and a few others managed to save the lives of countless survivors, Jews and non-Jews, who almost certainly would have starved or died of disease in the year immediately following the end of World War II. "We were just a couple of little guys who did what anybody else would do when they see injustice," he told me several years ago. "We stood up against the policies of our country and our leaders because we loved our country enough to make it more humane, to make it better than it was. That is true patriotism. If you truly love your country, you will change it for the better."[5]

Bob had grown up in Brooklyn, the son of European immigrants. After attending services at various churches and synagogues, he felt that organized religions spent too much time "praying to an amorphous being to do something rather than taking the responsibility upon themselves to solve the (world's) problems"[6]. Bob believed history was not for the watching, but for the doing.[7] So despite the long odds, Bob set out to change history.

After the Liberation Concert, Bob decided to take the plight of the DP's at St. Ottilien back to his fellow soldiers at Kaufbeuren. He first sought out his friend, Edward Herman. "Ed, we must do something. We must help," he said. Ed told Bob he had to see it for himself first. Before long, he did, and was greatly disturbed. "I couldn't believe it," Ed wrote. "These were people who were liberated *from* what? *To* what? People were literally walking death. They needed food. They needed clothing. They needed medication. At this stage, they weren't even existing."[8]

Bob and Edward watched with growing anger as the former Nazis and their German collaborators ingratiate themselves with the liberators. The Nazis and the Germans had lost the war, but in the eyes of the two young GI's, it seemed they were winning the peace, and at the expense of those who desperately needed help.

The history books rarely mention what happened to the hundreds of thousands of concentration camp survivors when the gates of Auschwitz, Dachau, Mauthausen, Buchenwald, Bergen-Belsen and the rest were thrown open. We are left to believe that liberation was the happy ending to one of the greatest tragedies in the history of mankind. Bob Hilliard and Edward Herman found out that liberation did not necessarily mean freedom. In many cases, it did not even mean an improvement in conditions for people who had, in some cases, suffered in camps for five, seven, even ten years. After liberation, many of the starving continued to starve. The sick continued to die. The prisoners, in many cases, kept wearing their striped concentration camp clothing, for they had nothing else to wear. These survivors, right at the time when they most needed food, warmth, and a welcome back into humanity, were often kept inside their former prisons, guarded now by American G.I.'s. They were no longer prisoners. Theoretically, they were free. They were now called 'Displaced Persons'. And displaced they were. They could not go home. Most had no homes to return to. Many had lost everything. They simply existed, waiting for help that never materialized.

Today, Bob Hilliard is a university professor at Emerson College in Boston, Massachusetts. He has worked in professional theatre, radio, and television, has been a federal government official, and is the author of over thirty books. He is trim and handsome, and can still fit into his old Army jacket. A Purple Heart is attached to that jacket, a Purple Heart that he won in the Battle of the Bulge. It was a wound that diverted Bob Hilliard from his path as an ordinary GI and sent him to the non-combat Second Disarmament Wing of the Army's Ninth Air Corps. It was there that Hilliard and Herman met. Edward had been a young entrepreneur before entering the service, and after the war continued in this role, specializing in global trade and international finance. Bob and Ed's unit, set up at an old Luftwaffe base on the outskirts of Kaufbeuren, fifty miles southwest of Munich, was charged with searching for any Nazi weapons which might prove useful to the U.S. military. Hilliard and Herman often saw DP's, Displaced Persons, wandering the sides of the roads. They saw lines of shuffling people, coming from everywhere and going nowhere, their few possessions carried or dragged along with them. Some of the weak, young, or old were carried or pushed in baby carriages. Few had proper shoes or clothing. If it hadn't been summer, Bob was convinced most of these displaced persons would have frozen to death.[9]

The situation at St. Ottilien was critical. People were dying there at an incredible rate, people who had survived in Auschwitz and Buchenwald and Dachau, who were now free. Two mass graves still exist near the hospital. The American military and the German townspeople were worried that the Displaced Persons carried serious diseases, such as typhus and tuberculosis. As a result, some of the camps were fenced with barbed wire, and American guards were posted at the entrances.[10]

"What's the difference between you Americans and the Nazis?" a concentration camp survivor asked Bob Hilliard, "except that you don't have gas chambers?" Indeed, conditions at St. Ottilien, and other camps for Displaced persons, were little better than the conditions in the concentration camps. Eisenhower's orders called for all DP's to get 1,200 calories a day, but most camps were getting more like 800 calories, maximum, per day, and many virtually no food at all. Zalman Grinberg had written dozens of letters pleading for help to relief organizations worldwide, including Jewish relief organizations, and had not had a single response.[11]

Meanwhile, the German civilian population received full rations from the occupiers. Bob and Edward became more and more angry about the American collaboration with former and still-active Nazis. They observed that in the early weeks and months of U.S. occupation, the Germans were afraid that the Americans would treat them the way they, the Germans, had treated those whom they had conquered. They took a fatalistic stance towards their occupiers, continuing to curse the Jews, sneer at FDR, and praise Hitler. Young American servicemen were lured into secluded areas by young German women and killed. Packs of German Nazi youths, known as Werewolves, roamed the countryside, killing the occasional GI. Over time, however, the Germans realized no serious reprisals were coming. They changed tactics. They decided "that they could defeat the American occupation aims most easily by guile, wile and smile than by confrontation."[12]

They noticed that many American GIs seemed to love Germany and the Germans in short order. A pack of cigarettes could satisfy almost any whim, from good schnapps to sex. Many GIs lost most of their initial anger with their former enemies, coming instead to believe that the German people had been forced to follow Hitler. Many also came to believe that most Germans knew nothing of the concentration camps. Many, to Bob's amazement, didn't seem to think it strange that they never met a German who had been a Nazi.[13]

Upon further investigation, Bob and Edward found that the Germans were not 're-educated', that the German students continued to learn from the same books and teachers as they had during the Hitler years. They saw that many of the Nazi officials remained in their jobs because 'they were the most qualified'. They noted bitterly how Hitler had called on German women to "win the peace" in the event the war was lost, and how many German women used their bodies and their intellect to do just that. High-ranking US officers all had German interpreters. These were usually attractive young German women.[14]

Of immediate concern for Bob and Edward were the suffering DP's at St. Ottilien. Together, they organized other GIs to pitch in and help out with food or other items. They began "appropriating" food from the base mess hall, with the help of one of the cooks. Ironically, they had to sneak the food past the American guards at St. Ottilien to get it to the starving inmates. They borrowed officers' uniforms, with the officers' permission, took off the insignias so that they wouldn't get court-martialed, and canvassed the area for supplies posing as US officers. One of the GI's who worked closely with them was Bob's assistant editor, Anthony "Dee" DiBiase, of South Philadelphia. They would go to a small town and demand that the burgermeister (usually the same person who was mayor under the Nazis) provide a hundred pounds of potatoes, and the next morning the burgermeister would have them waiting. They would bring them to St. Ottilien.[15]

As Edward has stated, "We hijacked trucks with food, with clothing, with GI clothes. We went around the camp, getting GIs to donate extra clothing if they could . . . And we wrote home immediately to our individual families . . . This was, in essence, the first stage in getting food to them any which way we could."

After many weeks in which the situation at St. Ottilien got even worse, with virtually no food, clothing, or medicines from any official source, Bob and Edward wrote a letter that would change history. It said, in part:

> "Friends:
>
> The Jews of Europe are a dying race. Even now, after the defeat of Hitler and Nazism, they are slowly being exterminated from the face of the earth.
>
> *YOU ARE TO BLAME!*
>
> If you consider yourself a human being, a member of the human race, then you are—although perhaps unwittingly, yet nevertheless certainly—a murderer.

For you are carrying out Hitler's plan of the destruction of the Jewish race. By your unconcerned neglect, you are just as responsible for the present death of the European Jews as the most diabolical of Nazis was in the past.

. . . thousands of . . . Jews in Europe . . . are today destitute, without food, shelter, clothing, or medical aid.

We understand that there are many things that you do not know; that you would be only too willing to help if you knew the facts . . . That is the purpose of this letter. To let you know what the Jews have suffered, what they are suffering and what you can—and must—do to help.

The letter recounts the successes achieved by Dr. Grinberg and the staff at St. Ottilien despite the lack of assistance from relief organizations, the U.S. military, or any other source.

"Today there are 750 people in the hospital, all of whom are receiving one-half of the food they need to recover properly, sixty percent of whom are confined to bed because they have no clothing to wear, others who are still wearing their concentration camp uniforms, all of whom are living with lice and disease because of the lack of bed clothing and equipment, and many of whom are not being cared for properly because of a lack of medicine.

In the next few pages you will find a speech given by Dr. Grinberg on May 27 of this year at what was called a liberation concert, a liberation concert at which the liberated people were too weak to stand, at which the liberated people still could not believe they were free.

Read this speech. Read it carefully. Put yourself in the position of the Jews you will read about. Every one of us knows that it could have been us.

Read it carefully—and THINK!"

Bob and Ed inserted the full text of Dr. Grinberg's speech, which the Doctor had translated from German to English for accuracy.

> "And it is not only this one hospital that we must help," the letter concludes, "There are dozens of survivor camps where the inhabitants do not even have that which those at this hospital have. Where conditions are a hundred times worse—and where there is also no help . . .
>
> These surviving Jews of Europe want to live. The fact that five children have already been born at St. Ottilien is proof enough. And the Jewish survivors can live if you will help them. We say they will live. WHAT DO YOU SAY?"

Bob and Ed gave the address of the Chaplain of the Kaufbeuren Air Base as the contact designated to receive and deliver donated supplies to St. Ottilien.[16] They bribed a German printer to print over a thousand copies of the letter. It was against regulations for them to write open letters while in the Army, but as there was nothing to prevent them from writing personal letters, they decided to address each letter to 'Dear Friend'.[17]

"We had the guys on the base send them out to wives, mothers, fathers, relatives, girlfriends, friends, *anybody* they knew who they thought might put CARE packages together," Bob stated.[18]

In their quest to feed and clothe the displaced at St. Ottilien, Ed Herman even managed to buy the base PX and give all its contents to the refugees, even arranging with the Colonel to have Army vehicles transfer the goods. When he heard about this, Bob told Ed, "Ed, you can't just buy a PX!" To which Ed responded, "I just did!"

"I was an entrepreneur," Ed says today. "I knew what I had to do and I did it".[19]

Ed Herman's brother, Leonard Herman, was a highly decorated war hero who had been on a national Victory Bond tour and had managed to make many important contacts across the nation. He distributed Bob and Ed's letter to the VIP's he encountered, and they made contacts of their own.

However, September of 1945 rolled around. It had been six weeks since the first letters had been sent, and not a single package had arrived.

Neither Bob nor Ed is sure who finally got a letter into the hands of the new American President, Harry S Truman. "We never really found out who got the letter to President Truman," says Bob. "Lenny (Ed's brother Leonard) got it to the two senators from Pennsylvania, one of whom might have gotten in to Truman. We also heard that Averill Harriman of New York got a letter and might have done so. Or Herbert Lehman of New York may have. It very well may have been a Pennsylvania senator. We just don't know for certain."[20] The fact is, the letter did reach President Truman. Apparently, Truman was upset by the allegations.

Former U.S. Immigration Commissioner Earl G. Harrison had been sent to Europe by Truman earlier that year to investigate the plight of the displaced refugees, particularly the Jews. Harrison had just returned when a copy of Bob and Ed's letter made it to Truman's desk. "Truman gave him the letter," says Bob. "Harrison visited my mother, to see who these two radical kids were."[21]

Bob got a letter from his mother. "Dean Earl Harrison came to visit me last month," she wrote, "He wanted to know about you. President Truman, he told me, was concerned about the letters you and Ed Herman have been sending all over the country. Dean Harrison said it was impossible to believe that all the things you wrote could be true, and he wanted to find out what kind of a person you were. You know what I did? You know all those letters you've been writing home these past months about St. Ottilien? I keep them in the top drawer of one of the little dressers in my bedroom. I gave him the letters. He sat down on the living room couch and began reading. After about twenty minutes he said, 'I believe it', and took those letters with him."[22]

The situation was getting larger-than-life for the two young Army privates. The fact that they had written a letter highly critical of U.S. policy in Europe, and critical of General Eisenhower, put them in a touchy situation. "I was not concerned," Bob says today. "We half *expected* we'd get in trouble, but we didn't give a damn. I'd been in the infantry and been wounded, and the war was over. What could they do to me? Sure, we could have been court-martialed, and throughout the whole process I expected maybe we *would* be court-martialed, but we felt it was important to do this, because it wasn't being done, and if they court-martialed us, so what? But they didn't, and I think they didn't because it would have been embarrassing to them."[23]

Earl Harrison returned to Europe on Truman's order to further investigate. "Ed and I met Harrison in Munich with the letter in his hand," Bob told me. "Rabbi Klausner, who had done great work at St. Ottilien, was walking with Harrison and Klausner stopped us and introduced us. Harrison said, "Oh, *you're* the boys who wrote this letter. We're going to do something about this". Bob turned to Ed and said, "Did he mean he's going to get us court-martialed?"[24]

A few days later, Bob was writing copy in the Special Services office when he was visited by a full colonel in the U.S. Army. The colonel had a SHAEF patch of a gold-handled flaming sword on a black V-shaped shield topped with a red-blue-green-yellow rainbow. His face was serious, almost angry. Bob knew it had to have something to do with the letter.

"'General Eisenhower asked me to stop by and see you and Private Herman while I was in the area', he said. "The general wants you and Private Herman to know he appreciates your calling to his attention, through those letters you sent to the States, the plight of some of the D.P.'s in some of the camps in Germany . . . Now that the General knows about the problems, he wants you to know that they will be taken care of. It won't be necessary for you to send out any more letters.' "'I've checked your records,' the Colonel said. 'I'm pleased that you have enough points to be going home soon. I'm sure you're looking forward to seeing your family and going back to college.'

"'Well, the General and I hope you'll be able to do so. We still have commitments throughout the world, and good soldiers like you, who take a special interest as you have in your country's affairs, are needed in places where we still have to keep our guard up. Like the Aleutians up in Alaska.' And he added, 'I note that you got frozen feet in the Battle of the Bulge.'"

Bob was struck by the fact that "the Commanding General of the greatest army in the world, which had just won a world war, sends a colonel to threaten to send a private to the Arctic!"

"'The letters will stop', said the Colonel. 'You and Private Herman should put your talents to better use and improve your positions in the army . . . If there are any more letters sent out, you had better put in for Arctic gear.' And then the intended coup de grace. 'And the papers needed for your discharge could get lost.'"[25]

The colonel then visited Ed Herman. "You may stop sending letters now. Packages have arrived. They will be relinquished. They will be allowed to come in." He repeated the threat about the Aleutians, adding "it gets pretty damn cold up there". Then, after warning Ed not to send out any more letters, he stalked out.[26]

"The fact that Ike sent a full colonel to warn us made us realize at that point we had someone on our side, and that was the President,"[27] Bob has said.

Instead of being intimidated by this strange course of events, the two privates celebrated. The fact that they were being threatened with Arctic duty was a very positive sign. "We must be doing something right!" Bob told Ed that evening when they talked it over.

"That night we sent out more letters."[28]

"Two hundred to be precise," Ed adds.[29]

Shortly thereafter, on September 16, 1945, MP's broke up a Yom Kippur service being celebrated at St. Ottilien. The Jewish Chaplain, Captain Klausner, was helping lead the service. Mixed in among the displaced persons at the service were a number of American GI's, many of whom had smuggled in food under their jackets for the hungry patients. The MPs kicked in the doors, charged into the room, and broke up the service because of the food smuggling, waving their rifles and knocking some of the older and weaker patients to the floor. One patient shouted, "You Americans are Nazis!" Another patient told Bob it reminded him of a similar event on November 9, 1938. He had been in a synagogue when the Nazis had burst in, destroying the Torah and other sacred objects. "It was called the Kristallnacht," the patient continued. "(At least) this time they didn't burn the synagogue."[30]

On September 30, the *New York Times* ran a front-page story titled "President Orders Eisenhower to End New Abuse of Jews: He Acts on Harrison Report, Which Likens Our Treatment to That of the Nazis".[31] Another story in the same issue contained the text of Truman's letter to Eisenhower. The letter was dated August 31, 1945.

> "My Dear General Eisenhower:
>   I have received and considered the report of Mr. Earl G. Harrison, our representative on the Intergovernmental Committee on Refugees, upon his mission to inquire into the condition and needs of displaced persons in Germany who may be stateless or non-repatriatable, particularly Jews. I am sending you a copy of that report. I have also had a long conference with him on the same subject matter."
>   While Mr. Harrison makes due allowance for the fact that during the early days of liberation the huge task of mass repatriation required main attention, he reports conditions that now exist and which require prompt remedy. These conditions, I know, are not in conformity with the policies promulgated by SHAEF, now combined displaced persons executive, but they are what actually exists in the field. In other words, the policies are not being carried out by some of your subordinates."

Truman goes on to discuss the lack of adherence to the policy on requisitioning billeting for displaced persons from German civilians. Instead, the policy has been to keep the DPs in the camps.

"Some of these camps are the very ones where these people were herded together, starved, tortured, and made to witness the death of their fellow inmates and friends and relatives."

"We must intensify our efforts to get these people out of the camps and into decent houses until they can be repatriated or evacuated. These houses should be requisitioned from the German civilian population. That is one way to implement the Potsdam policy that the German people 'cannot escape responsibility for what they have brought upon themselves'."

"We quote this paragraph with particular reference to the Jews among displaced persons:

'As matters now stand, we appear to be treating the Jews as the Nazis treated them, except that we do not exterminate them. They are in concentration camps in large numbers under our military guard instead of S.S. troops. One is led to wonder whether the German people, seeing this, are not supposing we are following, or at least condoning, Nazi policy'."

"'I know that you will agree with me that we have a particular responsibility toward these victims of persecution and tyranny who are in our zone. We must make it clear to the German people that we thoroughly abhor the Nazi policies of hatred and persecution. We have no better opportunity to demonstrate this than by the manner in which we ourselves actually treat the survivors remaining in Germany.'

"'I hope you will report to me as soon as possible the steps you have been able to take to clean up the conditions mentioned in the report.'

"'I am communicating directly with the British Government in an effort to have the doors of Palestine opened to such of these displaced persons as wish to go there.

Very sincerely yours,
HARRY S. TRUMAN'"[32]

The October 8, 1945 issue of *TIME* magazine picked up the story. A page 31 article carrying a photo of Earl Harrison read in part: "Jews, now driven by the need to save survivors from the European holocaust, were demanding the immediate reopening of large-scale immigration into the Holy Land . . . Into this explosive situation last week trod President Truman. As is his wont, the President simplified the complex situation. In Washington, he released a dynamatic report from former U.S. Immigration Commissioner Earl G. Harrison, whom he had sent to the Continent last June to investigate the fate of displaced refugees, particularly Jews. Harrison's report pulled no punches. He charged that displaced Jews are being held in unsanitary, barbed-wire camps, wearing hideous concentration-camp garb or German SS uniforms, with nothing being done for them by way of rehabilitation. Their guards are U.S. troops."

"Harrison went further. 'Beyond knowing that they are no longer in danger of the gas chambers, torture, or other forms of violent death, they see—and there is—little change . . . As matters now stand, we appear to be treating the Jews as the Nazis treated them, except that we do not exterminate them.'"

" . . . To General Dwight D. Eisenhower, the President sent a copy of this sizzling document, with an equally sizzling letter" calling for a change in conditions. An asterisk at the bottom of the page reads: "Reported the General's aides: the 'cleanup' had already started, camp conditions were already much improved."[33]

Papers picked up the story across the country.

In that same month, a displaced person at Feldafing sneaked out of the camp and went into Landsberg to try and find some food for himself and other starving survivors in the camp. The next morning, when he was reentering the camp, he was spotted by a U.S. MP who fired upon him without warning. The man was hit in the leg, and later that day the leg was amputated.

Dr. Grinberg went to see the captain in charge of the MP detachment, asking that the soldier be reprimanded as a warning to other MPs not to shoot "either deliberately or carelessly" at survivors.

"The American Military Police captain said," Dr. Grinberg told Bob, "that it was a shame that so many Americans felt so kindly toward the Jews as President Truman did."[34]

Hilliard praises the work of President Harry Truman with the Displaced Persons. "He did a lot of things FDR didn't do. There certainly was a degree of anti-Semitism in Germany on the part of the U.S. military. The State Department was clearly anti-Semitic, and FDR went along with State Department policy."

Are Hilliard's charges of anti-Semitic U.S. policies, or at the very least an appalling lack of concern for the suffering Jews, backed up by the historical record? In fact, they are meticulously backed up.

In his book, *The Abandonment of the Jews*, historian David Wyman (incidentally, a non-Jew) makes the following points concerning US policies:

1. "Authenticated information that the Nazis were systematically exterminating European Jewry was made public in the United States in November, 1942. President Roosevelt did nothing about the mass murder for fourteen months, then moved only because he was confronted with political pressures he could not avoid and because his administration stood on the brink of a nasty scandal over its rescue policies."

2. "The War Refugee board, which the President then established to save Jews and other victims of the Nazis, received little power, almost no cooperation from Roosevelt or his administration, and grossly inadequate government funding . . . 90% of costs were covered by Jewish organizations

3. "Only 21,000 refugees were allowed to enter the US during the three and one-half years the nation was at war with Germany. That amounted to 10 percent of the number who could have been legally admitted under the immigration quotas during that period."

4. Strong popular pressure for action would have brought a much fuller government commitment to rescue and would have produced it sooner. Several factors hampered the growth of public pressure. Among them were anti-Semitism and anti-immigration attitudes, both widespread in American society in that era and both entrenched in Congress; the mass media's failure to publicize the Holocaust news, even though the wire services and other news sources made most of the information available to them; the near silence of Christian churches and almost all of their leadership; the indifference of most of the nation's political and intellectual leaders; and the President's failure to speak out on the issue."[35]

Wyman continues: "Lack of knowledge was not a problem . . . The problem stemmed in part from plain bureaucratic inefficiency . . . By far the most important cause for State Department inaction was fear that sizable numbers of Jews might actually get out of Axis territory . . . This fear dominated the State Department's entire response to the Holocaust."[36]

In his book, *The Jewish Threat: Anti-Semitic Politics of the U.S. Army*, Joseph W. Bendersky, Professor of History at the University of Virginia and book review editor for the journal *Holocaust and Genocide Studies*, argues that "anti-Semitism permeated not only the State Department but also the thinking of the military officers and attaché's assigned to European embassies who attempted to influence Roosevelt administration policy in favor of Hitler and the Third Reich . . . anti-Semitism was pervasive among the officer corps. Prominent military leaders such as Mark Clark, George Van Horn Moseley, George Patton, Truman Smith, Albert Wedemeyer and Charles Willoughby, among others, combined social Darwinism with many of the same stereotypes about Jews that were promoted by European anti-Semites."[37]

Elie Wiesel, prize-winning author and former concentration camp inmate, wrote, "The truth must be stated and restated. The

suffering of the survivors did not end with the war; society wanted
no part of them, either during or after the war. During the war all
doors were closed to them, and afterward they remained shut. The
evidence is irrefutable. They were kept in the places where they
had suffered.[38]

A senior camp social worker writes, "People were thin, they
were ill, and they were bitter. If this was 'liberation', why survive?
People had kept themselves alive, barely so, in the concentration
camps, with the hope of going to America or Palestine. But neither
the Americans nor the British in Palestine said 'Welcome'".[39]

Things did not change for the better for the Displaced Persons
in the camps, and European Jews in general, until the arrival of
Truman. On December 22, 1945, he issued the so-called 'Truman
Directive' which stated that the United States would set an
international example by expediting admission of displaced persons
to the United States. For the first time since mid-1940, the U.S.
immigration quotas were open to full use. In addition Truman
called on Britain to permit 100,000 Jews to go to Palestine to help
relieve the DP situation.[40]

Within a few weeks of Truman's reprimand of Eisenhower, the
military released all the boxes of food and clothing it had been
holding for months while the Jews at St. Ottilien suffered. Bob, who
has been transferred to Oberpaffenhofen, got a call from Ed Herman,
still in Kaufbeuren, in mid-October. Mail trucks had been bringing
packages from the Munich train station to the Kaufbeuren air base
most of the day. By that evening, the chapel at Kaufbeuren was full of
packages from all over the United States. The floodgate had opened.[41]
Ed arranged for their delivery to the hospital.

"I made sure I was there," when the boxes arrived at St.
Ottilien, wrote Bob. "They were put on a cleared area on the floor
of one of the buildings. They contained clothes and food and
medicine, and even yarmulkes". Bob stated that he tried to act as
nonchalant as he could, but couldn't contain his excitement. "I
tried to cover my tears of joy with a broad grin. Ed and I stood
there watching, as one by one, two by two, ten by ten, staff and
patients of St. Ottilien came in. They approached cautiously,

carefully, as though it must be some kind of a trick . . . In a few minutes it seemed like the entire hospital had formed a semicircle around the pile of packages."

The DPs continued to stand silently and uncertainly, no one touching the pile of boxes "Then one man moved forward toward the packages, stood right in the center, then threw himself onto a pile of clothes, grabbed some in his hands, held them out as an offering to the crowd and shouted, dragging out each word as if he were proclaiming a great event, 'What . . . are . . . we . . . waiting . . . for?' and threw the clothes into the air with a shout of triumph, clapping his hands above his head. With one long cry of happiness . . . the people rushed toward the treasure."[42]

By the 21st of October over fifteen hundred packages had arrived for St. Ottilien, more than enough to meet its needs. The extra boxes were sent on to other camps. The Jewish Welfare Board, criticized for not responding earlier, had sent some of the biggest packages of all.

It wasn't until several weeks later that Bob and Ed learned that their letter had not only brought in the much-needed supplies, but that it had played a key role in changing U.S. policy.

After Truman's order to Eisenhower, food began to reach the DP's. This was in part because the shortage of food that existed in the immediate aftermath of the war was letting up somewhat. The DP's also received some new clothing, and the barbed wire was removed from around the camps. Things were still far from ideal, but it now appeared that the Jewish survivors would be cared for, would survive, and would have a chance to emigrate to the United States or Israel if they wanted to.

Bob himself left Germany in February of 1946. Ed Herman was discharged in May and decided to remain in Europe. He started a successful import-export business in Paris. He also occupied himself smuggling Jews into Palestine, including some of the St. Ottilien survivors.

In March, Bob became a civilian again. He was happy with his contributions, but wanted to put the incredible pressures of the war and the liberation behind him. He went on to have a successful career in the media, as a government official, and as a writer and professor. He married and had two children. He and Ed stayed in touch sporadically over the years. "If we'd wanted to, we could have capitalized on the contacts we made and what we had done with the letter, but we didn't. We accomplished what we had wanted to and then we went on with our lives."

"In the early to mid-nineties, I decided this story had to be told. We were getting older and won't be around much longer'," says Bob, "So I decided to write the book. I contacted Ed to be sure that what I remembered was accurate. We've stayed in close touch ever since."[43] Bob wrote the story of St. Ottilien, which he titled *Surviving the Americans: The Continued Struggle of the Jews After Liberation*. A German edition was subsequently published. He is now in the process of rewriting and updating the book with recently discovered new information and documents, with the new title *Miracle at St. Ottilien*.

On May 1-4, 2000, Ed and Bob arranged for a reunion of the survivors of St. Ottilien and their children. It was held in Florida and well attended. Sadly, Dr. Zalman Grinberg had passed away not long before. After the war, Grinberg emigrated to Israel, where he served in the Israeli government in their Health ministry. Eventually, Grinberg moved to the United States.

In the late nineties, Bob lectured for a journalism class of Professor John Michalczyk, Chair of the Fine Arts Department at Boston College and a prominent filmmaker. Michalczyk, who had done other documentaries on the Holocaust, was intrigued by the story, and decided to make a documentary film about it. This film premiered on November 10, 2002, in Cherry Hill, New Jersey, presented by the Delaware Valley Holocaust Education Center. Bob, Ed, and Leonard Herman were all in attendance, as were a number of survivors from St. Ottilien, and several children who had been born at the hospital, now in their fifties. The experience was moving, as the elderly survivors spoke of how the two young Army privates had come to their aid fifty-seven years ago.

The film has since been shown internationally, including at the Toronto Jewish Film Festival, The Miami Beach Holocaust

Memorial, the Boston Jewish Film Festival, at a number of venues in the northeastern United States, and as far away as Johannesburg, South Africa. It is scheduled to be shown at Yad Vashem, the Holocaust Museum in Isreal, and on U.S. public television.

Bob Hilliard looks back on the period when the concentration camp survivors needed so much and received so little, as a forgotten time in American and world history. He says, "If you look in the history books, you will find that in terms of the story of the survivors, the period from the end of the war in May, 1945 to late 1945 there is a missing period of history. It's an embarrassing era in American history and in British history. They just weren't prepared for what happened. Much of the world didn't care. Some degree of anti-Semitism was involved. Even though some supplies were sent to survivors, a lot of it disappeared in the Black Market."[44]

Today, on the occasions when Bob Hilliard speaks about his experiences in Germany, he always makes sure to hit his main point hard. "The point I try to make," he says, "is that two nobodies, two privates, the low men on the ladder, were willing to stick their necks out, and were able to change things. Many college students today don't even vote. It's like, 'I'm too cool for that'. Anyone, if they are willing to act on their beliefs, can even change government policy."[45]

A number of St. Ottilien patients and staff came to the premiere of 'Miracle at St. Ottilien' in November 2002, in Cherry Hill, New Jersey not far from Philadelphia. They came from all over the United States and Canada. In his remarks, Ed Herman quoted concentration camp survivor and author Elie Wiesel. "Elie Wiesel once said that for young Jews who survived the war, bringing a child into the world was a very great act of faith. Our survivors did not give up. Our survivors lived and flourished. Today we thank them. Each has a story to tell. Bob and I were catalysts. The survivors are the heart and soul of this film."

Dr. Moshe Ipp is one such child of hope. He made the trip from Toronto, Canada to attend the premiere. Dr. Ipp was born at St. Ottilien in November 1946 and left the monastery when he was one. His father was the chief physician at the hospital from

July 1945 to November 1947, when the family emigrated to South Africa. Though Dr. Ipp has no memory of St. Ottilien, he is grateful to Bob and Ed for helping him and his parents, survivors of the Kovno ghetto in Lithuania.

"They are both amazing individuals," he writes. "I feel very proud that they embarked on the course they took to inform the world about the ongoing plight of the Jews in the immediate postwar period. Their story is the 'power of two', the power and fortitude of two young men who defied the rules and showed the world that ordinary individuals can make a difference."[46]

Yetta Marchuck also attended the premiere. Like Dr. Ipp, Yetta is the child of Holocaust survivors and was born at St. Ottilien. Both her mother's and father's entire families were murdered in the Warsaw ghetto or Treblinka, with the exception of one of her mother's sisters. Yetta's mother and father married and returned to Poland after the war. However, after hearing of the Kielce pogrom, and other murders of returning Jews, they decided to flee back to Germany. They ended up in the British-controlled zone. By this point, Yetta's mother was pregnant, and they were uncertain where to go. "Just because the war was over did not mean that anti-Semitism was gone," Yetta wrote me. "A Jewish woman and her baby in the hands of German doctors was still a dangerous situation. The British told my parents that there was a hospital in the American zone that was started and being run by survivors. That was St. Ottilien, and that is where they headed."

"I was born at St. Ottilien and we lived in this area for the next four years."

Yetta's family eventually emigrated to the United States. "What Bob and Ed did for us all at St. Ottilien speaks for itself," she says now. "What they did for me personally at the reunion they organized and the documentary they inspired has helped me personally with closure. When we left on a military ship of June 15, 1950 and moved to the next part of our journey there was a part of my life, which always felt unfinished. Through Bob and Ed and all the 'St. Ottilien' family which I met I feel less alone and more a part of a very special family who understand the very special bonding of loss and suffering we have all experienced as survivors and children of survivors."[47]

A young Lithuanian named Morris Rich also ended up at St. Ottilien after liberation from Dachau. Rich's skill as a fourth-generation woodturner saved him from the gas chambers. When Ed and Bob first met Rich at St. Ottilien, the young boy weighed 64 pounds. Ed and Bob gave him the first orange the malnourished boy had ever eaten. After the war, Rich testified at a war crimes trial at Dachau. Four of his former tormenters were hanged. Many years later, Rich, now a successful woodturner in Miami, Florida, sent his two GI friends sets of hand-turned candle sticks to thank them. He also sent a photo of himself inscribed "Dear Mr. Herman and Dr. Hilliard: Thank you for saving thousands of lives including mine in St. Ottilien."[48]

Dora Heller survived the nightmare camp of Bergen-Belsen. After liberation, she got word that her boyfriend had also survived and ended up in poor health at St. Ottilien. "Thanks to people like you," she wrote Ed and Bob, "we had 32 years together in Pittsburgh, Pa . . . My unbound gratitude and respect to you two gentlemen for your above and beyond call of duty on behalf of our remnant . . . May G-d bless you for all you have done and especially for letting the world know!"[49]

After the premiere of 'Miracle at St. Ottilien' I saw Bob Hilliard standing in the small Holocaust Museum at the Katz Community Center, looking reflectively at the old camp uniforms, at the creased and yellowing photographs. Despite the fact that he had been the guest of honor that day, and spoke to a crowd of hundreds, he was now quite alone with his thoughts in the small museum. To a young person looking at the same displays the events surrounding the Holocaust must seem like ancient history. To Bob Hilliard, it is only yesterday. Bob Hilliard and the Herman brothers were not just passive observers of history. At a time when a suffering people dearly needed an outstretched hand, it was these young man who answered the call of their consciences, stuck their necks out, and, in so doing, changed history. How many of us can make a similar claim? How many of us are willing to?

"The world forgets," Bob writes in the last paragraph of his book. "Those of us who remember or who are concerned about what we have learned of the Holocaust must do everything we can to make certain that the rest of the world does not forget, and that genocide—whether deliberate or by neglect—should never happen again, to anyone, anytime, anywhere."[50]

Bob lives in the Boston area. Ed Herman lives in Florida. Leonard Herman lives in Georgia. They talk on the phone often.

Notes

[1]   Hilliard, Robert. *Surviving the Americans.* New York: Seven Stories Press, 1997, page 9
[2]   Hilliard, Robert, correspondence with author, August 19, 2003.
[3]   *Surviving,* page 8.
[4]   *Surviving,* page 21-22.
[5]   Hilliard, Robert. Speech at "Displaced: Miracle at St. Ottilien", Katz Jewish Community Center, Cherry Hill, New Jersey, Nov. 10, 2002.
[6]   *Surviving,* 37-38.
[7]   *Surviving,* 34.
[8]   "Miracle" Documentary.
[9]   *Surviving,* 28-30.
[10] "Miracle at St. Ottilien" Documentary.
[11] *Surviving,* 100.
[12] *Surviving,* 57-8.
[13] *Surviving,* 58-61.
[14] *Surviving,* 62-3.
[15] "Miracle" Documentary.
[16] *Surviving,* page 142.
[17] *Surviving,* page 134.
[18] Hilliard, Robert. Author Interview, June 21, 2003.
[19] Herman, Ed. Speech at 'Displaced: Miracle at St. Ottilien', Katz Jewish Community Center, Cherry Hill, New Jersey, Nov. 10, 2002.
[20] Hilliard, Author Interview, June 21, 2003.
[21] Hilliard, Author Interview, June 21, 2003.

22 *Surviving*, page 193.
23 Hilliard, Author Interview, June 21, 2003.
24 Hilliard, Author Interview, June 21, 2003.
25 *Surviving*, page 147-149.
26 Herman, Ed. Interview for film, "Miracle at St. Ottilien".
27 Hilliard, Author interview.
28 *Surviving*, page 150
29 Herman, Ed. Notes sent to Rob Morris, 2002.
30 *Surviving*, page 155-156.
31 *New York Times*, September 30, 1945, page 1.
32 *New York Times*, September 30, 1945 "Report is sent to Eisenhower".
33 *TIME* Magazine, October 8, 1945, page 31.
34 *Surviving*, page 158.
35 Wyman, David S., *The Abandonment of the Jews: America and the Holocaust 1941-1945* Pantheon, New York, 1984. Preface.
36 Wyman, *Abandonment of the Jews*, page 189.
37 Bendersky, Joseph W., *The Jewish Threat: Anti-Semitic Politics of the U.S. Army*, Basic Books. Reviewed by Jack Fischel in Forward, February 16, 2001, page 15.
38 Wiesel, Elie, *All Rivers Run To the Sea*, p. 145.
39 Greenfield, Howard, *After the Holocaust*. New York: Harper Collins, 1980, page 77.
40 Wyman, *Abandonment of the Jews*, page 273-274.
41 *Surviving*, page 188.
42 *Surviving*, page 189-190.
43 Hilliard, Author Interview, June 22, 2003.
44 Hilliard, Author Interview, June 22, 2003.
45 Hilliard, Author Interview, June 22, 2003.
46 Ipp, Dr. Moshe, Author E-mail interview, June 24, 2003.
47 Marchuck, Yetta G., Author E-mail interview, July 6, 2003.
48 Herman, Edward, Letter to Leonard Herman, June 21, 2003.
49 Heller, Dora, Letter to Edward Herman, June 16, 2000.
50 *Surviving*, 209.

Chapter Two

The Black Hell of Wauwilermoos

T he Swiss were, or proclaimed to be, neutral in World War II. Any Allied airman who happened to land in Switzerland during the war was interned for the duration. For some, this was an inconvenience, for though they were incarcerated, life was not terrible. For others, like Dan Culler, it was a descent into hell itself. Through a series of unfortunate events, he ended up in Wauwilermoos, one of Europe's worst prisons, a prison run by a Swiss Nazi. It is only through sheer will to live and the grace of God that he did not die there. The story of Dan Culler is disturbing on many levels, and is not an easy one to write. Dan Culler suffered greatly for his country, and to add insult to injury was categorically ignored by his military superiors and, after the war, by his government. The U.S. denied for years that any of the events in this story ever happened. In so doing, they denied Dan Culler treatment for wounds both physical and psychological, and at the same time, destroyed his chances for a job he loved in the post-war era.

Despite all this, Dan Culler is alive and reasonably well, living in Arizona with his wife Betty. He is a kind man who prefers to communicate through the written word because of his experiences. Writing a book of his Swiss experiences was a catharsis, a purging of many of the demons that had plagued him for nearly fifty years. A few years back, Dan returned to Switzerland to face down these same demons. The trip was anything but therapeutic, and is told in this story. Dan Culler is an American hero, not only because of what he did for his country, but because he has continued to love his country despite its lack of concern for him.

Dan Culler was born March 22, 1924 in rural Indiana, the tenth child to a farming family. The Culler family had been Amish in generations past, had then become Mennonite, and finally Church of the Brethren. The Brethren, like the Amish and the Mennonites, are pacifists, and Dan could have declared himself a conscientious objector when the U.S. entered the war in December of 1941. Dan, however, felt himself called to defend his country, and enlisted in the Army Air Corps in January 1942. He was a true country bumpkin, raised far from America's big cities. What little he knew of the outside world came to him via newsreels at the movies or over the radio.

His mother reluctantly signed the necessary paperwork allowing him to enlist. Dan was only seventeen. "My mother signed, but not willingly. She made the remark that she felt she was signing my death warrant", Dan writes. Her words were nearly prophetic, in ways Maude Culler could never imagine. And in ways he could never tell her.

Because of his mechanical aptitude, Dan ended up being trained as a flight engineer on a B-24 heavy bomber crew. At Lincoln, Nebraska, the crew was given a brand new B-24H bomber. "Just like the new automobiles of today, it even smelled new."

The crew flew the plane across the Atlantic Ocean to England, by way of Newfoundland, Greenland and Iceland, landing on October 18, 1943 at the 44th Bomb Group's base at Shipdam, England, where they were assigned to the 66th Squadron. The 44th was known as "The Flying Eightballs" for its propensity to attract enemy attention.

The plane was taken to the sub depot for modifications, and though they were told they would be getting it back, they never saw it again. It was the first of many disillusioning experiences young Dan would have to weather in the next few years. Their next would be a run-in with the squadron's operations officer, who tried to have the crew's heavy sleeping bags turned over to him and other officers. The crew appealed the confiscation, thus earning them the unending wrath of the operations officer, who from then on, according to Dan, assigned them the most decrepit, un-airworthy bomber for each mission.

Flying various rattling crates into combat, Dan was soon forced to confront his own Amish beliefs about war and killing, and the conclusion he reached was stunning and depressing. "I'm sorry," he writes in his book, "but if the Bible is the truth all humanity must live by, then there will be no place in Heaven for any of us who were forced to, or through love of country decided to take another human life. I only pray that there will be someplace besides Heaven that the Man up there has made for those of us who believed we were doing the right thing. I must admit that even believing this way, I still felt it was my duty to fight oppression. That is why, since World War II, I've felt a vacuum when praying to my God."[1]

He does, however, have fond memories of the kinship he felt with other airmen. "The feeling the closeness you got as you walked out of the briefing room and headed for your plane was something you never experience in civilian life. Maybe that is why war is so popular, and friends you meet in combat are friends forever."[2]

The crew managed, despite close calls, to make it back safely on twenty-four missions. If they could manage one more, they would have twenty-five, the magic number, and would be allowed to go home or be reassigned to less dangerous work.

On March 18, 1944, Dan's crew took off for their final mission. The target was a ball bearing plant on Lake Constance in Friederichshaven, Germany. It didn't look to be an easy mission. For one thing, the area along Lake Constance was heavily fortified because of its importance to Germany's steel industry. Because the mission was deep in enemy territory, there would be little fuel reserve. Since the Americans were unable to violate Swiss airspace, all approaches and departures had to be made in an east-west direction. The southern half of Lake Constance was in Switzerland. The Germans, aware of this, set up their anti-aircraft guns along the route that went east to west. The crews called it "Flak Alley".

"We were warned about crossing that thin line because the Swiss fighters and their anti-aircraft would shoot," recalls Dan. "The Swiss fighters and the anti-aircraft guns were the same as the Germans had . . . so we were sure they would be as deadly as the Germans. They were trained by the German military."[3]

On this mission, they flew a plane known as "Hell's Kitten" and would fly as group leader, carrying a special radar bombsight. All the bombs of the 44th Bomb Group would be released on their signal. Flying at 25,000 feet, a thousand miles inside enemy lines, the men breathed bottled oxygen at fifty below zero and waited for the bomb run. As they approached Friederichshaven, they could see dogfights between their escort fighters and the enemy. As the bomber stream approached the target, the sky filled with flak.

The mission became even hairier when the bombardier noticed, just before 'bombs away' that a group of B-17's was flying directly under the 44th's bomber stream. The bomb run had to be aborted. The plane took some terrific hits. But it was the second run that did them in. Seven planes from the 44th, slowly going around for the second time and with all the Germans gun trained on them, were shot from the sky on the second run.

During this go-round, there was a sudden explosion under the left wing and gas began running out in buckets. The left outboard engine burst into flames. As flight engineer, Dan scurried around inside the freezing plane, trying to keep it airworthy. The bombardier, flying the plane with the Norden bombsight, somehow managed to keep the crippled bomber on target until bombs away, and the squadron released their bombs on his lead. Had the crew elected to save the plane, the entire bombing run would have been thwarted. For his efforts to keep the plane airworthy long enough to initiate bombing, Dan Culler would receive the Distinguished Flying Cross fifty-nine years later. 'Hell's Kitten' now turned for home.

The pilot, George Telford, made a sharp turn to the left, hugging the Swiss border. Gas continued to stream from the wing tanks. Dan quickly transferred all the remaining fuel from the left to the right tank. The whole plane reeked of gasoline. He then checked the fuel gauges, and found the plane had a little more than two hours of fuel left. The oil pressure began to drop, and the oil temperature began to rise in both left engines. Flak had severed the oil lines as well. "Hell's Kitten" was doomed.

"During the briefing in England, the officers were told that if any plane was completely damaged, or had lost most of its fuel, and was close to the Swiss border, to try and make it there. There was nothing said about what would happen if we crossed into Switzerland, except that we would be interned, and since they were neutral, it was possible that we might be sent back to our own lines," Dan writes. The plane continued to lose altitude, alone somewhere over southern Germany. The pilot, knowing it was now or never, asked the navigator for the quickest route to Switzerland. They were soon intercepted by four Swiss Air Force Me109 fighters.

"Hell's Kitten" landed at Dubendorf, a short grass landing strip used by all incoming interned aircraft. The bombardier quickly destroyed the secret Norden bombsight, and Dan began procedures to blow up the rest of the aircraft by cutting the fuel lines and setting the plane on fire by firing his flare pistol. Word was that the Swiss traded partially damaged American aircraft for German fighters, and it was his responsibility to make sure the plane did not fall into Swiss hands. As he prepared to ignite the plane, several Swiss soldiers grabbed his ankle from below and pulled him from the aircraft, probably saving his life. He was drenched with gasoline and had he shot the flare pistol, Dan would undoubtedly have gone up with it.

The mission had been a costly one for the Air Corps. Thirteen planes, both heavy bombers and fighters, limped into Dubendorf that day. Regretting that he had failed in his duty to destroy his plane, but also glad to be alive, Dan Culler now faced an uncertain future as an interned American airman.

The interned airmen were taken under guard to a large Swiss theater. There, each was given a sheet of paper and told to write down personal information. Dan, in a uniform still soaked with aviation fuel, studiously avoided sitting near any smokers. His feet felt like they were on fire. They had been badly frostbitten during the mission. A Swiss officer haughtily told the men that Switzerland had never signed the Geneva Convention. As Dan and the others absorbed this absurd piece of information, they noticed an American brigadier general, dressed in a cavalry uniform, who was making no effort to hide his disdain for the downed airmen. He treated them, in Dan's words, as "scum and traitors". This was Dan Culler's first encounter with the American military attaché, General Barnwell Rhett Legge. It would not be his last.

The Swiss officer and General Legge both told the men that they would spend the duration of the war in Switzerland, and were not to attempt any escape.

"General Legge was at the hall that the Swiss placed us in to try and get us to answer questions about our mission and home base. All I wrote on the interrogation paper was my name, rank and serial number," Dan remembers. The airmen laughed when warned by General Legge not to escape. All their training had taught them to escape at all costs. This made Legge very angry.[4]

The president of the American Swiss Internees Association, Bob Long, himself a former interned B-17 pilot, confirms that there was a standard order given to airmen that they were to try to escape should they be captured. "Hell, according to the Articles of War we were under *direct orders* to seek to escape if the opportunity arose. This was a *code of conduct*,"[5] Bob insists.

General Barnwell Legge "had spent many years as Swiss military attaché, including riding out the war there. When American airmen entered Switzerland and were interned, it made this general's easy life more difficult. If we weren't here, he could have ridden out the war attending parties, impressing everyone with his polished cavalry uniform with a ton of medals across his chest. It was well known that he was more Swiss than American, and when he retired after the war, he stayed in Switzerland, never returning to America at all."

The internees were then taken by train to Frutigan. From there, they were loaded on a bus and driven up a narrow, winding mountain road to a town high in the Alps called Abelboden, southwest of Bern. The winding road was the only way in or out of

Abelboden, which in better times was a popular ski resort. The town was guarded and there was little chance of escape. Dan was assigned to a hotel, which was to be his new home. He found that in addition to American airmen, there were a number of British soldiers who had been taken prisoner in North Africa and imprisoned in Italy before that country fell to the Allied advance.

The life of an internee was tedious, but not hard. The American and British governments reimbursed the Swiss for all expenses of housing the internees, who were allowed to spend their time reading and walking. They were allowed to hike in the mountains as long as there was an armed guard present. Dan took advantage of this, despite his frozen feet. He soon came to the realization that it would be impossible to escape from Abelboden. "It was worse than a high wall. It was like a ten thousand foot fence surrounding us."[6]

The Swiss people struck Dan as sympathetic with the German Nazis. Many were members of the Swiss Nazi Party. He took French lessons to pass the time, theorizing that he would be able to use this language when he set out across France to make his way back to England. Escape was his duty, as he'd been taught in training. When he broached the subject of escape with other internees, however, they thought he was crazy. It was suicidal. Plus, life in Switzerland wasn't so bad.

Swiss citizens occasionally came to Abelboden to ski, though it seemed to Dan that their real purpose was to gawk at the interned airmen. He was befriended by a Swiss family. The father was an officer in the Swiss Army, and he had three pretty daughters. Dan was invited to go visit them in Lucerne, and was given a three-day pass by the commander in Abelboden. He found the trip relatively easy. The best way to escape would to get a pass out of Abelboden and then catch a train from there. He began to formulate his plan.

Dan planned to escape from Switzerland into Italy and meet up with the advancing American forces there. "One of the many things I hadn't counted on was that Germany wasn't going to retreat from Italy that easily. I let my eager mind get in the way of good common sense,"[7] he remembers. His plan was to take a bus to

Frutigen, board a train to Lucerne, and transfer to another heading south to Bellinzona, the largest city in southern Switzerland and one that was close to the Italian border. As he made plans to leave, he mentioned his plan to his ball turret gunner. "I wanted someone in my group to know where I was headed," he writes. He was surprised when the man told him that he, too, had been planning an escape to Italy with a British soldier and invited Dan to join them. The British soldier, in escaping from an Italian prison, had made contact with an Italian family near the Swiss border who would agree to hide them until the Americans arrived.

He also told the radio operator from his flight crew about the plan. This man tried to talk him out of it.

After each man bought a wide-brimmed black hat worn by many Swiss, the three caught an early-morning bus to Frutigen. The driver didn't ask to see their passes, and didn't seem curious as to where they were heading. As the bus descended the grade to town, it filled up with Swiss who seemed either unaware of or unconcerned about the three nervous escapees. They successfully purchased tickets for Bellinzona at the train station, and transferred to another train in Zurich. About three-quarters of the way to Bellinzona, their car filled with Swiss soldiers, who tried to make conversation in a variety of languages. "Every time I think about our great escape, I chuckle to think that we just happened to end up on a troop-carrying train," Dan writes. Still, they arrived successfully at Bellinzona, and made their way into the mountains. At this point, the plan began to unravel. The nights were cold and there was no food to eat. Dan's frostbitten feet begin to throb with pain. All three became weak and hungry after several days. In desperation, Dan ate some berries that poisoned him. Now too weak and sick to continue, the other two left him behind and disappeared into the mountains.

Dan staggered back into Bellinzona and showed his return ticket to Zurich, eventually boarding the train for the return trip to captivity. On the final short hop of his journey, the bus driver asked where the other two men were who had been with him going the other direction. He had traveled over five hundred miles on public transportation without capture, only to end up back in Abelboden. In two weeks, he had eaten little and looked like a skeleton. His feet were blackened and swollen. The radio operator welcomed him back, telling him "You're in a lot of trouble, not only with the Swiss, but with the American officer the Swiss put in charge of the internees".

Several days later, he was taken to meet the Swiss commandant. "When I was escorted to the Swiss commander's office, I soon learned he had no concern for my well-being. Instead, he was very upset over my escape, and once again reminded me that I and my fellow escapees had been the first people ever to escape from any of his camps, and that we would pay dearly for our action against him and the Swiss government."

"Every Swiss officer I met reminded me of the German SS officers I had seen in movies and on American propaganda posters. They were tall, blond haired, blue eyed, and cocky, and seemed to have a hatred towards Americans. I informed him of my duty as an American soldier to try and return to my own lines, no matter where I was. This fell on deaf ears. He told me that being captured by the Swiss, who were neutral, was altogether different from being captured by the Germans."[8]

After being locked in a small, dark room for several hours, Dan was escorted to a parked vehicle in back of the building. He spent the next ten days in solitary confinement in Abelboden. He was relieved when at the end of his stay he was returned to Abelboden. However, the following day he was awakened by gun-toting Swiss guards. He barely had time to wave good-bye to his friend the radio operator before being led away, "not realizing I was heading for a hell that would affect me for the rest of my life."

He was taken to the commandant's office and forced to stand at attention while the commandant dressed him down. "The more he accused me, the madder he got, until I saw a Hitler . . . a raving maniac standing in front of me. He was waving some thick book of Swiss Army Regulations as he paced back and forth in front of me. I was accused of everything possible under Swiss Military law. I don't remember ever being so confused and scared, even during combat. I was then informed that my punishment for escaping was not over, and that he had orders to send me to another prison. He said I was no longer a military prisoner, but was now classified as a civilian prisoner, and would be sent to a federal prison. He informed me that as a federal prisoner, I had no rights, that no one was allowed to know where I was going or why, or what prison I was being sent to. Thank God I never saw that Swiss officer again, but I met several more, even worse than he."[9]

Dan was loaded onto a train, guarded by three armed guards. "By daybreak, I was ushered off the train at a small station. Waiting for me were three much more professional looking soldiers, accompanied by two mean-looking German police dogs on leashes."

"One of the prison guards spoke very good English and told me I was being taken to Wauwilermoos Federal Prison. He asked me what I had done to be sent to this hellhole. I told him I'd tried to escape to Italy and return to my outfit. He laughed, and told me that the Americans were just getting a foothold in Italy, and that it would be months before their advance, if ever. He then told me that this was a very high security prison, and that only the worst of criminals from all over Europe—those who committed very serious crimes against the Swiss government or its people— were sent there. I asked him what type of crime a person has to commit to be sent to Wauwilermoos. His reply, 'Murder, rape, robbery, espionage or the black market'. He also informed me that he had brought many British soldiers here, but I was the first American."

Wauwilermoos was in the center of a large, grassy field. It had quite a few one-story barracks, and several very high barbed wire fences encircling it. There were guard towers and roaming guard dogs.

"As we walked through those gates, down the long narrow passageway that led to the prison commandant's office, the stares I received as I passed by each barrack sent cold chills up my spine. As we approached the commandant's office, the guard's last words were, 'I'm sorry to bring you to this hellhole. Watch your every step. There are some awful men in here, and you are so young."

The commandant reminded Dan of a B-movie French Foreign Legion commander. His name was André Beguin. In photos, Commandant Beguin looks like a softer, more corpulent version of George C. Scott playing Patton. Beguin wore high cavalry boots, horse-riding pants, and carried a horsewhip, which he cracked from time to time against his boot for effect. His comic-opera appearance reminded Dan of General Legge and his comments at Dubendorf: "Disobey this Swiss order, and you'll pay dearly."

Somehow, Dan worked up the nerve to reply to the camp commandant after the latter had finished raving and lecturing him. "I only take my orders from the American Army Air Force, and those orders are: when an airman falls into unfriendly forces, it is his duty to try and rejoin his own command."

Dan was then forced to strip, issued ill-fitting, dirty clothing and a blanket, and led to his barrack. None of the guards spoke English, or so it seemed. The building was about ten by thirty, with a ditch running inside one of the thirty-foot walls. This was the barrack toilet. The floor was covered with straw, which was used as toilet paper and sleeping surface. The barrack reeked of human waste. "One look inside and I knew that this was a place used to break prisoners down to nothing more than the lowest type of earthly creature", Dan recalls. Bugs crawled in the ditch and on the walls, and Dan, who had a fear of spiders, noticed the cobwebs hanging from the walls and ceiling.

Curiously, within minutes of his arrival, he saw a guard escorting a man in an Army Air Corps dress uniform, with sergeant's stripes. Dan yelled to him, asking if he was an American. He replied in the affirmative and asked if Dan also was. He said he'd been in Wauwilermoos before but had attempted to escape and was now going to be put in solitary confinement. He told Dan he would contact him when he got out. Dan never saw him again, and later, realized that the man wasn't American. "I found out later that the Swiss used many people in different uniforms for spy duty. Maybe this man, dressed as an American airman, was one of them."

He put off going into his barrack, number nine, until evening. As he worked his way through the narrow room to his blanket, he was stopped by several men, who pushed him into the ditch of human waste. He tried to talk and smile at them, and was met with horrifying stares. "What happened to me that night, and many more to follow, was the worst hell any person ever had to endure. Even death, though unknown, would have been more welcome than what I was about to face."

"To this day, I don't remember how many men were in Barracks Nine. But all of them participated in the things done to me while I was helplessly held down. It was a person's worst nightmare. I tried to scream, but they forced my mouth open and shoved straw into it. Coming from a small farming town, I had never heard of the things the men did to me. I was twenty years old and hadn't even been out with a girl, except to hold her hand and give her a light kiss on her cheek or mouth. I was bleeding from all the openings in my body, and for the first time in my life, I prayed to God to take my life from me, or give me some instrument to do it myself, so that I could end this torture."

Convinced that God was punishing him for disobeying His laws about killing, Dan crawled to his corner. He pulled his blanket around him and sat there all night in sheer terror. Too weak to make his way to the latrine trench, he had no alternative but to foul his pants.

The next day, the abuse continued. In addition to rape, he was held down while one man struck him as hard as he could on both sides of his head, with the flat parts of his hands, directly on his ears. After several slaps, he went unconscious. When he awoke, they jammed his mouth open with two sticks and shoved whatever they could find into his mouth. He felt blood running down the back of his throat, and he bit down so hard that he broke off one of his teeth.

Years later, Dan is still suffering from the beatings. "The doctor tells me my neck problem is strictly from the beatings I received at Wauwilermoos," Dan wrote me in November 2001. "They discovered that the vertebras in my neck have spurs on them and nothing can be done about it without the danger of paralyzing me. Right now, my neck, head, shoulders and both arms feel like a million little needles are running through them." [10]

The rapes and beatings continued. Most ended when Dan, dazed and beaten, was thrown into the ditch of human waste.

"They say," wrote Dan, "that if things are so horrible and painful at a time in your life, sometimes your brain will blank them out, and years later you will have flashbacks. To me, the flashbacks are as horrible as the real thing. I don't know how God saw fit to let my memory unlock those dark secrets of fifty years ago, unless it's for me to tell others of some of the inhumane things that people will do to each other."

Finally, in desperation, Dan stormed the commandant's office, letting loose with a barrage of profanity that he had never used in his life. "What I ended up calling the Swiss government, and everyone else, you wouldn't be able to find in a dictionary," he remembers. Each visit to the commandant only increased the wrath of the man and his guards. Eventually, he found that he could get out of the barracks at night, by crawling into the waste ditch and out under the wall. Nights were spent trying to stay away from his tormentors and hiding from the guards outside. Days were spent treating his rotting feet with fresh grass and lying near the fence perimeters trying to keep out of sight. Day after day he struggled to wash the human waste and blood from his clothing. He was bleeding from his rectum, there was blood in his urine, and he was constantly coughing and spitting up blood and bile. It was difficult to breathe. He had open sores all over his body. His buttocks were so raw he was unable to lie on his back, and could only sit with great pain. As days went by, he became weaker and weaker. His diet consisted of black bread and watery soup. "I had enough hatred by then that I could have killed, without remorse, everyone in that prison. My love and faith in mankind was rapidly disappearing, and only hatred remained," he wrote. [11]

Finally, looking like a scarecrow and nearly too sick to move, he knew he had to confront the commandant one more time. "I called him every bad name I could think of, and ended up with one I hadn't called him before, "you fucking Swiss". The commandant asked the guard, "Voss iss thiss focking?" The translator explained, and the commandant flew into a rage and sent Dan to the solitary confinement of a cramped room. This was the best thing that could have happened, for it meant that he was free from the men of Barracks Nine.

After one such confinement, he returned to the barrack to find that the men who had tortured him were all gone. His new barrack-mates, though still grubby, were much younger. And they recoiled from him. "In a few weeks, I had turned from a healthy American airman into a haggard-looking creature that somewhat resembled a human being. Even the guards seemed to treat me differently".

His new barrack mates were mostly Polish, Austrian and Hungarian. Though none spoke English, they did treat him with compassion. Finally, he could sleep at night in the barracks without fear.

He'd heard that there were British soldiers elsewhere in Wauwilermoos, and he requested that he be allowed to live with them, as none of his barrack-mates spoke any English. The commandant denied his request.

At this point, the man who would become Dan Culler's savior appeared one day at the gates of Wauwilermoos. "It was a real live spit-and-polish British sergeant-major. With him was a Swiss officer. I was so happy, I could have hugged him." The British sergeant major recoiled at the sight of Dan and began to make a wide detour around him. Dan spoke. The Brit froze, realizing that this animal was either a Canadian or American. "When I told them I was an American airman, they were even more surprised. The sergeant asked the Swiss officer, 'How did an American get in here?' He only received a shrug of the shoulders from the Swiss officer. In ten seconds, as they walked towards the commandant's office, I unloaded my story. I'm not sure if they understood me or not, but they never stopped walking towards the office, desperately trying to avoid me, while I was trying to tell them my troubles. I believe the Swiss officer didn't want to admit that anyone under their care

could be in my condition. I believe the British sergeant didn't
want to admit that any person who claimed to be a part of the
allied forces would be neglected like I was in a so-called neutral
country without them knowing about it."

The guards pushed Dan roughly to the ground, and the
sergeant turned, at the door to the commandant's office, and
promised to see him before he left. However, the man disappeared.
Though crushed, Dan was hopeful. If a British sergeant knew of
his existence, then maybe the American attaché, Gen. Legge, would
be notified and would take the steps necessary to rescue him.

Days later, the sergeant returned. He told Dan that the
commandant would not agree to reassign him to a barrack with
British prisoners. The commandant didn't like the British or the
Americans, said the sergeant, and the commandant "has nothing
but hatred for you". He told Dan that the section of the camp in
which he was incarcerated was isolated due to the fact that it held
the camp's most dangerous prisoners. He couldn't believe that Dan's
only crime had been to attempt escape.

The sergeant took him to the commandant's office, where the
commandant allowed Dan to speak. He asked why he'd been put
in Barrack Nine with the worst prisoners. Why had the American
attaché never been informed of his incarceration? Why did he have
to wear these filthy clothes? Where was the Red Cross? Why didn't
anyone speak English in this camp? The commandant got madder
and madder, and the sergeant and the commandant argued loudly.
Then Dan dropped his pants to show his sores, boils and infections.
Before they could stop him, he tried to show them the skin
protruding from his rectum and the burning red infected skin
around it. He then was wracked with terrible coughing, catching
blood and saliva in his hand so as not to foul the floor. Instantly,
the commandant, the sergeant and the translator jumped back.
The commandant said he thought Dan had tuberculosis. "I was
informed that I was not a prisoner of war, and Wauwilermoos was
not a prison camp, but a federal prison. The Red Cross had no
authority over federal prisons. Furthermore, I was told that the

American attaché, and the brigadier general in charge, weren't concerned about me since I had disobeyed orders and attempted to escape. The sergeant shook his head in disbelief when he relayed the message from the commandant telling me I wasn't considered an American soldier by the American Attaché in Bern anymore."

The sergeant also told Dan that this camp was much worse than any of the Italian or German POW camps he'd seen. "It was beginning to become clear to me," remembers Dan, "The America that I loved, fought for, and was willing to die for, was abandoning me. I now felt more alone than I ever had."

The British sergeant brought more unwelcome news on his next visit. The American Attaché did not recognize the existence of Wauwilermoos because the Swiss refused to admit to the Americans that the prison existed. General Legge would offer him no assistance, telling the sergeant's superior, "This soldier broke Swiss law, so he is in the hands of the Swiss government".

When he left, the Brit warned Beguin that nothing had better happen to Dan. Speaking to Dan, he turned grim. "Those dirty bastards, putting you through hell and never even giving you a trial!" He assured Dan that all hell was going to break loose, and Dan watched him walked purposefully away from the prison until he was no more than a speck, hoping against hope that the sergeant was right.

Several days later, with no notice, Dan was given some cleaner clothes, allowed to clean up and shave, and loaded onto a train with three guards and two viscous-looking dogs. The other passengers stared at him in disbelief, giving the little band a wide berth. The train entered the station at Baden, and as Dan, the guards, and the dogs walked through the station, the people parted in horror and curiosity, staring at this fearsome human skeleton who must be a very dangerous criminal to have such an escort.

In Baden, Dan was finally given the hearing he had been denied. The ball turret gunner and the British soldier who had escaped from Abelboden with him were also there, though none of them had a chance to speak and Culler never saw either of them again. The proceedings were held in German, arranged, as far as Dan could ascertain, to "clear the records, just in case someone, sometime, might question my sentencing and treatment without a court trial".

At trial's end, Dan was sent back to Wauwilermoos. "With the same soldiers and dogs, this very sad and sick American soldier was escorted back to more hell in Wauwilermoos. How I was going to survive the duration of the war—or longer—under that sadistic commandant at Wauwilermoos? I was ever so down in body and spirit as I was on the train ride back."

A few days later, the British sergeant major was back at the camp. He went to Commandant Beguin's office and when he returned, he walked with Dan back toward Barrack Nine and told him that he had threatened Beguin. The sergeant had told Beguin that if Dan were to die as a result of the lack of medical treatment, the British government was officially going to have the Swiss government and the commandant charged with his death.

"Why should you or the British care about this American," Beguin shot back, "if his own government doesn't?"

"Because he is a human being and one of our allies who fought against Hitler," the sergeant shot back.

As Dan walked with him to the gate, the sergeant warned him that Beguin was not above treachery. He was fearful about what would happen if Dan were released from prison and told of his treatment. It would be in the best interests of Commandant Beguin to see to it that Dan never left Wauwilermoos alive.

A few days later a young American airman was moved into Barracks Nine. He told Dan he was from Kansas City, Missouri and had been a tailgunner on a B-17. Dan was so glad to have someone to talk to that he would have gladly talked to Hitler's brother. But something about the airman did not ring true. The conditions did not seem to bother him. He went and visited the Commandant's office several times a day. And then, one night, Dan's coughing fits got so bad that he was moved to solitary, probably to protect the other prisoners from tuberculosis. The next day, he was called into Beguin's office, where Beguin gave him a four-hour pass to visit the nearby village of Nebikon. An

English-speaking guard told him "the commandant, out of the goodness of his heart, wants you to visit a restaurant in Nebikon. Some good Swiss restaurant food may help bring back your health and be good for the boils that cover your body."

Dan, dazed, offered that he had no Swiss money. The commandant reached into his own pocket and pulled out a Swiss paper bill equivalent to a five-dollar bill.

Dan staggered out of the commandant's office, threw some water on his face, and made for the gate. His fellow prisoners looked equally confused, except for the American airman, who waved and wished him good luck and good eating.

He stopped halfway to the village to stuff fresh grass inside his shoes. As he did so, the thought struck him that he had not told the American airman where he was going or what he was doing. He also began to have the distinct feeling that he was being followed.

As he was entering Nebikon, he heard a woman's voice. Turning, he saw a lovely young woman hiding behind a large tree. The woman pulled him behind the tree and asked if he were the young American from Wauwilermoos. She proceeded to tell him that she and her mother were Austrian and had fled to Switzerland to escape the Nazis. She admitted that the Swiss used her to gain information on undesirables. Because she was only fifteen, she was also used to trap undesirables in compromising situations.

He remembered seeing a Hungarian prisoner being led away to a life term in a Swiss prison. He had asked a guard what the man's crime had been, and the guard had told him that the man had forced an underage girl to have sex with him. "Are you the underage girl that the Swiss used to trap the Hungarian prisoner?" he asked her. Her answer was yes. "Are you working for the commandant of Wauwilermoos?" Dan pressed.

"Yes, and I'm also the commandant's girl," she added.

"Why did you warn me?" he asked her.

"You look like you've had enough punishment," she replied. "I will tell the commandant that you were too dirty, and I was afraid I might catch a disease and pass it on to him".

He spent the remainder of his pass time walking and talking with the girl, and then she helped him back to the path leading to the prison. He never saw the American airman again, and was thrown back into solitary confinement.

Realizing that Beguin had tried to set him up, Dan knew his chances of escaping Wauwilermoos alive were nearly nil. One day he tried to commit suicide by stuffing straw down his throat and into his lungs. He vomited and passed out. When he awoke, he saw the British sergeant looking down at him. The Brit had just returned to the camp armed with an order from the British government and signed by a high-ranking Swiss official saying he was to receive medical treatment at once.

"Even to this day, I don't remember how I got to the hospital in Lucerne, or what happened after I got there, but when I woke up, I thought I was dead. I was in a white room, lying on a bed, and all I could see was a very large cross on the wall at the foot of the bed."

The Swiss now began to destroy the evidence of abuse presented by Dan's diseased, skeletal appearance by nursing him back to health. Eventually, it dawned on him that he was in a tuberculosis ward in the hospital.

One day, he heard a familiar voice, and the British Sergeant Major came into his room, dressed in a white gown. "His head was covered with something that resembled a white sack, with only holes for his eyes. He looked ridiculous, and I told him so—and for the first time in months, I laughed, and so did he. The laughter was contagious, and soon the whole room was laughing."

The Sergeant told him he had been taken in a heated mail train car to Lucerne, where a doctor operated on his rectum, which had been torn by the men of Barrack Nine. The doctor also told him there was nothing that could be done for the beatings to his ears and head. Both of his lungs were partially collapsed. He had also lost a tooth. In addition, he had tuberculosis, and would soon be sent to a TB sanitarium in Davos. The doctor said he'd never seen a man so close to death, and was quite proud of how the hospital had been able to save his life. The TB would always be inside his body. Fifty years later, Dan contracted pneumonia working on his Arizona ranch. A doctor discovered that the TB virus was still in his body and that his lungs showed the damage done fifty years before.

The British Sergeant Major wished him the best and told him he could only stay a very short time. He told him he was proud and happy that he was recovering. Dan took his hand and thanked him, told him how without his help he would have died. His only reply was that he had a very different view of the American military, seeing how they had neglected one of their own warriors when he needed help so badly. He then departed through the swinging door, and Dan never saw or heard from him again.

As Dan slowly healed, he worried about what would happen to him once he was well enough to be released. He also found that he was terrified when left alone in a room with other men, a manifestation caused by his experiences in Barrack Nine. It is an affliction he still suffers from. He told one of the doctors who treated him that if he was returning to Wauwilermoos, he hoped the doctor would kill him. The doctor shook his head, said he'd heard of the place, and that the patients who had been sent from there had all been in very bad shape on arrival. He later was told by a nurse that the doctor, who was also in the Swiss military, had gone to the authorities and told them "If this man is sent back to Wauwilermoos, you are going to have a dead American soldier to explain to the Americans after the war".

He was issued some used clothing, including some decent shoes. He was then moved under guard to a TB sanitarium near the town of Davos. Several days after his arrival, a young man came to visit him. He identified himself as a representative for the US Army Attaché in Bern, and said he had come on the insistence of Dan's pilot, who had been searching for him since he had been imprisoned at Frutigen after his first escape attempt.

The man warned Dan, out of earshot of others, that he was in grave danger, and not to trust anyone. The pilot had paid a lot of money to the Swiss underground to finance Dan's escape out of Switzerland. The man gave him forged passes and train tickets to

Geneva. At the border, he would meet his pilot, copilot and navigator, and together they would be smuggled across the border to rendezvous with the French underground.

The railroad tickets would get him from Davos to Bern and then from Bern to Geneva. Despite his fears of what might happen if he were captured trying to escape a third time, Dan agreed to meet the rest of his crew at the assigned location.

In the meantime, he continued to heal and to help other TB patients sicker than himself.

On the day of his escape, he packed a few items into an old handkerchief and into his pockets. One was the sheet of paper he'd received at his trial in Baden. It named Wauwilermoos, on government stationery, and was signed by the six Swiss judges at his trial. Many years later, when he wrote the Swiss Embassy, the Swiss still denied that Wauwilermoos existed.

He met up with his bombardier and the two continued on together by train. Near Geneva, a Swiss military man approached and questioned them. He took the bombardier off somewhere but let Dan continue his journey.

He rendezvoused at the assigned location, a small café in Geneva. It didn't take long for him to figure out this was a smuggler's hangout.

His pilot and copilot were already there. Together, they were loaded into a taxi and taken out into the countryside. The taxi sped into the Swiss countryside, headed towards a spot along the border where there was a shelf along the barbed wire border that could be leapt over. The taxi screeched to a halt a quarter mile shy of the agreed escape point and the driver ordered the three escapees out of the car. They dashed across an open field towards the low spot in the barbed wire, a full quarter-mile away.

Halfway between the car and the border, shots rang out all around them. It was a setup. Bullets whizzed by their heads.

They approached the escape spot, where true to plan, the French side was a good deal lower than the Swiss side. Three rolls of barbed wire were piled up in a pyramid to prevent crossing. They would have to leap across the rolls to make it to freedom.

They leapt at about the same time, bouncing across the wire before rolling into France. Looking back, Dan could see that the barbed wire was at least twelve feet high. Other than the one spot they had crossed, there was no way they would have cleared it at any other point.

The pilot had been hit in the ankle. As they got up, the Swiss border guards approached them on the Swiss side, guns drawn, but it was over. The Swiss officer said something to his men. They lowered their guns. The three Americans began slowly walking away from the border. The pilot said he didn't think the Swiss would dare shoot them in the back this close to the border.

It wasn't until they were some distance from the border that they stopped to assess their injuries. Other than the pilot, none of the Swiss bullets had pierced their flesh. However, Dan counted ten bullet holes in his baggy suit. "That baggy suit had saved my life. With my unbuttoned coat and baggy trousers flopping in the wind I made a very large target."

The three men rendezvoused with the French underground, and after a few days, an American C-47 landed at a remote grassy field, picked the men up, and took off. Dan Culler was a free man.

Back in England, an incredulous doctor refused to believe that Dan's terrible condition was the result of time in a Swiss prison. The Swiss were neutral. Weren't they head of the International Red Cross?

Though the crew had completed their missions, Dan rejoined them at the 66th Squadron's Quonset to await return to the States. He spent hours each day soaking in a hot bath and getting slathered with medication for his boils. A trip to his old hut revealed that all his belongings had been stolen after he'd been reported interned. None of the crew ever recovered a single item.

Dan was interrogated in London about his experiences. He told a young military interrogator his entire story, leaving out nothing. He also said that he planned to make public back in the States what the Swiss had done, and how he had been abandoned by the U.S. military attaché in Bern. The interrogator listened intently, but soon stopped taking notes.

A few days later, Dan was called in for a follow-up session. This time, there was another man there as well, dressed in the uniform of military intelligence, who identified himself as a captain and a minister in the Church of the Brethren, Dan's faith. The door was locked from the inside. The captain looked Dan in the eye. "I don't believe this story to be true," he said. "The Swiss are a gentle people." Dan responded that being surrounded by Axis powers can change the way people act. The captain said he didn't believe there was such a place as Wauwilermoos, and accused Dan of making it up. Dan had the paper from his trial, signed by the judges, and pulled it out as proof. The captain attempted to take the paper, saying he was going to put it in Dan's file. Dan refused to give it to him.

In the next session, the two interrogators were joined by a third. Again, the door was locked from the inside. The new man was a full colonel. Dan was told to stand at full attention while the others sat. Finally, the colonel waved the interrogation papers in Dan's face and yelled, "Sergeant, you are a God-damned liar! There is no such place as Wauwilermoos in Switzerland, and if there were, the Swiss would not put someone in there for attempting to escape. The American government is paying the Swiss large sums of money to care for internees!"

Dan was scared to death, and when he was permitted to speak, he began a coughing spell and threw up the usual blood and phlegm into his hat. "I tore off my jacket and shirt, showing them my remaining sores and boils. I dropped my pants below my waist and exposed the many festered boils and sores along my waistline. I removed my shoes and the bandages, exposing two very tender feet with no toenails, just callused skin." He didn't know if the shape of his body shook them up, or if they were just shocked that a Tech Sergeant had just dropped his pants in front of them. He asked them if he looked more like a prisoner or an internee who had been treated humanely.

"If you broke the law by trying to escape, then you deserved your treatment at Wauwilermoos," the colonel snapped. He then confiscated all the interrogation paperwork. He informed Dan that the US had mistakenly bombed Switzerland on several occasions, with some loss of life and great loss of property. The American government was working on a ten million dollar compensation plan right now, and that they didn't want negotiations harmed by any bad press about the Swiss or Swiss mistreatment of internees. He informed Dan that he must never speak of the issue again. If he did, the Swiss and American governments would deny all charges, classify him as unstable, and give him a Section Eight discharge. A Section Eight could mean placement in an Army or VA mental institution for years.

As a coup de grace, the colonel told Dan that if he continued to press the issue, he would be returned to the Swiss to serve the remainder of his sentence, and that charges would be filed against his pilot for helping him to escape from Switzerland.

All papers relating to Dan's experiences were to be purged from every existing military file. "When I think of it now, fifty years later, and hopefully as a more mature person, it makes me so damn mad," Dan writes. "The colonel got his way. Nothing was placed in my record about my treatment at Wauwilermoos, or any other treatment I received there or after my return to American authority. My discharge papers never mentioned my internment, and all my records, including my medicals, were destroyed in a fire. It was as if I spent from 1942 to 1945 in the US Army Air Force doing absolutely nothing. Against the colonel's orders, I did keep one piece of evidence—my papers from the trial in Bern. I still have them in my possession today."

Dan ended up back in the States working as a line chief on aircraft for the Air Force, until during medical treatment, it was discovered he had tuberculosis and other serious medical problems, none of which showed up on his medical records. After extensive treatment, a doctor pressed him on how he gotten so many diseases and injuries. Dan had also panicked in an enclosed room with another man, a result of his Wauwilermoos experience, and had beaten the orderly up, and they were concerned about his mental state. Dan, aware of his agreement not to talk, at first refused to answer. Finally, he gave a general answer about having spent time in a prison in Europe during the war. As a result of divulging this information, his military career was over. When he was given his honorable discharge, the pay sent home during the time he had spent in Wauwilermoos was deducted. There was no such place. Instead, he was classified as AWOL—absent without leave—during his time in prison. Surprisingly, or perhaps not surprisingly, the AWOL never showed up in his military records.

After the war, the Swiss government tried Commandant Beguin. It was found that he was a former member of the Foreign Legion and a member of the Swiss Nazi Party, and that he had been appropriating large amounts of the funds coming into Wauwilermoos to pay for his mistresses and his own lavish lifestyle. According to the account on the Swiss Internees website, "although serving in the Swiss Army, Beguin was also a Nazi, as member of the National Front. He was known to wear the Nazi uniform and sign his correspondence with 'Heil Hitler'. He was given his command at Wauwilermoos despite his prior dismissal from the Swiss Army in 1937 for financial fraud and various confrontations with the police. While in command, he publicly berated Americans, sentenced them to solitary confinement, and denied requests for Rules of Conduct required under the Geneva Convention on the basis that Switzerland was not a signatory. In 1946, Beguin was court-martialed in a trail that lasted 149 days. He was convicted of administrative misdemeanors, dishonoring the Swiss and her army, embezzlement, and withholding complaints from inmates. In its decision, the court described Beguin as a "crook, embezzler, con-man and inhuman." Beguin was sentenced to several years of inprisonment, fined, and stripped of his civil rights."[12]

The American military attaché, Barnwell Legge, never returned to the United States after the war. He preferred to remain in Switzerland with his Swiss wife. The two OSS men who ordered Dan Culler's story suppressed were Allan Dulles, OSS chief in Switzerland at the time, and William Casey, head of the OSS in London. Both went on to distinguished careers as public servants for various administrations.

Dan went on to live a successful life, married, had children, and is now retired and living in Arizona, where he continues to write. Though in very poor physical health, he manages to get from day to day. He always answers his emails, always writes back. Our planned meeting for the summer of 2003 fell through when he became too sick to meet with me and spent a good amount of time in the VA Hospital. He has come a long way towards regaining his mental health, but the scars will always remain.

In a final note, Dan was invited to return to Switzerland in 1994 by the President of Switzerland. He was given a formal apology by Swiss President Kaspar Villager, both in person and in the form of a letter. The letter, dated March 9, 1995, states in part, "I received your account of the experience you made during your internment in Switzerland as a member of the US Armed Forces from the Swiss Embassy in Washington. I read your portrayal with great interest and regret that the memory of your internment in 1944 and, in particular, that of your detention in Wauwilermoos is colored by such traumatic experience. I appreciate that it is difficult for you to understand why you were assigned to the Wauwilermoos detention camp. Together with innumerable other young Americans, you came to Europe to rescue the continent from facist aggressors . . . Your attempt to flee and rejoin your unit was not defamatory, though such behavior was in fact contrary to Swiss orders . . . From today's point of view, the Swiss military court punished you very severely . . . This sentence reflects the important pressure exercised by other countries on Switzerland which was then surrounded by war. The Swiss authorities were afraid that a less severe attitude toward attempts of interned military personnel to escape would be interpreted as preferential treatment by the other warring party."[13]

Dan and Betty visited Switzerland in late October of 1995. The trip was paid for by a Swiss news station that smelled a good story. However, after their arrival in Switzerland, it became very apparent that the news people were using Dan for their own purposes. Soon after their arrival on the whirlwind tour, they were informed they would be interviewed not just by SF DRS TV but also by the *24 Heures* newspaper.

The first stop was Abelboden, where Dan had started his detention. "This place brought back good and bad memories," wrote Dan in a story later. They found an old bus, the same one he had made his first escape attempt in, and "we completely reenacted my escape from Abelboden". Dan was beginning to feel uneasy, the repressed memories starting to resurface. To make matters worse, the press of interested news people and curious gawkers bothered his claustrophobia.

Next, three news crews accompanied Dan and Betty to Frutigen. The news people had prepared a surprise for Dan—"a surprise I could have very much done without". The 'surprise' was the prison cell where he had been placed after his escape attempt. The flashback was so intense that it caused Dan to collapse. All the while, the Swiss news cameras kept running.

The next day, the news crews had scheduled to take Dan Culler to Wauwilermoos, or what was left of it. Dan by this point just wanted to get on a plane and go home, but he tried to be a gamer about it. He spent the night plagued by nightmares. In the morning the group headed to the village of Wauwil. The camp itself had been destroyed by the Swiss right after the war. Built on the spot was a new drug treatment center. Though greeted warmly by its director, Dan was subjected to a harsh interview by the village newspaper reporter. "I could feel the hostility towards me by this person, like many in the area. He refused to believe that there was ever a place called Wauwilermoos or that it had a commandant named Beguin. Just like the people around the Jewish death camps in Germany who denied their existence, the citizens around Wauwilermoos denied its existence."

The rest of the trip was somewhat better. On October 30, Dan and Betty met with Swiss President Kaspar Villager for thirty-five minutes in his office. "President Villager was the most pleasant and sincere person I had ever met. Everything he said came from his heart." After the meeting and some obligatory photographs, Dan and Betty spent time at the American Embassy, where they met with the Marine Corps guards and discussed Dan's experiences.[14]

The trip was both a catharsis and a nightmare for the Cullers. The insensitivity of the Swiss news people was incredible. However, the sincere meeting with President Villager did salve some of Dan's long-term mental wounds.

A final note to this already complicated and fascinating story. In December 2000, Dan received an unusual Christmas card with a Swiss postmark. He opened it with great curiosity. Dated December 8, 2000, it read: "Dear Mister Dan Culler, I learnt your story and the hard trials you went through. They make my heart bleed, awfully bleed, because I am the youngest daughter of Captain André Beguin and I'm born on the eve of my father lawsuit (17-2-1946). After so many sufferings for everyone of us, for you, for my sister and for my father too, after so many sufferings . . .

I BEG YOUR PARDON

and with the most sincerity, I send you all my best wishes for better health, a Merry and peaceful Christmas and a Happy New Year.

God bless you,
Jacqueline-André Perissinott"[15]

Though denied by both the Swiss and American governments for many years, one can now find information about this mysterious place, long since covered over and otherwise forgotten, on the Swiss Internees Website. Through the efforts of individuals like Dan Culler and his fellow internees, the truth is beginning to emerge. What follows is the little remaining history of the place Dan Culler thinks of as his own personal hell.

"Established in 1940," reads the report, "Wauwilermoos Military Prison was located in Lucerne, Switzerland. The prison held many nationalities, including Swiss criminals. Surrounded by several rows of barbed wire, the compound was patrolled day and night by armed guards with attack dogs. The barracks were wooden single-wall construction, and prisoners slept on boards covered with dirty straw. Lice and rats also inhabited the barracks. The latrines consisted of slit trenches inside or outside of the barracks, and no hygiene facilities except the chance to be hosed-off every few weeks. Food was poured from slop pails into troughs or tin pans. Internees lacked medical care, proper nutrition, Red Cross contact, or access to any mail or aid parcels. Most prisoners left Wauwilermoos severely underweight, and covered with boils or other ailments. American internees were sent to Wauwilermoos without any trial or legal due process, and were kept there indefinitely until the American Legation found out and petitioned their release. Although the Red Cross inspected the camp on a few occasions, they simply noted that sanitary conditions could be improved, and prisoners were not aware of the length of their sentences or why they were in the camp in the first place."[16]

Notes

1   Dan Culler, *Black Hole of Wauwilermoos*, Circle of Thorns Press, 1995. Page 102

2   Culler, *Black Hole*, 105

3   Culler, *Black Hole*, 150

4   Dan Culler, Author Interview, December 2001.

5   Bob Long, Author Interview, September 1, 2001.

6   Culler, *Black Hole*, 169.

7   Culler, *Black Hole*, 173.

8   Culler, *Black Hole*, 198.

9   Culler, *Black Hole*, 203

10   Culler, letter to author, (11/25/01)

11   Culler, *Black Hole*, 218.

12   Swiss Internees Website. <http://swissinternees.tripod.com/adm/ad/popup_source.shtml?member_name=swissinternees&path=wauwilermoos.html&client_ip=198.81.26.79&ts=1081119640

&ad_type=POPUP&search_string=andre+beguin+wauwilermoos&id=
af5d5fde2ebc1d17de00d48 581635396>

13   Letter from Swiss President Kaspar Villager, dated March 9, 1995, from
     the collection of Dan Culler.

14   Dan Culler, "Dan and Betty Culler Trip to Switzerland", written by Dan
     Culler in November, 1995. Author's collection.

15   Photocopy of original Christmas card from Jacqueline-André Perrissonett
     to Dan Culler, December 8, 2000 in author's possession.

16   Swiss Internees Website. <http://swissinternees.tripod.com/adm/ad/
     popup_source.shtml?member_name=swissinternees&path=
     wauwilermoos.html&client_ip=198.81.26.79&ts=1081119640&
     ad_type=POPUP&search_string=andre+beguin+wauwilermoos&id=
     af5d5fde2ebc1d17de00d48581635396>

Chapter Three

Memphis Belle and Hell's Angels: First to Finish

The early history of the U.S. Eighth Air Force in England was not one to instill confidence in the hearts of Americans back in the States. The American forces had committed themselves to daylight bombing, against the advice of their British counterparts, who considered it suicidal and had long since switched to nighttime bombing. The Eighth still held to the theory that a tight formation, or combat box, of B-17 Flying Fortresses, each bristling with guns, was capable of defending itself from enemy fighter attack without the aid of long-range fighter aircraft. And the Eighth was finding that this was a mistake. Daylight bombing of Europe was very much a work in progress, with an incredible number of factors to work out. Engineers in the States struggled to improve the defensive and offensive capabilities of the B-17. At the same time, they labored to create a long-range fighter aircraft capable of escorting the slow-moving bombers all the way to the target.

Equipment in the aircraft proved inadequate. Many men lost limbs or lives at fifty below zero due to poorly designed equipment. The Americans, only forty years beyond the first tentative flight by the Wright Brothers at Kitty Hawk, worked to improve the odds for the men and machines who flew the dangerous missions over Europe. As they did so, thousands of young men awoke each morning throughout England and boarded their Forts, each knowing full well that it could be the last day of their young lives.

It became apparent to Eighth Air Force command early on that the odds of any man finishing up a tour of duty in a B-17 over Europe was next to zero. Morale began to suffer. In the first three months of American involvement, fully eighty percent of all aircrews were shot down. High command decided to institute a rule mandating that flight crews had only to survive twenty-five missions to complete their tour. In my conversations with the men who flew in the very early stages of the American air war over Europe, I am struck by the recurring statement that those who remain are few and consider themselves very, very lucky. Many of those first idealistic, gung-ho aircrews who flew their new B-17Fs over to England in 1942 and 1943 have found permanent rest in cemeteries across Europe. Many more became prisoners of war in Germany. And a few, lucky or blessed or both, managed to survive and return home.

This is the story of two airplanes: Hell's Angels and The Memphis Belle. It is also the story of their crews. Both planes and crews managed to survive what had begun to seem impossible to the young men who flew those early bombing missions over Europe. They were the first two heavy bombers to complete twenty-five missions over Europe in 1942 and early 1943. Of the staggering 12,750 Boeing B-17s built, one of these two—the Memphis Belle—went on to become the most famous B-17 of all time. It became the topic of an acclaimed war documentary and returned to the US for a heralded victory tour. It winged into legend along with its crew. A Hollywood movie about it became one of the top films of the early nineties. Its pilot, Robert Morgan, is one of the most famous B-17 pilots of all time and recently wrote a best-selling memoir. The plane itself, after years of neglect, has finally gotten the love and respect she so deserves and is on display on Mud Island in Memphis, Tennessee.

On the other hand, the B-17 "Hell's Angels" and the men who flew her disappeared from the pages of memory shortly after the war, despite the fact that she finished her tour several days before the Belle. Her men did not hob-nob with the rich and famous. No movies were made about her. And she was eventually scrapped.

The crew of the Memphis Belle never tried to grab the limelight away from Hell's Angels, the plane that actually finished first. It was simply the work of fate, the War Department, and a young moviemaker named William Wyler. And the fame accorded to the men of the Memphis Belle was not always a positive. Ironically, it cost pilot Morgan the chance to marry the love of his life, the woman for whom the plane was named.

Christmas 1942 was not a bright time for Robert Morgan and the crew of The Memphis Belle. As he remembers, "Nobody was in a festive mood, not with all those empty tables and chairs at evening mess . . . the awareness of death always in our midst. Thirty-six B-17s had crossed the Atlantic from the United States to England to form the original 91st Bomb Group. Of these, twenty-nine had been shot down, a casualty rate of eighty-two percent."[1]

The Memphis Belle, officially plane #41-24485, flew with the 92nd Bomb Group under Robert Morgan's command in those early months of daylight bombing. During her tour, the Belle shot down eight enemy fighters, possibly destroyed five others, and damaged at least a dozen more. She dropped more than 60 tons of bombs over Germany, France and Belgium. During her 25 missions she flew 148 hours, 50 minutes, and covered more than 20,000 combat miles. When the Belle finished her tour, she was bullet-ridden and flak damaged; on five separate occasions she'd had engines shot out and once came back with her tail nearly shot off. Other than a cold-related injury to a gunner, Captain Morgan pulled his crew through with no major injuries, an incredible feat. She flew for 10 months from November 7, 1942 to May 19, 1943, completing her twenty-fifth mission on May 19, 1943 and, with her crew, made a glorious return to the States to tour the nation and prove the capabilities of the Flying Fortress in combat over Europe.

The 303rd Bomb Group's B-17, named "Hell's Angels", was piloted by an unassuming man named Irl Baldwin. The aircraft, originally known only as #41-24577, was named "Hell's Angels" on the forth or fifth mission after Captain Baldwin solicited names for the aircraft on the interphone on the way home from a mission. One crewman suggested "Hell's Angels", after a World War I movie. Another crewman piped in that the name was appropriate, as the mission they had just completed was "the closest to hell that angels will ever get!" Hell's Angels completed its tour of duty on May 13, 1943, six days before the Memphis Belle's wheels touched the welcome pavement of England after its twenty-fifth mission. No film was made of the crew, and the victory tour was delayed until after Hell's Angels had flown forty-eight missions over Europe. In fact, Hell's Angels did not return to the States until January of 1944, long after the Memphis Belle had cemented her place in the hearts and minds of the American people.

Time has taken its toll on both crews. Only a few men from either crew still survive. And as the warriors make ready for their final missions, it is fitting to examine this intriguing story of the two planes and crews who, in the deadly skies over Europe in early 1943, struggled not for fame, but simply for survival, and how one found fame and fortune while the other stayed in relative obscurity for the next sixty years. In the course of writing this chapter, the goal has been to interview as many of the surviving principals in the story as possible, and to honor them all, laying out the facts and the arguments of both sides. There are many ways, it is evident, to arrive at that magical 'first to complete twenty-five missions' claim. The fact that one plane may have finished a few days ahead of the other diminishes the courage and sacrifice of these young men not one iota. All are heroes. All deserve accolades. As does every single man who ever climbed into the confines of a B-17 to risk his life over the continent.

The records clearly show that Hell's Angels was the first aircraft to finish twenty-five missions over Europe. In his book, *The Mighty Eighth*, long considered the Bible of all matters Eighth Air Force, British historian Roger Freeman writes, "May 14, 1943 was a milestone for the Eighth. For the first time, over two hundred heavies were dispatched. Another notable occurrence was the completion of twenty-five missions by the Molesworth Fortress Hell's Angels."[2] Later in the book, Freeman writes "Hell's Angels, that had been the first B-17 of the Eighth to reach 25 missions, had by 4th October completed 43."[3]

Harry Gobrecht, 303rd B-17 pilot and former historian of the 303rd Bomb Group is an ardent defender of the Hell's Angels. Over the years, he has written letters to many historians about the Belle/Angels controversy. He has been successful in having some historians change the historical record in their books. He also discovered that Captain Morgan completed his twenty-fifth mission on May 17, according to the 92nd Bomb Group's 324th Squadron Record, but that the Memphis Belle itself did not complete its twenty-fifth until May 19. "The Belle had been grounded several times for repairs due to battle damage and on several of these occasions, the Belle's regular crew had been assigned to fly combat missions on other aircraft. Therefore, in order to bring the plane's mission numbers up to the crew's, the Belle was sent out on combat missions with other pilots and crews," he writes. Another history of the Memphis Belle notes that on May 19, 1943, "the battered plane that had carried Bob Morgan and his crew through flak and fighters so many times, and had taken her share of a beating on several occasions while dishing out more than her share of war, flew her last combat mission. This time, since most of her crew had completed their twenty-five missions, it would be Lieutenant C.L. Anderson, who had flown her on another mission, at the controls with his own crew."[4]

Irl Baldwin, the pilot of Hell's Angels, who has since died, wrote to Gobrecht that he, as a pilot, had completed his 25th mission on May 14. He also said in later letters that at least part of his crew finished their twenty-fifth mission on the same day. The plane itself did not complete its 25th mission until May 17.

Why so much contention about being the first to finish twenty-five missions, some readers might wonder? At the time, the magic twenty-five was the US Eighth Air Force's Holy Grail. The twenty-five-mission rule had been instituted in late 1942 by the Eighth Air Force's new leader, General Ira Eaker, who was concerned about the high losses and the effect it was having on morale. According to Bob Morgan, "What a masterstroke of psychology that announcement was! . . . We eagerly fastened on this new incentive. Twenty-five missions? We can do that! Was a thought that raced through the mind of every pilot and crewman."

And yet, as the missions continued, it became apparent that even achieving twenty-five missions would be nearly impossible. Many men became convinced even twenty-five was unattainable. Still, it was the goal, and one all hoped and prayed for. It became a sort of talisman, a number with quasi-mythical status, and those who achieved it first became living proof to the rest of the men that survival was, indeed, possible.

As the B-17s of the Eighth Air Force mounted the intensity of their missions over Europe, the Eighth began to attract the attention of the U.S. press corps. "We noticed," writes Morgan, "that more and more U.S. journalists—and British as well—were showing up at our bases in England, writing us up, trying to cadge rides on our sorties".[5]

"The journalists paid particular attention to the planes and crews whose mission totals had started to pile up toward the magical twenty-five. The Memphis Belle attracted its share of press attention, especially given its eye-catching human-interest angle—being named for the pilot's girlfriend".[6] The crew did not always welcome the attention. A rumor began floating around the Eighth that the Luftwaffe was reading the news accounts and its pilots were gunning for the Belle.

"It was only a matter of time before film-makers began showing up, too," writes Morgan, and indeed, he began to see a "trim, fairly cocky fellow in an airman's flight jacket and billed leather cap bustling around, waving his hands in the air, a cigarette burning from the middle of his lips and a couple of cameramen dogging his footsteps".[7]

If one event can be identified as the defining moment when the Memphis Belle and its crew would be pegged for fame, it was the arrival of this cocky young film producer. His name was William Wyler, nicknamed "The Hollywood Colonel", and he already had an impressive Hollywood film resumé. He had come to England to produce a war documentary about the Eighth Air Force, and he decided Bob Morgan and his crew were just the men he needed for his project.

Wyler brought with him 200 small 16-millimeter cameras, which he handed out to flight crews with the directive "Take as much film as you can, and after you turn in the film, you can keep the camera". He convinced Bob Morgan to let him accompany the crew on missions, and he ended up flying five missions with the Belle.

Wyler played down the significance of the Belle in the film. The narrator says in a dramatic monotone that the film is about "just one mission of just one plane and one crew in one squadron in one group of one wing of one Air Force out of fifteen United States Army Air Forces." Still, he must have known that by choosing this plane and its men, he would be catapulting them into national fame back home.

By the time he was done, Wyler and his cameras had taken nearly twenty thousand feet of film footage. On the Belle, he used hand held 16mm and 35mm cameras to give the perspective of the crew.

The Memphis Belle and Hell's Angels each continued to eke out one agonizing mission after another. There were few milk runs. Most missions resulted in the loss of close friends. The men began to find themselves becoming defensively numb to the terrible losses and carnage. "We'd mention it, and then change the subject," remembers Morgan.

The men of the 303rd, including those of Hell's Angels, spent time trying to figure out ways to improve their odds. They were the first to install twin-.50's in the nose of the B-17 to ward off Luftwaffe frontal attacks, for example. "This pioneering and experimental spirit was about all that kept the morale of officers and men from taking a nose-dive," remembers 303rd pilot Harry Gobrecht. "At the base, men were trying to ignore the growing number of empty bunks in the Nissen huts. Airplanes were wearing tin-can patches over ragged holes and flying on parts that made crew chiefs prematurely gray. The 303ʳᵈ was at low ebb."[8]

Trips to London helped. There was a shortage of young men, and a man in an Eighth Air Force uniform attracted plenty of female attention. Some of the men drank to forget what they had seen. Morgan found himself on several occasions partying with Clark Gable, who spent time as a B-17 waist gunner while shooting another war film.

"The Memphis Belle kept flying and coming back," writes Morgan. A few other crews were also edging their way toward twenty-five. "We tried not to know who they were. We tried not to keep count, to keep score. We tried not to think about it."[9]

As the time grew short, it became a logistical nightmare to figure out how everyone on the plane, and the Belle herself, could finish twenty-five at the same time and on the same mission. It soon became apparent that this would be impossible. On some missions, the Belle was being repaired and the men flew another plane. Then there were the usual comings and goings typical of any flight crew. The crew of both the Belle and Hell's Angels had turned over in a number of the positions. Men had come on board for as little as one mission, others had flown more and left, and others were new. This confusion led to additional problems later when proponents for the Belle or Hell's Angels made their arguments about who 'really' flew twenty-five missions first.

Wyler may have chosen the Memphis Belle as the star of his show, but he was a smart man and hedged his bets. He knew the odds were against any ship finishing twenty-five, and so unbeknownst to Morgan and his crew, he put a backup film crew aboard Hell's Angels, assigned to take the same footage, just in case the Belle—and Wyler himself—were to go down before the magic twenty-five.

On May 13, 1943, Captain Irl Baldwin took Hell's Angels up for its twenty-fifth mission, a run to Meaulite. The same day, the Memphis Belle flew a mission, its twenty-first. When the wheels of Hell's Angels touched the tarmac back in England, she became the first plane to complete the magic twenty-five. However, in the absence of film crews and journalists, the event, though celebrated by the men of the 303rd, was little remarked upon elsewhere. This suited Captain Irl Baldwin fine. He was just happy to be done and alive. As the crew celebrated, the ground crew made the aircraft ready to fly again. Unlike the Belle, Hell's Angels would continue to fly missions for the aircraft-poor 303rd. In fact, she would go up the very next day, May 14, to bomb Kiel, and the day after as well.

The Memphis Belle flew its twenty-fifth mission on May 19, 1943, to Kiel. Bob Morgan had already completed his twenty-five, but the plane and some of the crew needed the mission to reach twenty-five. The Belle's pilot that day was Lt. C.L. Anderson. It was a day of celebration for the men of the Memphis Belle. They had done it. They could now go home.

Bob Morgan showed his ability to think from a promotional angle after the mission. A non-smoker, he put a Camel cigarette in his mouth for the cameras. "I was getting pretty good at this media business," he writes. "I'd studied those full-page ads in *Life* and the *Saturday Evening Post*—the ones that showed famous ballplayers and movie stars smoking Camels. I figured if Wyler's camera caught me smoking . . . I just might get in on some of that endorsement money". For his efforts, the non-smoking Morgan almost lost his lunch after the first puff, and never got the endorsement.[10]

The crew and plane were instant media stars. They were visited by the King and Queen of England. Morgan had a date with Olivia de Havilland. This was just a hint of what was to come when they returned to the States.

William Wyler had his footage and his story. He had survived five missions with the Belle crew and earned their respect for his courage under fire. He now returned to Hollywood to put together his film. His goal was to show the goings-on of a typical bombing mission over Europe, from start to finish. Though he had footage from five missions, plus the additional footage shot by men to whom he had given free cameras, he decided to present the footage as if it all happened on just one mission. To make it more dramatic, he decided that the mission must be the Belle's twenty-fifth. In the finished cut, it appears that the Belle's twenty-fifth mission is a tough one. In actuality, the Belle's twenty-fifth was a milk run with no casualties and no difficult landing. He staged the shots of the men running from the plane after the mission. The voice-overs during combat were done back in Hollywood after the war, because all the footage Wyler shot was silent.

From October to March 1944, Wyler edited the 20,000 feet of film down to a 45-minute color film. He added voice-over narration to tell the story of the 10 crewmen as examples of simple average American boys doing a tough job.[11]

The film was a huge success in the States, and is still considered one of the best documentaries to come out of World War II. The film, and the highly publicized victory tour of the Memphis Belle crew, vaulted the ordinary men into extraordinary heroes. Morgan returned to find himself a celebrity. The crew toured over thirty cities around the States. During the tour, Morgan and crew had the opportunity to meet Wilbur Wright, who less than fifty years before had taken that first shaky flight at Kitty Hawk.

Sadly, this Victory Tour proved the undoing of a romance that had survived all the hardships that the war had thrown at the Belle. Robert Morgan proposed to Margaret Polk, the Memphis Belle herself, shortly after the return to the States. "As Margaret and I made plans for a hasty, blissful wedding, we were brought up short—not by parents, not be second thoughts, but by the War Department . . . in the person of a public relations officer assigned to our tour." The marriage, explained the officer, would have to wait until after the victory tour, at least several months. It would add 'human interest' to the tour.[12]

Though Morgan tried to get her to elope while on the tour, Polk refused to do so. And finally, after hearing loud female voices in the background over the telephone from one of Morgan's tour parties, the relationship was terminated.

Offered a variety of positions by the brass after the victory tour, Morgan instead chose a second combat tour as a B-29 pilot in the Pacific. "I couldn't see myself behind a desk or training pilots," he says. Taken with the new B-29 Superfortress, which he had seen while on the victory tour, he asked to be assigned to one. In 1944 he took command of the Twentieth Air Force's 869th Bombardment Squadron, where he led the first B-29 raid over Tokyo on November 24, 1944. After cheating fate a second time and completing twenty-five missions in the Pacific, he retired from active duty in 1945. However, he has been known the world over ever since as the pilot of the Memphis Belle, and is still in demand as a speaker and signer of autographs. His crusades now are to find the sunken wreck of his B-29, Dauntless Dotty, and animal rights.

As for Hell's Angels, after completing 47 missions over Europe, she too returned to the States. Her original crew had long departed, however. All her original crewmen, with the exception of the only surviving Hell's Angels crewman, Navigator Harold Fulgum, completed their twenty-five missions. Fulgum, who only flew one mission with the Hell's Angels, was shot down with another crew and became a POW on his third combat mission. His replacement, 1st Lt. Parley Madsen, flew twenty missions with the Hell's Angels crew and two with other crews, and was shot down May 29, 1943 and became a POW. Therefore, the Hell's Angels crew can not make the claim of being the first crew of which all members completed twenty-five missions.

The Memphis Belle also had many different crewmen. According to 303rd Historian Harry Gobrecht, those who flew with Captain Morgan included ten copilots, three navigators, two bombardiers, five flight engineers, three radio operators, four waist gunners, four ball turret gunners and four tail gunners. Morgan's copilot, James Verinis, flew five missions with the Belle, and actually became the first 8th Air Force pilot to complete twenty-five missions. The first enlisted crewman to fly twenty-five missions was Sgt. M. Roscovisch from the 306th Bomb Group, on April 6, 1943. In all, forty-four different crewmembers flew the Memphis Belle to her twenty-five mission total: four pilots, eleven copilots, four navigators, two bombardiers, six engineers, four radio operators, six waist gunners, four ball turret gunners and four tail gunners.

Of course, this was an entirely normal occurrence at the time. Crews were far from static. Men were asked to fill in on account of illness or injury, men were occasionally in the brig for a mission or two, and there were many other reasons why crews were fluid.

In fact, there are so many variables in deciding what is a 'crew', and what constituted 'twenty-five' that the argument will never be completely solved. Morgan points out that some members of the Hell's Angels crew had not finished twenty-five missions while all on the Belle had. In an e-mail he sent to me, Bob Morgan writes "we were the first crew to complete twenty-five missions for each man—some of the Hell's Angels crew had not completed 25 missions even though the plane had."[13] Gobrecht admits that the word 'crew' has never even been fully defined, and he concedes that Hell's Angels never claimed to be the first plane on which all crewmen had completed twenty-five. Still, he counters with a question of his own. Who was the real Bob Morgan crew? "Is it the *original* Bob Morgan crew, crewmen who *flew* with Bob Morgan with the Memphis Belle, or the crew that flew the Memphis Belle back to the States? In my opinion, this question has no legitimate answer that can be verified."[14]

Gobrecht is also bothered by the fact that "there have been many publications that have repeated the claims that the Memphis Belle was the first in the 8th Air Force to complete twenty-five missions . . . The United States Air Force Museum at Wright Patterson Air Force Base in Ohio continues to persist in its claim that the Memphis Belle was the first B-17 to fly twenty-five missions in their Memphis Belle exhibit."[15]

This frustrates Harry Gobrecht. As a proud member of the 303rd Bomb Group, he strives to uphold the honor of his group's most famous ship. As a historian, he chafes at the historical inaccuracy. "In May, 2001, I had several long visits and dinners with Bob Morgan and his wife Linda at the 8th Air Force Historical Museum in Savannah", he wrote me. "I purchased a copy of Bob Morgan's book *The Man Who Flew the Memphis Belle*. He autographed it for me as follows: 'To Harry, My good friend of the

303rd Bomb Group—a great outfit with Hell's Angels, the first B-17 to finish 25 missions'".[16]

Colonel Morgan lives in North Carolina today, and is still active in writing and traveling. In his eighties, he still holds an active pilot's license and works full-time in the real estate business and makes personal appearances around the world. "Yes, I knew about Hell's Angels," he wrote me in 2004. "I don't feel she got overshadowed by the Belle. We were the first crew to complete twenty-five missions for each man. Some of the Hell's Angels crew had not completed twenty-five missions even though the plane had. I have met some of her crew and still stay in touch with them".[17]

The decision to spotlight the Belle, he adds, was made by High Command. And while some of the 303rd people were disappointed over the Belle's publicity and the lack of publicity over Hell's Angels, "it was the decision of the War Department to chose the Belle over Hell's Angels," he wrote me. Captain Morgan and his men were simply the men who went along with the PR campaign.

An email correspondence between Harry Gobrecht and Bob Morgan's wife Linda resulted in a mutual agreement. "We did reach a concession with them (The 303rd) where we say 'Memphis Belle, 1st to complete 25 combat missions and return to the U.S'," adds Morgan.[18] True to his word, Morgan's website and business card now identify the Memphis Belle as "the first Eight Air Force WWII Bomber to complete 25 missions and return to the United States."

The site also says in the biography of the Belle: "On 17 May 43 the B-17 Memphis Belle and her crew made military history as the first WWII bomber to complete 25 combat missions & return to the United States. They flew the Belle home in June 1943 and for three months flew her to 32 American cities to thank the American people for supporting the war effort."

In the end, the old warriors seem more inclined to compromise and share the distinction, realizing that in the chaotic world of early 1943, with shifting crew assignments, shifting planes, and enterprising brass and Hollywood producers, there are many ways to define 'first'. A photo Gobrecht sent me shows him with Bob Morgan, arms around each other, two men who together bravely served their nation in the skies over Europe at a time when most men never returned. And Harry Gobrecht, while willing to defend the honor of Hell's Angels as the first to finish to the end, has mellowed enough to write "I believe that the entire 8th Air Force family can be very proud of the Memphis Belle and Captain Bob Morgan for what they accomplished. Bob Morgan has been a wonderful ambassador for the furtherance of the heritage of the 8th Air Force." Still, he ends with a lament for his friend Irl Baldwin, who never got the credit Gobrecht feels he deserved in life. "Irl Baldwin also had a proud record during his lifetime. He was a very modest and laid-back type of individual and didn't enjoy the limelight as much as Bob Morgan."

Perhaps, then, it all worked out for the best.

As for the Belle herself, in 1945 an enterprising reporter found her in an aircraft boneyard in Altus, OK. He wrote a story and contacted the Mayor of Memphis. The City bought her for $350 and on July 17, 1946, she was flown home to Memphis.

In 1950 the Belle was placed on a pedestal near the Army National Guard. Unfortunately, the plane was not protected from vandals and souvenir-seekers and was allowed to deteriorate outdoors. In November 1977, she was moved to the Air National Guard area at the Memphis airport. Some concerned citizens attempted to raise funds to restore the Belle to her former glory but it took a last ditch effort by a local businessman to save her. The city of Memphis donated a piece on land on Mud Island where the historic bomber could be displayed. Federal Express and Boeing each donated $100,000 toward restoration and the City donated $150,000. An appeal by Hugh Downs of TV's 20/20 resulted in $576,000 in donations from around America.

On May 17, 1987, roughly 44 years after she flew her 25th mission, the Memphis Belle Pavilion was dedicated. With twenty-five thousand in attendance, a formation of seven B-17's, the largest formation since World War II, flew overhead in salute and "bombed" the pavilion with thousands of rose pedals. Margaret Polk and the Belle crew looked on as the crowd cheered. The Air Force declared the Belle a national historic treasure.[19]

Sadly, due to a lack of funding and non-support by the city of Memphis, the Belle has been allowed to further deteriorate in the past few years. She is now located at the Jim Weber Restoration Center near the Millington Municipal Airport in suburban Memphis. The Memphis Belle Association plans to restore her as time and money permit.[20]

And what of the fate of Hell's Angels, the first B-17 to complete 25 missions out of England? After completing 48 missions on November 26, 1943, she retired. On January 7, 1944, the 303rd Bomb Group honored her by adopting the name "Hell's Angels" as the Group's official name. On January 20, Hell's Angels departed Molesworth for the last time with hundreds of names scrawled in white paint all over her fuselage. Before the plane left for the States, she was visited by the actor Ben Lyon, one of the stars of the 1930 movie that inspired the crew to name their B-17 "Hell's Angels". Twelve crewmen made the flight to the United States with Captain John M. Johnson as pilot. Six members of the ground crew were also aboard. Gobrecht adds proudly that "this was the first Eighth Air Force ground crew, and to my knowledge the only ground crew, to return to the U.S. together and make a tour of the U.S."[21] After arriving at Tinker Field, Oklahoma City, Oklahoma on January 29, the plane was reunited with its old pilot, Irl Baldwin, and the plane and crew embarked on an industrial morale tour of the United States covering 18 cities. The tour ended on May 19 at March Field, Riverside, California. The plane was transferred to the USAAF Training Command where she was used to train many crews until the end of the war. On August 7, after the Japanese surrender, Hell's Angels was transferred to Searcy Field, Oklahoma, and the first plane to fly twenty-five missions out of England met the same end as all but a handful of its siblings—it was scrapped.

Compare the Numbers:

COMBAT MISSIONS FLOWN BY 303rd Bombardment Group (H) *Hell's Angels* & Captain Irl Baldwin and 91st Bombardment Group (H) *Memphis Belle* & Captain Robert K. Morgan

MISSION DATE	TARGET	303rd BG MISS#	HELL'S ANGELS MISS#	CAPT BALDWIN MISS#	91st BG MISS#	MEMPHIS BELLE MISS#	CAPT MORGAN MISS#
07-Nov-42	Brest	—	—	—	01	01	01
09-Nov-42	St. Nazaire	—	—	—	02	02	02
17-Nov-42	St. Nazaire	01	01 BR(1)	01 BR(1)	03	03	03
18-Nov-42	St. Nazaire	02	—	—	04	—	—
22-Nov-42	Lorient	03	02 BR(2)	02 BR(2)	05	—	—
23-Nov-42	St. Nazaire	04	—	—	06	MA	MA
06-Dec-42	Lille	05	03	03	07	04	04
12-Dec-42	Rouen	06	RP(3)	—	08	—	—
20-Dec-42	Romilly	07	—	—	09	05	05
30-Dec-42	Lorient	08	FTO(4)	FTO(4)	10	06[B]	—
03-Jan-43	St. Nazaire	09	04	04	11	07	06
13-Jan-43	Lille	10	05	05	12	08	07
23-Jan-43	Lorient/Brest	11	06	06	13	09	08
27-Jan-43	Wilhelmshaven	12	07	07	14	RP	—
02-Feb-43	Emden (Hamm)	13 GA(5)	GA(5)	GA(5)	15(5)	RP	
04-Feb-43	Emden(Hamm) (U)	14	08	08	16	—	09[X]
14-Feb-43	Hamm	15 RE BR(6)	09 RE BR(6)	09 RE BR(6)	17 RE(6)	10 BR	10 BR
16-Feb-43	St. Nazaire	16	10	10	18	11	11
26-Feb-43	Wilhelmshaven	17	11 [A]	—	19	—	12 [X]
27-Feb-43	Brest	18	12 [A]	—	20	—	13 [X]
04-Mar-43	Rotterdam	19	13	11	21	MA	MA
06-Mar-43	Lorient	20	14	12	22	12	14
08-Mar-43	Rennes	21	15	13	23	MA [C]	—
12-Mar-43	Rouen	22	16	14	24	13	15
13-Mar-43	Amiens	23	17	15	25	14	16
17-Mar-43	Rouen	RE BR(7)	RE BR(7)	RE BR(7)	RE BR(7)	—	—
18-Mar-43	Vegesack	24	18	16	26	—	—
22-Mar-43	Wilhelmshaven	25	19	17	27	15	17
28-Mar-43	Rouen	26	20	18	28	16	18
31-Mar-43	Rotterdam	27	21	19	29	17[D] BR(8)	—
04-Apr-43	Paris (Billancourt)	28	22	20	30	MA	—
05-Apr-43	Antwerp	29	23	21	31	RP	19 [Y]
16-Apr-43	Lorient	30	—	—	32	18	20
17-Apr-43	Bremen	31	—	22 [B]	33	19	21
01-May-43	St. Nazaire	32	—	—	34	20	22
04-May-43	Antwerp	33	24	23	35	—	23 [Z]
13-May-43	Meaulite	34	25	24	36	21 [E]	—
14-May-43	Kiel	35	26	25	37	22 [F]	—

15-May-43	Heligoland	36	27	—	38	23	24
17-May-43	Lorient	37	28	—	39	24	25
19-May-43	Kiel	38	—	—	40	25 [E]	—
21-May-43	Wilhelmshaven	39	—	—	41	—	—
29-May-43	St. Nazaire	40	—	—	42	—	—

FOOTNOTES

[A] *Hell's Angels* Pilot—lst Lt. James H. McDonald on 26 Feb & 27 Feb 43—Captain Baldwin on leave

[B] *Memphis Belle* Pilot—Lt James Vernis (Morgan Crew CoPilot) on 30 Dec 42—Capt Morgan was sick

[C] *Memphis Belle* Pilot—Capt E.D. Gaitly, CoPilot & Col Stanley Wray on 08 Mar 43

[D] *Memphis Belle* Pilot—Capt H.W. Aycock on 31 Mar 43

[E] *Memphis Belle* Pilot—Lt C.L. Anderson on 13 May—Capt Morgan in London & 19 May 43—Capt Morgan had completed his combat tour

[F] *Memphis Belle* Pilot—Lt J.H. Miller on 14 May 43—Capt Morgan in London

[W] Captain Baldwin flew in #41-29644 *Jersey Bounce, Jr.* 358th BS (VK-C) on 17 Apr 43

[X] Captain Morgan flew in #41-24515 *Jersey Bounce* 324th BS (DF-H) on 04 Feb, 26 Feb & 27 Feb 43

[Y] Captain Morgan flew in #41-24480 *The Bad Penny* 324th BS (DF-C/B) on 05 Apr 43

[Z] Captain Morgan flew in #41-24527 *The Great Speckled Bird* 324th BS (DF-Y) on 04 May 43

FTO—Failed to take off due to mechanical problems

RE—Division recall due to bad weather

GA—Group aborted mission due to bad weather

RP—B-17 stood down while under repair

MA—Mechanical abort after takeoff before target reached

BR—Bombs returned to base

U—Exact target unknown—Group Navigator believed that six 303BG B-17s bombed Groningen

(1) Group unable to locate target—Credited mission

(2)	Bomb rack malfunction over target—Credited mission
(3)	Bomb release intervelometer test requested
(4)	#3 Engine failed to start
(5)	Recall 30-40 miles off Dutch coast. Non credited crew sortie
(6)	Recall between coast & Dokkum Holland—Credited mission
(7)	Recall between beacon 8 & 10—Non credited mission
(8)	Weather obscured target—Credited mission

Chart compiled by Harry D. Gobrecht, Lt. Col., USAF (Retired)[22]

Notes

[1]   Robert Morgan, with Ron Powers, *The Man Who Flew the Memphis Belle*. New York: New American Library, 2001, page 132.

[2]   Roger Freeman, *The Mighty Eighth*. London, Cassell & Company, 2000 Revised Edition, page 47.

[3]   Freeman, *The Mighty Eighth*, page 74.

[4]   Menno Duerkson, *The Memphis Belle-Home at Last*. Memphis: Castle Books, 1987, pages 234-235.

[5]   Morgan, Man Who Flew Memphis Belle, p. 172.

[6]   Morgan, p. 173.

[7]   Morgan, 173.

[8]   William A. Feeny, editor, "And the Angels Struck", from *The First 300— Hell's Angels*, January 1945.

[9]   Morgan, 185

[10] Morgan, 207.

[11] http://history.sandiego.edu/gen/filmnotes/memphisbelle.html

[12] Morgan, 225

[13] Col. Robert Morgan, Author interview, January 3, 2004.

[14] Harry Gobrecht, Letter to author, January 13, 2004.

[15] Harry Gobrecht, Letter to author, January 13, 2004.

[16] Gobrecht, Letter, Jan. 13, 2004.

[17] Col. Robert Morgan, Author interview, Jan. 3, 2004.

[18] Col. Robert Morgan, Author interview, Jan. 4, 2004.

[19] Memphis Bell Website, largely written by Robert Morgan's wife, is summarized in the previous two paragraphs.

[20] Harry Gobrecht, Author email, January 31, 2004.

[21] Gobrecht, Author email, January 31, 2004.

[22] Chart can be found at the Hell's Angels website < http://www.303rdbga.com/h-ha-mb.html> Used with the permission of Harry Gobrecht.

Chapter Four

The Star of David over the Swastika:

Jews over the Reich in World War II

F light crews in the Army Air Corps had the highest casualty
rate of any branch of the armed forces in World War II.
Casualty figures for the Eighth Air Force alone were staggering. Of
the 210,000 air crewman who flew out of England, 26,000 were
killed. This is fatality rate of 12.38 percent. An additional 21,000
Eighth Air Force airmen ended up as Prisoners of War in Germany
or Nazi-occupied Europe. Of those who flew the original twenty-
five-mission bomber tour in 1942-1943, just 35 percent survived.
The Eighth also lost over 6,500 B-17 and B-24 heavy bombers
and over 3,300 fighters.[1] Figures for the Fifteenth, the other main
Air Force charged with bombing Europe, were little better.

In the early months of the air war, in 1943 and early 1944,
the chances of a crewman completing the obligatory twenty-five
missions were almost non-existent. Assuming a loss rate of four
percent per mission, no aircrews would survive to complete their
tours. Even at a loss rate of only two percent per mission, a man
had only a fifty-fifty chance of survival. Early in 1943, aircrews
over Europe were suffering losses of 8 percent per mission, "meaning,
on average, no one could expect to complete his thirteenth
mission".[2]

Why begin a chapter on Jewish airmen with these statistics? Every man who climbed into a heavy bomber and flew over Europe in World War II knew as the plane's wheels left the runway in England, North Africa, or Italy, that there was a very real chance that he would never live out the day. And if he did, he might do so only after bailing out of a mortally wounded aircraft, possibly wounded himself. If he survived the descent, and wasn't pitchforked by angry German civilians, he might have the 'luck' to be captured by the Luftwaffe and sent to one of its many Stalag Lufts to sit out the remainder of the war as a POW.

The Jewish airman had an additional worry. Every time he strapped on his parachute harness, he knew that in a few hours he would be flying over land controlled by an enemy who thought of him as a sub-human 'untermensch'. He also knew that the enemy was sending millions of Jews to concentration camps across Europe. Though few airmen knew the truth about Hitler's death camps or 'The Final Solution', they knew from relatives in the old country that pogroms and deportations of entire Jewish populations had been going on for years. And in missions where he flew over Germany itself, the Jewish airman knew that he was an enemy to almost every person on the ground, civilian or military. What was worse, death in the air or death on the ground? It took incredible bravery for these Jewish airmen to fly, day after day, mission after mission, knowing full well that the chances of survival were near nil, and that the chances of a fate worse than death after capture were great.

This chapter will deal primarily, but not exclusively, with the lives of four Jewish airmen who flew over one hundred and fifty combined combat missions over Nazi-occupied Europe. Three of these men flew in the early months of U.S. air combat in Europe, Leonard Herman and Gus Mencow, and Robert Rosenthal. Bombardier Leonard Herman was part of the original 95th Bomb Group, and flew his first mission of May 13, 1943, finishing November 3, 1943. Navigator Gus Mencow was part of the original 390th Bomb Group, assigned in late March of 1943, and flew his missions between late-July of 1943 and mid-February of 1944.

Pilot Rosenthal flew his missions in late 1943 and 1944 with the 100th Bomb Group. All three men survived tours of duty when the chances of survival were slim. Leonard returned to the States a decorated war hero, sold bonds, and ended up returning to Europe and flying a second combat tour. Gus was promoted to group and later wing navigator. Robert Rosenthal, also known as Rosie, became a legend in the Eighth Air Force and in air war history in general.

The fourth Jewish airman, Jerome Jacobson, flew later in the war, as a bombardier with the 15th Air Force out of Foggia, Italy. Though by this time the P-51 Mustang was providing fighter escort all the way to the target, many of the Fifteenth's targets, such as Vienna and the oil refineries of Eastern Europe, were heavily flak-defended. By the time of Jerome's experience, flight crews were flying 35 rather than 25 missions. The odds were better, but they were still frightening.

Like most World War II veterans, these four men are masters of understatement. None feels that what he did is anything out of the ordinary, and none feels that his experience warrants retelling. After the war, all returned to their normal lives. Two became successful businessmen, one became a lawyer, and one became a doctor. Now in their eighties, one could easily pass any of them on the street without the slightest inkling that these are men whose courage is beyond anything most Americans will ever know.

"Leonard Herman," wrote his former Operations Officer in a book published after the war, "was the most visibly fearful of any crewman within the limits of my memory. I think being Jewish added to his fears, because I believe that fear of Nazi torture was much worse than death itself should he have to bail out over Germany and be captured. But Leonard never missed a briefing, and he never missed a tough assignment. In spite of his apparent and visible fear, Leonard truly had the courage that makes men great . . . He overcame fear to serve his country well."[3]

Leonard is a diminutive man, a few inches over five feet tall. The photos taken of him during his nationwide War Bond Tour in late 1943 show a young man who looks rather like Alfalfa from the old "Little Rascals" comedies. However, Leonard's Air Corps uniform is covered with an array of medals, including the Air Medal, Three Oak Leaf Clusters, a Purple Heart, and a Distinguished Flying Cross. These days, Leonard faces all of life's challenges with a sense of humor. He dealt with his fears during the war with humor as well. "The joke going around at barracks at the time was 'What is the fastest thing in Berlin?'", he remembers, "and the answer was 'Leonard Herman on a bicycle after he gets shot down'". Leonard's sense of humor sparkles through in any conversation, and was a key to his survival as a Jewish airmen during the war. On one mission, he shot down an attacking German fighter as everyone on the plane screamed for him to hit it. After the mission, and at reunions years later, every time Group Commander Dave McKnight ran into him, he thanked Leonard for saving his life. "What are you talking about?" Leonard would invariably tell McKnight. "I wasn't saving your life. I was too busy saving *mine*!"[4]

The mission that sticks out in Leonard Herman's memory is the mission to the submarine yards at Kiel, Germany on June 13, 1943. It was his sixth mission, six hours and twenty minutes long, and came only two days after a six-and-a-half-hour mission to Wilhelmshaven. "We had seven B-17's from our squadron on that mission," says Leonard. "Only two came back. And on the very next mission, the other plane went down. That left just us."[5] Seven planes down on the Kiel mission meant seventy men, including the first US General to become a combat casualty in Europe, Gen. Nathan Bedford Forrest.

For Gus Mencow, there were also many terrifying missions. Greatest of them all, perhaps, was the legendary mission to Munster on October 10, 1943. According to General Thomas Jeffrey, the Deputy Group Commander of the 390th at the time of the Munster mission, "this mission was one of the toughest, if not the toughest flown from England by the Eighth Air Force during World War II. It certainly was from the point of view of the thirty crews (300 men) that went down."[6] Gus also flew on the infamous "Black Thursday" Schweinfurt mission of October 14,1943. On this mission, commonly accepted as the most savage air battle ever fought, almost six hundred airmen went missing in action, some killed and some POW. Sixty of the 228 B-17's attacking that day were lost.

Gus Mencow agrees that humor was important to any air crewman. "Humor was a defense mechanism," Gus told me. Even on the hairiest missions, there were moments of great levity that broke the tension of the men on board. There had to be, the odds against survival were so minuscule. Though Gus's famous plane, 'Betty Boop Pistol Packin' Mama' was not shot down during Gus's tour, one of his waist gunners was killed during an air battle. After Gus's tour ended, the reliable old 'Betty Boop' herself went down, killing most of the crew and leaving the rest POW.

Despite his knowledge that to be captured a Jew in Nazi-occupied Europe would be a terrible thing, Gus refused to hammer out the "H" signifying that he was a Hebrew that had been imprinted on his dog tags. "I was raised to be proud of being a Jew," he says. He was willing to take the risk and acknowledge his faith.

Perhaps the most famous Jewish airman who flew the heavy bombers over Europe in World War II is Robert Rosenthal. Pilot of the B-17 "Rosie's Riveters", Rosenthal flew with the famous "Bloody Hundredth" bomb group, piloting the 100th's only B-17 to survive the infamous Munster mission. According to 100th Bomb Group navigator Harry Crosby, "Robert Rosenthal seemed to have a charmed life. He flew his first mission on October 8, 1943, where he saw eight planes go down. Two days later he saw the entire group go down (on the Munster Mission). His was the only plane that returned from Munster."[7]

"He finished his tour, during his first twenty-five missions moving his way from the wing up to flight leader, and then to low squadron lead. At the end of his tour, most of his crew went home, but he stayed on, first as squadron operations officer. He started his second tour. He volunteered especially for the tough ones. Eventually, he became squadron commander of the 418th."

"What made him fly? The story is that his family was a part of Hitler's Holocaust. His grandparents killed on Crystal Night. I never knew for sure, and I didn't ask."[8]

Rosenthal got shot down on a mission to Nuremberg, though he managed to nurse the plane to a crash-landing in Belgium. He then evaded capture and returned to Thorpe Abbotts three weeks later. He was then made Squadron Commander. Three weeks later he was shot down again and was returned to US troops by the French resistance, making his way back to Thorpe Abbotts yet again.

On Rosenthal's 52nd mission he was shot down a third time while leading the entire task force over Berlin. On March 1, Crosby got a phone call from Russia. It was Rosenthal. He had gone down and been captured by Russian troops, who sent him to Moscow. After dining with U.S. Ambassador Averill Harriman, he returned yet again to the 100th to lead his squadron.

After the war, Rosenthal served at the Nuremberg War Crimes Trial and went on to a long career as a successful lawyer. Rosenthal wrote to me in 2001 after I contacted him for his story for this chapter, saying "I have received more than my share of recognition. There are so many aviators who served in the Air Corps who have been overlooked and whose stories deserve to be told. I would urge you to contact Dr. Jerome Jacobson, who was an early lead navigator in the Fifteenth Air Force. He was very young when he entered the Air Corps and was promoted quickly because of his ability."[9]

I contacted Dr. Jacobson by mail and, after modestly insisting he had nothing really exciting to share, he agreed to be a subject for this chapter.

A number of missions stick in Jerome Jacobson's mind. Perhaps first and foremost is the one he wasn't on. On Feb. 24, 1944 he went on an R&R to Egypt and Palestine for 10 days. The very next day his crew—with his assistant squadron bombardier flying in his place—was shot down over Linz, Austria. Fortunately they all bailed out safely and became POWs. On another mission, flak exploded in the nose section, shattering a glass map case over his head and showering him with wood splinters from the navigator's table. The plane returned perforated by over a hundred flak holes. Like the other two men, he watched planes filled with his comrades explode in mid-air, leaving nothing more than an oily smudge and tiny scraps of metal. He prayed as flaming planes hurtled earthward, urging the men inside to hurry and jump.[10]

Did the Jewish airmen feel they were on a special mission to rid the world of a society devoted to their destruction? Though most had only vague ideas of the Holocaust going on below them, many still knew that they were, in effect, fighting for their own people as well. Leonard Herman remembers being approached by his commander before one mission. "He said he realized that the mission fell on a Jewish High Holy Day," remembers Leonard, "And he asked me if I wanted to fly. I didn't even hesitate. It was Yom Kippur. I said, 'the best thing I could do right now for my people is to go and bomb the hell out of those bastards', and that's exactly what I did."

Leonard told his folks back in Philadelphia of his decision, and his father stood up in the synagogue the following week and told the story to the congregation. "Because of that, the temple had a huge number of donations," remembers Leonard. "About the most they'd ever had."[11]

Many Jewish airmen flew over Nazi-occupied Europe in World War II. A significant number were killed, though many beat the odds. And hundreds, possibly thousands, did fall into the hands of the Germans or their Axis partners. The next chapter deals with the Jewish airmen who became Prisoners of War in the Third Reich. Leonard Herman, Gus Mencow, Robert Rosenthal, and Jerome Jacobson may have been four of the lucky ones, but their courage and willingness to put their lives and their faith on the line against Adolph Hitler is the stuff of legend.

Notes

[1]   Astor, Gerald. *The Mighty Eighth*, Dell, 1997, p. 486.

[2]   Boyne, Walter J., *Clash of Wings*, Touchstone, 1994, p. 306.

[3]   Hawkins, Ian (Editor), *B-17's Over Berlin*, Brassey's Books, page 250.

[4]   Herman, Leonard, Author Interview, July 7, 2003.

[5]   Herman, Author Interview, July 7, 2003.

6   Jeffrey, Thomas S., as quoted in Hawkins, Ian, *Munster: The Way it Was*, Robinson Typographics, Anaheim, CA, 1984, pageviii.

7   Harry Crosby, *A Wing and a Prayer*. New York: Harpercollins, 1993, page 171.

8   Crosby, p. 319.

9   Robert Rosenthal, Letter to Author, August 21, 2001.

10   Dr. Jerome Jacobson, Letter to Author. December 15, 2001.

11   Leonard Herman, Author interview, January 17, 2004.

Chapter Five

Jewish POWs: Prisoners of the 'Master Race'

E very Jewish airman had a dog tag around his neck that he knew could also be a one-way ticket to a concentration camp. Every tag listed the religious affiliation of its wearer—'RC' for Catholic, 'P' for Protestant, 'H' for Hebrew, or Jew. Jewish airmen knew that being captured wearing the 'H' could result in death. For this reason, some hammered out the 'H' on the tag. Others, as they dangled from their parachutes, ripped their tags off and cast them to the winds. Most, however, kept the 'H', and suffered the consequences.

There were tens of thousands of Jewish airmen flying over the Reich in World War II. An unknown number, certainly several thousand, were shot down and ended up as prisoners of war in German Stalag Lufts. As airmen, they were more fortunate than their ground-fighting counterparts. The Stalag Lufts were run by the Luftwaffe, under the direction of former World War I ace Herman Goering. The Luftwaffe was a professional military organization made up of career military men, not the quasi-military Nazi zealots so commonplace in the SS. Goering and the officers under him believed the romantic notion that all airmen belonged to a fraternity, similar to that of the medieval knights. Goering saw American airmen as competitors and adversaries, not as the 'luftgangsters'—or air gangsters—that most Germans believed British and American airmen to be. Treatment of airmen, whether

Christian or Jewish, was a cut above treatment of other POWs, in almost every instance. The Luftwaffe tried hard to round up American and British airmen after they parachuted to earth. In many cases, Luftwaffe troops saved them from the murderous rages of German civilians. Late in the war, Luftwaffe prison guards even used the American and British POWs as a kind of human shield, to protect against the fanatic SS as it attempted to round up troops for a final suicidal stand at Hitler's Bavarian redoubt.

Some Jewish airmen who ended up as POWs report that their experiences as guests of the Germans were nearly devoid of anti-Semitism or mistreatment. Mozart Kaufman, a fighter pilot who was shot down on his 74th mission (24 against the Japanese in the Aleutians and 50 against the Germans in France) says, "I was not treated in any way badly because I was a Jew." While in transit to the camps, Kaufman was approached on a train by a German civilian who asked him if he was Jewish. Kaufman, who is proud of his heritage, said that he was. The German "said 'okay' and walked away." The Luftwaffe, Kaufman thinks, took care of all airmen, regardless of background, because of the belief in the fraternity of airmen.[1] In fact, after the war, Kaufman became a good friend with Hans Scharff, his German interrogator at Dalag Luft.

However, there were instances where Jews were mistreated. In at least one case, the Jewish kriegies were isolated from the rest of the men, possibly for execution. In one camp, Stalag Luft I, Jews were relocated to a compound next to the ammunition dump where a stray bomb could have finished them off. However, in instances where the Germans did separate out the Jewish kriegies, non-Jewish POWs refused to stand idly by, instead making sure that the Germans realized that there would be hell to pay if anything happened to their fellow airmen.

The following is the story of Jewish airmen who became prisoners of war in Nazi Germany. Though the Third Reich was a system dedicated to the complete destruction of the Jewish race, almost all the Jewish aircrew POWs lived to tell the tale of their captivity.

Few Jewish airmen flying over Europe were aware of the specifics of the German death camps. The American government was fully aware of the camps' existence early in the war, and the information did make it into the papers. But by this time many of the young Jewish airmen were already in training or overseas. "We knew Jews were dying," says Gus Mencow, a Jewish navigator who was not shot down. "But we didn't know about the camps."

Today, Edwin Herzig lives in Monsey, New York. As a young man, he enlisted in the Army Air Corps. He ended up in the Fifteenth Air Force in the 98th Bomb Group, 415th Squadron, stationed at Lecce in the heel of the boot of Italy. "We were supposed to do fifty missions," he remembers. "After flying two or three times, I realized we would never do our fifty missions, because we didn't have fighter escort all the way to the target and we had some pretty rough targets, including the Ploesti oil fields . . . all the way up to air fields in Hungary."[2]

"At Lecce, I received a visit from G-2 (Intelligence) where they got together all the Jewish fellows in the bomb group and we were told by a colonel that if we were conscious and had to parachute out, to throw our dog tags away because the dog tags had an 'H' on it for 'Hebrew'. But, being twenty years old, I thought I was Jimmy Cagney. I thought I was the toughest thing there was, and not only did I ignore that message, but besides my dog tags, I carried in my wallet a little plastic mesuza. A mesuza is a scroll with the Ten Commandments on it, and usually they are on doorways of Jewish families."

Edwin flew twenty-six missions as an engineer/gunner on a plane named 'Sky Virgin', piloted by Phillip Ball. On the twenty-sixth mission, the aircraft was shot down over Castel Maggiore, about twenty kilometers north of Bologna, Italy. Of the ten men aboard Sky Virgin, eight were killed. The only survivors were Edwin and the ball turret gunner. "I was extremely fortunate," says Edwin, "not only to get out of the plane alive, but also by not being separated from the other POWs and taken away and shot. I know some people were. Originally I was also reported as killed. I had ten different wounds from flak and aircraft fire, plus severe burns as the plane had been on fire. It burned off one of my ears."

Still, he had the presence of mind to bail out of the dying aircraft. "When I jumped from the burning aircraft, I was semi-conscious. I woke up at the hospital. Sitting next to me was a man in a monk's robe, and I thought 'Sure enough, I'm in heaven'. But he was an Italian chaplain . . . He told me I was not in heaven, but in an Italian Catholic hospital somewhere between Ravenna and Bologna.

"The battle line at that time was at Anzio. The Germans were still fighting but their spirit was gone. The Chaplain told me that the Italian Blackshirts had found me, (and) they had gone through my belongings and found my mesuza. They didn't know what it was. They thought it was some kind of secret writing. They wanted to turn me over to the Gestapo to be shot as a spy. The Catholic chaplain intervened. He smuggled a card to the International Red Cross in Geneva registering me as a Prisoner of War."

When his wounds had healed enough for Edwin to be moved, he was taken by train to Stalag Luft IV in Poland, a non-com prison camp housing American fliers and a few British. "As far as Jewishness goes, I was taken off trains twice and beaten up by Germans. A lot of Jewish fellows were beat up this way," he remembers.

Bruce Bockstanz shared the nose of his B-17 with his good friend, Joel Bernstein, a Jew. "When we were shot down and taken prisoner in July of 1944, he was treated more severely than the rest of the crew. All of us were threatened and called 'terrorfliegers' and 'luftgangsters' by our civilian captors, but he was singled out for racial slurs. While waiting at the Frankfurt train station, a businessman approached and hit him with a briefcase." This experience, and Bernstein's further experiences in prison camp, left scars. "After he died, his wife told me of the nightmares and sleepless nights that bothered him for years after his return".[3]

Lt. Paul Canin's B-24 was shot down over Auschwitz in 1944. After his capture, he, like all new POWs, was sent to Wetzler for interrogation. "My first encounter with the interrogating Nazi

officer was intimidating. He wore a swastika armband, behind him
was a huge swastika flag. I suspect he was an American traitor who
left the U.S. to make his fortune by participating in the Third
Reich. He spoke with an American accent and used occasional
slang expressions." Canin gave him no information, but the
interrogator shocked Canin with his intimate knowledge of Canin's
background.

A few days later, Canin had a bizarre experience. He was led
from his cell and asked to join five high-ranking German officers
in uniform for dinner. There was a table of mouthwatering food
nearby, and the officers asked Canin to help himself.

"Perhaps I was the evening's diversion for a group of bored
officers," Canin thought to himself. "I instantly felt a responsibility
as a Jew not to reinforce any of their ideas of stereotyped Jewish
behavior . . . If they expected to witness a glutton attacking their
food they were going to be disappointed. I replied, "No, thanks.
I've sufficient food."

After he had been seated, one of the Nazi officers said, "You
must be curious why we brought you here. You see we seldom
find any Jews actually doing the fighting. They always manage to
get others to do that for them."

Canin said that in his experience, this was not the case. He'd
trained with many Jewish officers.

The officers then asked him if he had heard about the condition
of Jews in Germany. "We know they are treated horribly and are
placed in concentration camps," Canin replied.

"This is not true and your own propaganda," an officer replied.
"Do you know that eighty percent of all the lawyers in Berlin were
Jews, and sixty percent of the judges were Jews? Don't you think
we have a right to our own country?"

Canin stayed silent. They asked him if he knew any good jokes
about Hitler. Canin said he did, but he couldn't remember them
at the moment. "Seemed the safest response at the time," he wrote
later.

They then asked him about the new Mickey radar which he
had been operating when he was shot down. He proceeded to

make up an elaborate lie about how the men trained on this new device. Years later his son, a Navy pilot, told him this was the best way to avoid torture.[4]

Harvey Greenfield was a bombardier on a B-17 when he and other crewmembers had to bail out after losing a dogfight over Germany. He jumped from 18,000 feet, free-falling most of the three miles before pulling open his parachute. He was wearing dog tags with the Hebrew 'H' inscribed on them. "Since it was always the other guy who is going to get shot down and not me, I did keep mine on," he said. He was captured after hiding in a barn for a day.

"When I was interrogated by a young captain who had been a former employee of some rayon lining company in New York, seeing my dog tags, he said, 'You know we can make a lot of trouble for you.' At which point I said, 'I have been starved for three days, fought many hours before that trying to stay alive, jumped from 18,000 feet, and now you're going to make trouble for me?'"[5]

Mozart Kaufman was held in solitary for over a month. During this time, "I was a son of a bitch. I wouldn't tell them anything," he chuckles. After the war, when Kaufman met master interrogator Hans Scharff, now a fellow Southern Californian, Scharff admitted that there had only been three men out of whom he had gotten absolutely nothing of value. One of them was Mozart Kaufman.

Once in the hands of the Luftwaffe and in the Stalag Lufts, the Jewish airmen enjoyed the same rights and privileges as the other men, and there was no discrimination by the camp officials or by American officers in charge. "We had very little contact with the Germans," writes Harvey Greenfield. "They would just as soon shoot a Jew as a non-Jew who happened to poke their heads out of the windows during an air raid or who was late getting someplace." According to Greenfield, some of the Luftwaffe commandants actually protected their Jewish charges. He learned later that the camp commandant, a career soldier, had refused an order to send all the Jews from the camp. He said he will always remember the prison commander for this courage in refusing that order. Though

I was unable to corroborate this account, there are similar instances that make it believable.

Each camp had American officers in positions of direct leadership over the men. The Americans were answerable to the German camp command but were given free reign in the distribution of food and coal and in the daily administration of discipline. Many American officers did all they could to make the Germans' job as difficult as possible. They also stood up for their men—all their men—whether Gentile or Jew, Black or White.

One interesting story shows how the non-Jewish kriegies stood up for their friends in the camp. The scene occurred at Stalag Luft One. A room with forty men in it was threatened by a German officer and two armed guards. The officer ordered all Jewish POWs to step forward on the count of three. On the first order, none did, though two men were Jewish. On the second order, with the officer infuriated, the Jewish airman was about to step forward when all forty of the men in the room stepped forward.

Sy Hatton recounts how a German officer demanded that all the Jews in the barracks step forward. "We all stood at attention and he says, "I'm here for a specific purpose. I know there are some Jewish soldiers in the room and I'm going to count to three. I'd like them to take a step forward!"

The officer counted to three, and no one stepped forward. There was a deathly silence in the room. The officer got very angry, and stated that if nobody stepped forward on the second count, the German guards would be ordered to open fire.

As Hatton and the other Jew began to step forward, an amazing thing happened. "As soon as he starts to say "drei", I start to take a step forward, and . . . MY GOD! . . . I look around and there's forty men taking a step forward! All forty men are taking a step forward! All forty without an order!

"Now here's American Airmen from all over the country," Hatton recounts. "I never met any of them. Every one of them, at the count of three, took that step forward. You could say it was just American ingenuity!"

"This sergeant became livid! He started to curse again in German. His face turned purple. The veins were sticking out on both sides of his neck. I'm sure that he'd never come across anything like that before. The two privates put their guns back on their shoulders; each of them grabbed and arm and dragged him out of there. They just left and nobody ever bothered us again about being Jewish."

"I tell you, I really felt proud to be an American. If you planned something like that, we probably would have screwed it up!"[6]

After the assassination attempt on Hitler, life in the camps became more severe. At one point, according to the Stars and Stripes, Hitler gave an order that all American POWs were to be deprived of their boots and marched to their deaths. The American camp officers did not back down.

Stalag Luft I, located at Barth on the North Sea, had a peculiar incident in January of 1945, that has been well corroborated. Fighter pilot Mozart Kaufman recounts it this way. "A few days after Christmas, we were notified that all of the Jewish POWs in the entire camp would be moved out of their barracks and consolidated in one compound. On January 10 I left my friends behind and moved out of North No. Two Compound to No. One Compound, where I met new 'Kriegies', all Jewish. The Germans told us that Hitler had given the order that we were all to be annihilated. My attitude towards danger had always been to ignore what I couldn't control, and I hadn't given a damn about their threats before . . . None of the other men in the barracks carried on or seemed worried, either. Of course, later history told us of Hitler's grand plan—the annihilation of all the Jews in Europe. Our fate was only a small step for him".[7]

Paul Canin remembers that the segregation happened at about the same time as the Battle of the Bulge, and was the result of "an upsurge of optimism that they (the Germans) might win the war. Anti-Semitic pamphlets began appearing in our library . . . One night, guards went through the rooms in all the barracks, telling the Jewish officers that we should prepare to leave the following morning. This was ominous, with the possibility of our being sent to an extermination camp under SS control. My roommates with whom I had bonded over the past four months were as distressed as I was. One of two of them said they'd be sure to track down whatever would happen to me. A few gave me some of their personal rations."

"The following morning, all the known Jewish officers were placed in a separate compound. The Germans announced this was done in accordance with the Geneva Convention that required 'separate compounds for each nationality'. In other words, they were saying that we weren't Americans, we were Jews. Being isolated in a separate compound put us in a precarious position with a very uncertain fate."[8]

Joel Bernstein's friend Bruce Bockstanz writes "I believe the Germans were following orders from a higher authority but realized the war was all but lost and that they would be held personally accountable for anything they did to this group. Actually, the barracks where they were confined was one of the original in the camp and much better constructed than the rest of us had. Their treatment and food continued to be the same as the rest of us received."[9]

One non-Jewish POW remembers "the Jewish compound was kind of isolated from the rest of the camp and it was right next to the ammunition dump so that any misplaced bomb on a raid from the British or U.S. could result in their destruction. Fortunately that never happened."[10]

Aaron Kupstow remembers the day well. "One morning in early February, at roll call, they called out a bunch of our names and told us to remain after dismissal. After the others left, we were marched through the camp to another barracks and were told that this was our new home. I was in a room with thirteen others, and after talking for a few minutes, we realized that we were all Jewish. Checked the other rooms—the same thing. We then realized that this was a Jewish barracks. We were in a distant corner of the camp, had our own barbed wire, and were sort of isolated. Rumors started to spread that, during one night, we would probably be marched out and sent to death camps and no one would know. The decision was made to notify the Geneva Convention through our top American officers, Colonel Hubert Zemke and Lt. Colonel Francis Gabreski."

When Zemke and Gabreski found out about it, they were furious. The German commandant had issued a list of names of Jewish prisoners to Colonel Zemke, informing him at the same time that the Geneva Convention allowed the segregation of prisoners by race. Zemke sent a letter of protest to the Geneva Convention, which some men credit with saving the Jewish airmen. He also threatened the German camp leaders that any action taken against the Jewish airmen would be held against them as war crimes after the war. On one occasion, when Zemke heard a rumor that the Germans were considering moving the Jews out of the camp, he threatened the commandant with a general uprising.

Mozart Kaufman, who'd grown up in Vicksburg, Tennessee, received a cultural education as a result of the segregation. The hungry POWs in all camps talked and lusted over food far more than women. "Now that I was with Jewish men, I began to hear a new menu being discussed. In Vicksburg, I had not been exposed to the wonderful ethnic Jewish food that one found in New York. There were coffee cakes and sponge cakes, humentachen, honey cake and honey balls. Some of the foods I had never heard of—lox and cream cheese on bagels, marinated herring, pickled onions, pickled tomatoes, lauchen kugel, matzo ball soup."[11]

Another protector of the Jews, at least in one instance, was a Roman Catholic Chaplain by the name of TJB Lynch. Captured at Dunkirk, the Germans wanted to repatriate him, but Lynch insisted on staying. "He felt his mission would be with the men in the camps, and he stayed to the end," says Edwin Herzig. "He was about forty years old at the time, tall, balding, and a great man." Father Lynch worked tirelessly to attend to the spiritual and physical needs of the prisoners. One young American prisoner, Joseph Sellers, was nursed back from near-death by the daily visits of Father Lynch, and as a result of Lynch's example, became a Catholic priest after the war.

Lynch intervened when an order came down to put all the Jews into a barracks and burn them alive by torching it. According to Edwin Herzig, "Germans tried to put all us Jewish guys in one building and burn it down, but they were stopped by Father Lynch . . . when he intervened with the commander and told him that if he did anything to the Jews, he would go down as a war criminal. Father Lynch actually saved the day for us in January, 1945." This incident has been corroborated by Joseph Sellers to the author.[12]

The separation of Jewish prisoners did not happen just at Barth. Sidney Thomas became a POW at Stalag Luft VIIA at Moosburg, near Munich, in December of 1944. "As a Jew and an American prisoner of war in Stalag Luft VIIA . . . I encountered no overt discrimination for several months. However, early in 1945, an order came down from the camp administration segregating all Jewish prisoners and forbidding them to go to Munich on work details with the other prisoners. Whether this was meant as a first step in future measures against Jewish prisoners, we never learned. Fortunately, nothing further came of this order, and after some time, as I recall, we were able to take part, once again, in the regular routine of the camp. I would assume that this abortive attempt at special treatment of Jewish prisoners had its origin in a directive from higher Nazi authority and was not confined to Stalag Luft VIIA." In the end, Thomas contends, "the Jewish airmen were saved "by fears, certainly in the lower echelons, at a time when Germany was clearly losing the war, of future punishment as war criminals."[13]

It is impossible to say what might have happened to the Jewish airmen had the war gone more Hitler's way. Many Jewish airmen, and their Gentile counterparts, are certain that the Jews would eventually have been exterminated. That they survived is a result of a combination of factors. First, there was Goering's World War I Luftwaffe mentality that didn't distinguish Jews and Christian 'knights of the air'. Second, many of the camps were staffed with career military men who didn't share Hitler's fanatical ideas about the Master Race. Third, there was the aggressive intervention on the part of the American officers in the camps, such as Zemke, Gabreski, and Spicer. Fourth, there was the feeling among the German camp staff that the war was lost and that war crime trials would await if anything bad happened.

One has only to look at the tragic story of Berga to see that the American Jewish airmen were lucky. Stalag 9B, northeast of Frankfurt, was a German prison camp for Allied ground troops. The camp swelled during the winter of 1944-45 with American POWs from the Battle of the Bulge. As the Americans were processed, their SS interrogators noticed "a sizable number of Jewish-sounding names" and the Germans soon demanded to know which of the 4,000 American POWs were Jewish.

"In our country, we don't differentiate by religion—we are all Americans," stated Hans Karsten, the German-American POW designated as an intermediary. For his insolence, he was thrown down a flight of stairs. He returned to the men and told them that under no circumstances were they to reveal who was Jewish. At the lineup the next day, no one stepped forward when an SS officer requested Jews to do so. The Germans, enraged, decided to make the selection themselves, based on who had Jewish-sounding names or looked Jewish. They selected 350 men and separated them from their fellows. Among the men identified as Jews were men named Watkins, Acevedo, Young and Griffin. Of the 350 selected, only 80 were Jewish.

These 350 were then shipped to Berga, a satellite camp of Buchenwald in eastern Germany. The new prisoners arrived in February of 1945. Their job was to help dig 17 underground tunnels to make an armaments factory safe from Allied bombs. For the first time, a large group of American troops witnessed the Holocaust first-hand.

Two per mattress, four per bunk, the conditions the Berga prisoners faced were hellish. They never changed clothes. Lice crawled over everything. Food consisted of watery soup and one loaf of bread divided among twelve men. There was dysentery and typhoid, but no medical care. The POWs spent twelve hours a day digging underground alongside other Jewish slave laborers. The quartz ripped their lungs out in pieces when they coughed. Hans Karsten was singled out for even worse treatment. "The only thing worse than a Jew is a German traitor", one SS man told him.

During the time the 'Jewish' contingent was at Berga, 70 died. Those who survived would never be the same. "The bodies were all over the place," remembers one survivor. "They didn't bury them. There was death all over the damn place."

Another survivor, Gerald Daub, remembers that Berga was "what I imagined hell to be."

In April of 1945, the Germans force-marched the survivors, now no more than living skeletons, out of the path of advancing U.S. troops. As they marched, Daub saw a roadside lined with the corpses of inmates who had been shot by the Germans. They were finally liberated a few weeks later.

The Jewish airmen may have been more fortunate overall, but they still had to spend months or years in the hands of a nation that thought of them as subhuman, wondering whether they would survive should Hitler have another whim or should the tide of battle turn. Mozart Kaufman sums up his feelings as a former POW eloquently. "I realized (after the war) that the German people felt that they were innocent. When our men went into Barth (after liberation) and talked to the people, those Germans were shocked to learn that this terrible concentration camp had really existed right outside their small town. They claimed the German soldiers never told any of them what they were really doing there every day. What did the German people really think when hundreds of thousands of their fellow Germans, their neighbors, were rounded up and shipped away in trucks and freight cars, never to be heard from again?"

"They were told that they were a superior race of people, and they believed it."

"When they bombed Poland, they were told it was right, and they believed it."

"In 1940 when they bombed England and the innocent cities and towns, they were told that was right and they believed it."

"When the British and the Americans bombed their factories and cities years later, they said we were gangsters. They not only believed this but tried and actually did kill unarmed airmen who parachuted into their midst."

"How could such a 'civilized' people be so right?"[14]

Notes

[1] Mozart Kaufman, Author Interview, December 7, 2003.

[2] This and all future quotes from Edwin Herzig are the result of author interviews on September 25, 2001 and August, 2002.

[3] Bruce Bockstanz, Author email interview, June 30, 2002.

[4] Paul Canin, POW Diary, Online at <http://www.merkki.com>

[5] Harvey Greenfield interview, find source.

[6] S/Sgt. Hy Hatton, 392nd BG http://www.b24.net/pow/luft1.htm

[7] Mozart Kaufman, Fighter Pilot: Aleutians to Normandy to Stalag Luft I, San Anselmo, CA: M&A Publishers, 1993, page 149-150.

[8] Canin, POW diary.

[9] Bockstanz, author interview.

[10] Paul Haggerty, email posting, 7/27/2001.

[11] Mozart Kaufman, Fighter Pilot, 156-157

[12] Edwin Herzig author interview and Fr. Joseph Sellers, OSB, author interview.

[13] Sydney Thomas, Letter to New York Times, April 12, 1990.

[14] Mozart Kaufman, Fighter Pilot, 181.

Chapter Six

The Hand

Lee Kessler is a survivor. The bumper sticker on the back of his car says, "I've Survived Damn Near Everything", and if anyone is qualified to have that sticker, it is Lee. He has survived four plane crashes. The first was during training when he was an aerial gunner. The pilot was killed. The second was the crash of his B-17 into the Irish Sea on the crew's arrival in England. All crew survived but Lee spent three hours in the freezing water before rescue. The third was when the crew took out two wheat fields in England after a landing. No crew injuries but the plane was totaled. The last was the when his B-17 was shot down on a combat mission over Wilhemshaven, when he became a POW.

Lee survived bailing out of a crippled plane, parachuting into enemy territory, capture, interrogation, imprisonment, and a forced march. He survived open-heart surgery. At eighty-three, he still fights his daily battles with a variety of ailments. But one of the defining moments of his life involved the death of an anonymous Hungarian Jewish prisoner. Lee Kessler's knack for survival ensured that this moment was not lost in time. As a result, the moment has been preserved and treasured by thousands around the world.

Lee Kessler's defining moment came one day in late March 1945. Kessler was part of a group of American Air Corps POWs who were being force-marched away from the advancing Russian Army late in the war. As the rag-tag formation of weary POWs passed the Austrian town of Mauthausen, about 12 miles from the city of Linz, they crossed paths with a formation of Hungarian Jews from the German concentration camp at Mauthausen and who were being slowly worked to death in a quarry nearby. In the account he wrote up after the war, he tells the story that inspired 'The Hand'.

"With the onslaught of the Russian advance through Hungary and the approach toward the Danube River in late March of '45 the Germans evacuated our camp and put us on the road marching toward the west. After a couple of weeks on the road we were marching past a place called Mauthausen. We learned it was a concentration camp, altho (sic) at the time we knew little about them. Approaching us from down the road a group of these prisoners from this camp who we learned later were working in a quarry. They were Hungarian Jews and were guarded by the SS. We were halted at the side of the road for these walking skeletons to pass, but when they came even with us their guards stopped them. One of our guys threw a cigarette over towards them which was a mistake as they were like a pack of hungry dogs. The SS beat them back and of the one who was too weak to get up a spectacle was made for our benefit.

> "As we moved on we heard shots, mostly pistol, and we knew what they were for. Those who could not get up because of weakness were shot. Two prisoners followed in a wagon and loaded the bodies. As I approached one of the bodies at the side of the road, I noticed a crinkled photograph by his hand. As he lay with one arm stretched out as if reaching for the picture, I saw that he had been shot in the head. I moved off the road to get a better look at the photograph and was about to pick it up when a guard hollered for me to get back."

> "The picture was of a woman and two children. As I looked back, a butterfly landed on him. I was numb the rest of the march. Here was this man, dead by the side of the road, probably the last thing he looked at was his family, a

photo which was his only possession, and where were they? Dead or in some other camp. At that moment I could only think that everyone has the right to die with dignity and here was this poor soul who died with such obscurity."

"Some time in the fifties I started and outlined the drawing but finally put it away as I felt no one would understand what I was trying to portray. Then twenty years later after a severe heart attack and out of IC recovering, I needed some form of therapy and at the suggestion of a nurse who knew me and my association with art, I had my wife hunt for the layout, bring me my ink and pens and with the encouragement of the staff I finished the picture."

"Like other pictures, I put it away and until two years ago it lay in a drawer. I still felt that no one but me could really understand it. Then at the POW Convention when another POW was being interviewed, he related a story of how he saw this man lying on the ground, pull a picture from his pocket and as he kissed it a guard shot him."

This is the story of a young man who witnessed a moment in which, somehow, unbelievable human cruelty, incredible love, and overwhelming beauty all happened simultaneously. It was a moment that epitomized the horrors of war, the power of the human spirit, and the eternal renewal of nature. Because of this young POW's ability to draw, his experience would become universal. The picture it inspired—called simply "The Hand"—is displayed in museums, galleries and synagogues in all fifty states. It hangs in the U.S. Prisoner of War Museum in Andersonville, Tennessee. It has hung in the National Holocaust Museum in Washington, D.C. It hangs in Yad Vashem, the most famous Holocaust museum in the world, at the Mauthausen Concentration Camp Museum in Austria, and in many other foreign nations. 'The Hand' has inspired letters of thanks and gratitude from Israeli Prime Minister Yitzhak Shamir, from Nazi Hunter Simon Wiesenthal, from Yad Vashem Holocaust Martyrs' and Heroes' Remembrance Authority in Jerusalem, from the Anne Frank Center in New York, and from former Mauthausen concentration camp survivors. Lee Kessler has also been a guest speaker on many occasions, relating that single encounter, including an address at the University of Notre Dame.

Yet for the first thirty years of the drawing's existence, it lay in the drawer of its creator, who was convinced that no one else would appreciate it or understand his motivation for having invested so much of himself in it. It was a work of art that took years to complete. The seed of the idea that formed the basis for 'The Hand' was planted in the mind of a young twenty-one-year-old prisoner of war on a forced march when he saw a scene that seared itself into his soul. The idea's germination took several years, but the young man laid out in rough form the original drawing after his return from the war. 'The Hand' only bloomed into completion after the young man, now older and recovering from a near-fatal heart attack, ate a dinner of boiled potatoes that took him back to his time in solitary in a distant German prison camp and convinced him and others of his need to deal with the moment that forever changed his life.

He talks of 'The Hand' with modesty, as if he is still unable to believe that it has touched others so profoundly. At times, its success puts stress on him. "I've been talking about it for ten years now, in schools and other places," he says, "and I get tired of it. But I also look at it as kind of a mission. I'm proud that people are interested in my story."[1]

Lee loves to draw. He's been drawing pretty much his whole life, and at times hoped to make a career of art. He won some art contests as a young man, and several of these even led to paid projects. His first paid project was a picture of a girl holding a glass, commissioned for a bar, for which he received ten dollars.

Lee kept drawing and entering art contests. His big break was winning a contest where one of the judges was from New York City. This judge was in the calendar business, and he called Lee and asked him to freelance for his company. Lee did calendar paintings, "mostly busts, things like 'green-eyed brunette with a tennis racket". Even the military recognized his artistic talent. They offered to send him to the Military Heraldry Department, where he could make signs and design the art for squadron patches. "But I wanted to win the war," chuckles Lee. He turned down the chance for safe service and instead went into the Army Air Corps. "While in the Air Corps, I did the nose art for seven different planes. Only one of them didn't get shot down."

Lee's World War II scrapbook is filled with photos, paintings in watercolor, news clippings, and other memorabilia. The cover is skillfully painted with the highlights of Lee's Air Corps career— his swearing-in, training, ditching in the Irish Sea, air combat, including the German plane he shot down the mission before his fateful mission, his capture and march as a POW, and his liberation. The scrapbook, bound with a Nazi belt and buckle that Lee got on one of the final days of his captivity, also lists the number of Lee's friends, including his best friend, who never came home.

Lee was a very young man when he went off to war. He enlisted eleven days after Pearl Harbor, and flew with the 306th Bomb Group as a Flight Engineer/Top Turret Gunner on a B-17. It was early in the war when Lee's crew began flying missions. Germany was still winning the war. The Army Air Corps had yet to establish air superiority. There was no long-range fighter to escort the bombers to and from the targets. Consequently, many of the young men who flew the heavy bombers early in the war failed to return. "The average life expectancy at the time was four to five missions," Lee remembers. He flew his first mission on October 9, 1942. One a mission to Bremen in April of 1943, his entire squadron was wiped out, except for his plane. On May 21, 1943, while on his nineteenth mission, his plane was shot down on a mission to Wilhelmshaven, a city near the North Sea.

A flak burst killed the bombardier and navigator. Lee helped the pilot, who had also been hit and had shattered his shoulder, out of his seat, and the two jumped together. The ball turret gunner made it out safely, only to be pitchforked on the ground by angry Germans. Lee landed in the harbor and swam ashore, where a farmer took pot shots at him. Rescued by several Luftwaffe officers, Lee was marched through town as German women spit on him and children threw rocks at him.

Loaded into a boxcar, Lee spent several harrowing days locked inside, including one night while an Allied bombing raid raged around him. He spent ten days in solitary at Dalag Luft in Frankfurt, where he was stripped naked, beaten and interrogated.

The last day, the interrogator came in and showed Lee all the clippings from the Akron Dayton papers of his service career. "The Germans were winning the war at that point, and I thought 'if they know this about me, a nobody, how can we win this war? We can't win this war.' It was the lowest point for me. On the way out, the interrogator turned and said, 'Oh, and by the way, congratulations on winning the Distinguished Service Cross'. He knew about it before I did."

Lee was sent to Stalag Luft VII-A in Moosberg before being moved later in the war to Stalag 17-B near Krems, Austria. "My enemies in POW camp were disease, loneliness and hunger," he remembers. He remained there until February of 1945.

In November of 1944 Hitler ordered all the US soldiers held POW executed. Stalag XVII-B was evacuated and the men were marched east. They ended up marching 500 miles. "I try to tell kids today about that," says Lee. "That's like marching from Canton, Ohio to Chicago".

On the march, Lee carried the camp's only US flag, which was issued to be used at military funerals. As the march progressed, he got tired of carrying it. Everyone was soaking wet, and the flag got heavy. However, the flag ended up saving the entire column several times. Allied planes occasionally flew over the prisoners on the road. The men would yell "Flag!" and Lee would run up and lay it out on the ground, and the planes would swoop over and waggle their wings and not strafe them. The flag became Lee's friend as well. He used it as a pillow at night. When it got unbearably cold, he used it for a blanket. Some mornings he awoke to find he was covered with snow, the flag shielding him.

Sometime in March, the POW column reached Mauthausen. The plan, possibly, had been to exterminate them in the camp, but they were marched on past. Why? "There was such a backlog of prisoners there that they were storing bodies for disposal", says Lee. The efficient Nazi killing machine had outstripped the camp's ability to destroy the evidence.

It was here that Lee encountered the column of walking skeletons and witnessed the event that would forever change his life.

Of all the inmates held at Mauthausen, the two groups treated worst were the Hungarian Jews and the Russians. These two groups were housed separately, in the open air, surrounded by barbed wire.[2] The camp itself had been built in 1938, near a granite quarry, in order to use the forced labor from the camp in quarry work. Mauthausen was one of the most feared camps in the entire Third Reich. Inmates at Auschwitz shuddered at the thought of being transferred there.[3] Mauthausen was classified as a so-called "category three camp". This was the fiercest category, and for the prisoners it meant "Rückkehr unerwünscht" (return not desired) and "Vernichtung durch arbeit" (extermination by work).[4] 118,000 perished there out of a total population of less than two hundred thousand.[5] Some were gassed but most were simply starved or worked to death.

The Hungarians were returning from a stone quarry, known as the Wiener Graben. In the Wiener Graben the prisoners were divided into two groups; one hacked into the granite and the other carried the slabs out of the quarry. Prisoners were forced to carry granite blocks up 186 steps. The small blocks weighed between thirty and forty-five pounds each, while the larger blocks could each weigh more than 75 pounds. Any prisoner assigned to the quarry could expect to be quickly worked to death.[6]

Two columns of prisoners meet on an Austrian road. One man is murdered. Another young man sees, and cannot forget. Lee couldn't put an age on the man who lay before him, his grimy hand outstretched towards his last possession. "Everybody looked old to me then. I was just twenty-one myself. The kids in the photo looked maybe nine or ten years old. I only got a quick glance. And the photo was beat up and wrinkled." He walked over to the body to get the photo. Who were these people? Where were they now? Would they ever know that in his dying moment, this man had held them in his hand? He glanced back one last time at the scene, and as he did so, a butterfly landed on the man's grimy, outstretched hand, fluttering its wings lightly.

When the POW column halted later, Lee found another prisoner in the column who had witnessed the man's final moments. According to him, an SS soldier shot the man at point-blank range in the head with a pistol. As he lay there, he pulled the photograph from his pocket, held it up to his face, and kissed it. The guard fired again into his head, killing him, and leaving him lying on the side of the road, the photo not far from his hand.

The image haunted Lee Kessler. He could not get it out of his mind. "I thought, if I die, somebody will get back to my mother and father. But nobody was going to know about this guy." If the family were alive, they would never know where or how their husband and father had died, an anonymous inmate, shot on the side of a road in Germany. Or that in his final moments, he had thought of them, looked upon them, and kissed them tenderly.

The American prisoners kept marching. Instead of ending up in Mauthausen, they spent two weeks living in a forest until they were liberated by Patton's Third Armored Tank Division.

Lee returned to Canton, Ohio after the war. He sat down and drafted the first draft of the drawing that would become "The Hand". It was a rough sketch, showing a large, battered hand in the foreground clutching a photo, a butterfly on the thumb. In the background, the man's fellow prisoners and their guards continue to march toward an uncertain fate. "I didn't do any of the detail work at that time. I put it away in a drawer. I didn't realize at the time that most of us guys (combat veterans) had Post Traumatic Stress Syndrome. I would wake up and think about this experience with the man on the side of the road. But it took me another twenty-five years to get around to the detail work," he says.

In the meantime, he went to college on the GI Bill, at Ohio University in Athens in 1946. An athlete, he went out for the football team. However, his two years of incarceration in German prison camps had taken a toll. "I admire your guts," the coach told him, "but I can't afford to have a guy die on the football field." From there, he went to Hoover Sweeper Company. "My father had been there. I got into a program there. Got married. Somebody found out I was a college grad and I got bounced out of the program. During Korea I worked in a factory. Then I got laid off, and bounced around. Spent some time working for Ford Motor Company. Then a position opened up with the school system in Canton. They needed somebody to be in charge of the stadium and the Canton sports program." Canton is also the site of the Pro Football Hall of Fame, and Lee was connected with that organization as well during his career.

Like many veterans, Lee Kessler returned from the war and built a normal life. He got married, had three kids, and held a job, working hard and moving up as things opened up for him. But he never forgot the man with the photograph on the side of the road.

It was 1974. Lee Kessler was in the hospital after undergoing open-heart surgery. He was on a doctor-ordered bland diet. "One night, they gave me boiled potatoes, just like I'd had to eat in solitary confinement back in the prison camp, and it took me right back to solitary. That night, I had a very bad night. I don't know what all I said that night, but I didn't want to talk to anybody. My son had just gotten back from Vietnam. He came in to see me. I proceeded to snap at him, too. I told him to just leave. 'What's wrong?' he asked me. I proceeded to tell him that my nerves were shot. My son talked to one of the nurses. It happened the nurse was taking a psychology class and asked her professor about my situation that evening. The next day, she came in and sat down next to my bed. We talked. Her psychology professor had told her that I needed to get it out. My wife got my pen and ink and brought it to me in the hospital. I got out the drawing of the hand and I finished it there in the hospital."

"While I was working on the picture in the hospital, there was a Catholic priest who'd come by and visit. One day he brought in a guy while I was working on the picture. The guy looked at the picture and he began to cry. He was a rabbi." It was the first inkling to Lee that his drawing had some sort of universal appeal. However, after finishing the drawing in the hospital, he put it away in a drawer again. It had been thirty years since Lee had seen the nameless prisoner on the side of the road. Now, the drawing would sit in a drawer for another twenty.

It was the American flag that brought the picture out of the drawer for good. In the mid-seventies, Lee was invited, along with several other POW friends, to be on a Cleveland, Ohio morning television show, called "Morning Exchange". He brought the American flag he had carried during his years of imprisonment. While at the taping, one of the other men who had been on the march told Lee that he had also seen the anonymous man with the photo, and told Lee the story of what he'd seen. The show was a big success, and the men were invited to appear on 'Good Morning America' with David Hartman, in conjunction with the Cleveland POW Convention for a similar segment.[7] Lee again brought the flag, but this time, he also brought along his drawing to show to his comrade who had also seen the man with the photograph.

The 'Good Morning America' show was a big hit. Thousands of veterans from around the United States watched the program, and many wept as it brought back similar memories of man's inhumanity to man in wartime.

The story of 'The Hand' would not be complete without the story of a Jewish World War II veteran named Leonard Herman. Herman, himself a survivor of two combat tours over Europe, believed in the power of the drawing from the moment he first saw it, and it was his persistence that turned the drawing into an internationally recognized testament to the brutality of the Holocaust.

Leonard Herman is eighty-seven years old. He lives in Columbus, Georgia, but spent most of his life in Philadelphia, where he was a successful businessman with an eye towards promotion. Leonard was a bombardier on a B-17 in the 95th Bomb Group early in the war, at the same time Lee Kessler was flying his missions. He completed his tour, and despite the fact that every mission terrified him, he volunteered for a second tour of duty and completed it as well. Leonard had good reason to be afraid on missions over Hitler's Third Reich. He is Jewish.

In conjunction with the 50th Anniversary of the B-17 Bomber, being held by Boeing Aircraft in Seattle, Washington in 1985, Leonard arranged to have the 95th Bomb Group's annual reunion in Seattle, so that the veterans could enjoy both activities simultaneously. He had been instrumental in getting the history of the 95th Bomb Group into print a few years before, and had even arranged for an internationally known aviation historian, the Englishman Ian Hawkins, to serve as Editor. Leonard hoped to promote the book, *Courage, Honor, Victory* (later renamed *B-17's over Berlin*), at the reunion and at the Boeing anniversary bash.

One afternoon, Leonard and some other volunteers had set up Dictaphones in a room at the hotel where the reunion was being held. "Some guys will never write down their stories because they say they don't know how to write well, so we set up and were recording everybody that came in," Leonard told me.[8] "This fellow named Upchurch came in. He'd been a POW with someone named Lee Kessler, and he brought Lee's sketch of 'The Hand' with him and said 'Hey, look at this.' I looked at it and asked if I could make some Xerox copies of it. I asked him where the original was. He said Lee Kessler had it. So I got Kessler's phone number and gave him a call."

He gave Lee Kessler a call. "Kessler didn't think much of it. He downplayed the drawing and said it had very limited appeal."

"I said, 'Lee, first of all, are you Jewish?'"

'No,' he said. 'I'm Catholic.'

'Well, *I'm* Jewish. And *I'll* get you the exposure.' I told him.

Lee was uncertain. Leonard was not to be deterred. He knew 'The Hand' was an important piece of work.

Remembering Leonard's persistence, Lee chuckles. "He could squeeze blood out of a turnip. He wanted to produce the drawing. I told him I didn't have any money. I had a house and kids going through school. Leonard said he'd handle all that."

Leonard saw his involvement as a personal mission. "It is a very touching and emotional picture," he says. "You don't have to be Jewish to understand it. Amongst the Jews it has a very emotional appeal. It's sad. A lot of people can relate to it. So many who are not Jews have related to it. People who are not art lovers, people who have no interest in history or World War II, they still take to it because it so graphically depicts the situation and the politics and policies of the Nazis in World War II."

"I talked him into sending the original to me. I took it to an engraver to make plates. Then I arranged to have it reproduced. The initial run was somewhere between five hundred and a thousand. We chose the type of paper to put it on, a thick white stock that looked good."

Leonard asked Lee to write up an account of his experience surrounding 'The Hand' to be used with the print. Lee sent him one, figuring Leonard would then get someone to rewrite the story. No particular care was made to get it grammatically correct. Lee regarded his draft of his experience as just that—a draft. But when Leonard's secretary read Lee's words, she began crying. Leonard read it, and decided to use it just as it was.

Leonard arranged to have one of the master forgers from the Great Escape do the calligraphy on the story that would accompany each print of 'The Hand'. John Wells had been an art teacher in New Orleans before the war. After ending up in the 95th Bomb Group in England on a replacement crew, the U.S. and British decided to utilize his art skill and send him to forgery school in England. "They were looking for specialists and heard John was an artist, so they sent him to forgery school, then put him on a plane in hopes that if he got shot down, he could use that skill,"[9] says Leonard. Sure enough, Wells' plane went down and he became a

POW at Stalag Luft III, where he became a master forger in the mass breakout known as the "Great Escape", preparing fake German documents for the escapers.

Years later, Leonard met Wells at a 95th Bomb Group Reunion, and enlisted his help in hand-lettering Lee's story as well as the print's Certificate of Authenticity.

Leonard's plan was to send the print itself, the story behind the picture, written in calligraphy, and a Certificate of Authenticity, as well as a letter from Rabbi Arthur Rutberg, to art museums around the world, especially museums dealing with the Holocaust or Judaica.

"Once we had the litho, I started to take it to different places, and talk to people on the phone. I asked Rabbi Arthur Rutberg (of Shearith Israel Synagogue in Columbus, Georgia) at a Holocaust Memorial Service if he would write a letter explaining the Holocaust to accompany the lithograph. We sent the letter and litho to about forty synagogues and museums and that started the ball rolling."

The letter from Rutberg, written on Shearith Israel Synagogue letterhead, read, in part, "We would like to share with you a poignant piece of Holocaust art for your exhibit and/or resource center. <The synagogue> became the proud owners of this drawing that traveled from Germany to Ohio and now to Georgia. We believe that this drawing reflects the need to continue to study and teach about the Holocaust, to remember what was witnessed not only by the people of Europe but by American soldiers as well."

"As you read the story . . . you can sense the simple but powerful message found within this artwork. While it depicts and actual event witnessed by an American POW, we can see so many elements of the Holocaust. The photograph symbolized all the families and communities that were lost . . . The hand symbolized the suffering of more than six million individuals. And the butterfly symbolizes the hope that still survives."

"We trust you will find a proper place and usage for this piece of art. It is registered in the art collection of the Yad Vashem in Jerusalem under number 2732. It is our pleasure to send it to you free of charge."[10]

In time, Lee was invited to come and appear at different events commemorating the Holocaust. Leonard continued to send out the lithograph of 'The Hand' as promotions, gifts or prizes.

And what did Lee Kessler think of the sudden interest in his drawing? "He didn't believe it", says Leonard. "We sent the prints everywhere, even overseas. We contributed them, never sold them. That started the ball rolling. It got so the *big* museums, like Yad Vashem in Israel, and a major museum in Hungary, were displaying 'The Hand'. We began getting calls from people. One guy called from Texas saying his father had been on that march at Mauthausen. He'd been one of the Hungarian Jews. Another wrote that he himself may have been on that same march.

That man, a Mr. Jacobs of Dallas, Texas, wrote Lee in November of 1993:

> "Dear Mr. Kessler:
>   I received a copy of your touching drawing from Leonard Herman. This drawing . . . will remind people about the Nazi atrocities. The drawing shows that people cannot say that the Holocaust never happened. Your drawing provides proof that the Holocaust happened, concentration camps, gas chambers and crematoriums were real. That those people cannot deny and say it never happened. Thank you very much for drawing the picture. I am a Holocaust survivor liberated from Mauthausen on May 5, 1945."[11]

From Austria, Nazi-hunter Simon Wiesenthal wrote:

> "The Simon Wiesenthal Center in Los Angeles forwarded the print you so graciously gave to me . . . Thank you so much; I was very touched by it. The scenes which are described on the back of the print are so very familiar to me because I lived through similar ones on the marches I was forced to go on."[12]

"It touched Jewish people deeply," Leonard says, "Many Jews who saw the lithograph and learned the story of 'The Hand' didn't just look at it and read it and say 'Nice article'. They were *interested.* They *investigated.* 'The Hand' memorialized all the people who suffered. It created a flood of interest. Lee was so surprised. He became internationally known."

Leonard Herman is happy that 'The Hand' has become a symbol of the Holocaust. And he is happy that he was able to be partly responsible for its worldwide success. He finds the quirks of fate remarkable that led up to 'The Hand' becoming such an important work.

"If Lee hadn't been shot down, there would have been no picture. If I hadn't talked to Upchurch at that reunion, I don't know if 'The Hand' would have gotten the attention it deserved. Lee Kessler is dedicated to many things. He cares about many things. But he doesn't like to talk about it." Leonard Herman, a lifelong promoter, was just the man "The Hand" needed. The friendship that began with 'The Hand' continues to this day.

"Lee and I stayed in touch over the years," says Leonard. "Then, a few years ago, both our wives passed away. We didn't talk for a long time. I'd call the number and no one answered. I thought I'd lost track of him. Then, earlier this year, we got back in touch again."

Today, Lee Kessler gets up most days and heads over to the MAPS Air Museum at the Akron/Canton Airport. MAPS (Military Aircraft Preservation Society) is made up of one building that houses a small gift shop, a small but amazingly comprehensive, artifact-rich museum, and a large shop area where the teams reconstruct vintage aircraft to flying condition.

Lee admits, at 82 he's "too old to buck rivets" and his job right now is painting the logos of all the Air Forces in WWII to hang high on the walls of the hangar. Lee has his own small office to work from, but does a lot of the work at home in his basement. He shows us through the museum with obvious pride. "There aren't enough hours in the day," he says, to do all the work that needs doing on this new museum. It is getting ready to move into larger quarters. "This is a labor of love," Lee says on several occasions. Nobody gets paid to work on the planes.

In Lee Kessler's back yard, there is a tall flagpole. The American flag flies from the top, as well as the Ohio flag and the POW/MIA flag. He no longer has the flag he carried on the long march in 1945. Shortly after liberation, the flag almost ceased to exist. The POWs were getting fumigated and had to relinquish their possessions. Lee refused to give up the flag to be burned. He took it home, had it dry-cleaned, and stored it in a trunk. It flew for the last time at a POW reunion in Florida in 1980, and is now on display at the National Prisoner of War Museum in Andersonville, Tennessee.

Lee Kessler continues to live modestly, doing what he can to preserve the memories of World War II through his work at the museum. He still paints and draws, in addition to his museum work. "Circumstances don't make the man. They only reveal him," he says. In a death march in 1945, three men were revealed. One showed he loved his family to the end. Another showed he was a cold-blooded murderer. A third remembered the scene and had the talent to bring it to life for thousands.

Epilogue: Lee Kessler died in the fall of 2003, shortly after I met with him for our interview at his home in Canton, Ohio.

Notes

[1]   This and all subsequent quotes from Lee Kessler come from an author interview from March 2003 and an author interview at Lee Kessler's home in Canton, Ohio in July 2003.

[2]   http://www.jewishgen.org/ForgottenCamps/Camps/MauthausenEng.html

[3]   http://www.remember.org/camps/mauthausen/mau-quarry01.html

[4]   http://www.jewishgen.org/ForgottenCamps/Camps/MauthausenEng.html

[5]   http://www.remember.org/camps/mauthausen/mau-quarry01.html

[6]   http://www.us-israel.org/jsource/Holocaust/mauthblocpic.html

[7]   http://www.pownews.com/THE.HAND.htm

[8]   This and all subsequent quotes from Leonard Herman come from an author interview of 6/17/2003.

[9] Herman, Leonard. Author Interview, June 17, 2003.

[10] Rutberg, Rabbi Arthur, Letter to Holocaust Education Center and Memorial Museum of Houston, November 30, 1995.

[11] Jacobs Letter, 11/28/93, to Leonard Herman.

[12] Wiesenthal, Simon. Letter to Leonard Herman, June 5, 1990.

Chapter Seven

The Carson Twins at War

A mother's misgivings, a brother's love, and one man's will to live despite all odds form the framework of the story of the Carson brothers. It is a story that, though true, is so incredible that it sounds more like a motion picture or a novel. It already forms the basis for one book, and it may yet end up as a movie. In the meantime, the twin brothers, Gene and John Carson, continue to enjoy life with the same passion they've evidenced throughout, oblivious to the passing of nearly eighty years lived hard in war and peace. Gene enjoys the sunsets from his large home in Hawaii with his wife and a parrot named Claiborne, and John and his wife Wanda get out and travel on their Harley Davidsons, accompanied by their pet sugar glider Pockets, who may well be the world's only motorcycling marsupial. Both men are at peace, but it's been a long and sometimes arduous road. Gene escaped from the confines of the base bakery to fly not one but two tours of duty over Europe as a tailgunner and engineer on a B-17 at a time when finishing one tour had odds of one-in-three. John was shot out of the sky, became a POW in a German Stalag, survived a rudimentary emergency appendectomy and a brutal eighty-day forced march of over three hundred miles between February and April of 1945. Both men made the military a career, becoming Lieutenant Colonels and serving in Vietnam. John has survived all three of his children, including his oldest son, John, a Marine Second Lieutenant who was killed in Vietnam. Theirs is a story of perseverance, family loyalty and love.

In 1848, their grandfather John Carson immigrated to the coal country of West Virginia from Kerry City, Ireland, to escape the potato famine. At sixty-one, widower John married fifteen-year-old Effie Wickline. The couple had two sons, Patrick and Thomas. In 1917, Thomas was shipped to Europe to serve his country in the First World War, where he was wounded and inhaled phosgene gas, and was originally listed as Killed in Action. When Thomas returned from the war, he moved to rural Pennsylvania and began a career as a fireman, shoveling coal on the Delaware, Lackawanna and Western Railroad. He met a young schoolteacher named Esther, and they were married. In 1924, Thomas and Esther became the proud parents of twin sons, Gene and John Carson. Less than three years later, Thomas Carson was dead of consumption, a result of the poison gas inhaled while fighting in the trenches of the Great War. Esther was left alone to raise her two energetic and occasionally mischievous sons.

John and Gene grew up in the relative security of the Milton Hershey School in Hershey, Pennsylvania. The school had been set up by the chocolate magnate, Milton Hershey, to serve as a model school for orphaned or half-orphaned boys. Both boys loved airplanes from an early age. They devoured issues of pulp aviation magazines such as G-8 and his Aces, Bull Martin and Nippy Weston as they outduelled the Germans in World War I. They built rubber-band-powered Spads and Fokkers and launched them from a third-floor window. According to John, they often set the German Fokkers on fire to ensure that the Spads would be victorious.

John remembers that "Gene could talk me into anything and usually did. I recall nearly being electrocuted when he unscrewed a light bulb and had me insert a horseshoe magnet into the bare socket to 'recharge the magnet'." Gene could get himself into interesting situations as well. On one occasion, he nearly immolated himself when he lit a 'strike-anywhere match' on the celluloid toilet seat while using it. But Gene also showed a capacity early on for caring for his twin brother. He pulled John five miles "over some sizable hills" on a sled after John broke his leg when they were ten. "His deed always comes to mind when I see a picture of a boy helping his brother with the statement: 'He is not heavy, he is my brother'", writes John. "These words define my brother Gene in every respect."

It was a scene of brotherly devotion that would be repeated on a grand scale in World War II. Upon returning to the States after surviving twenty-five missions as a tail gunner over Europe, Gene found out from his mother that John had been reported Killed in Action. His response was to re-enlist and go back to Europe for a second tour, knowing deep down that John was still alive and that he would find him. And in the end, he did.

I have never met Gene Carson, but have corresponded with him quite a bit over the Internet and he was an early respondent to my calls for stories. In June of 2001, I met his brother John Carson at his home in a pine-shaded, hilly subdivision near Spokane, Washington. He and his second wife Wanda live in a large house on several acres. They have a utility building next to the house that holds some of their impressive collection of motorcycles and a four-wheeler. A motor home is parked next to the building, and a white Cadillac and a Toyota sports car sit on their drive-through driveway.

Both John and Wanda look much younger than they are. John is nearly eighty but looks sixty despite recently having angioplasty. Wanda looks even younger.

John was the first of the twins to enter the service on June 23, 1942, the day after his high school graduation. His mother, remembering what war had done to her husband, was distressed but understanding when first John, and then Gene, enlisted in the Army Air Corps with dreams of flying. After completing gunnery training, John was assigned as an assistant radio operator/gunner on a B-17 heavy bomber. However, the assistant radio operator on a B-17 was required to fly in the ball turret, and John's claustrophobia and airsickness made that job impossible. He traded positions on the crew with the tail gunner.

While engaged in low-level training in the Black Hills of South Dakota, "I made one of the dumbest moves of my life by having my girlfriend come out from Chicago so we could be married," writes John. Shortly after the big event, John was shipped out with his crew to fly their new plane to North Africa, and the new Mrs. Carson returned to Chicago to live with her mother. They flew by way of Bangor, Maine; Newfoundland; Prestwick, Scotland; and Casablanca, arriving in August of 1943 at an airfield near Tunis, Tunisia. They were now officially part of the 2nd Bomb Group, 96th Squadron.

While there, John flew some tough missions and also received word from Gene that his brother was stationed in England with the 8th Air Force. Gene had flown his first mission in September 1943 as a member of the 388th Bomb Group, 560th Squadron.

In December of 1943, John's group moved to a base on the European continent, at Foggia, Italy. John took this opportunity to change crews and positions, becoming a radio operator once again. He had flown 23 missions as a tail gunner.

It seemed to John that his new crew was destined to have bad luck. On each of the five missions John flew with this crew, something bad happened. On his fourth mission with the new crew, the tail gunner got careless and let the German fighters in too close. As a result, he was wounded and the fighters could now approach the tail with impunity. The plane was riddled with machine gun fire, the wing tip was shot off, the hydraulic system was damaged, and jagged holes a foot long creased the fuselage. Miraculously, the pilot managed to nurse the plane back to base.

On the next mission, they would not be so lucky.

On December 20, 1943, the crew flew a B-17 named 'Eager Beaver' on a mission to Aloysis Airdrome at Athens, Greece. Just as they approached the target, the plane took several direct hits from German 88-milimeter flak guns. The third hit split the plane apart and the tail, severed from the rest of the plane, fell off into space. Engines screaming, the 'Eager Beaver' rolled over on its back and began its death dive.

Temporarily trapped by centrifugal force and his own gun, John knew he was going to die. "I tried to faint. That didn't work. So I prayed," he says, "I said, 'Please, God, I don't want to go to hell'". Somehow, he managed to break free and ran out of the gap in the plane where it had come apart.

"I landed in a field near the target. I didn't have any chance to escape. Two German soldiers ran up and captured me right away," John remembers. All he had time to do in the brief moments before capture was to get down on one knee and thank God for letting him live.

Incredibly, other members of the crew had also managed to escape from the shattered plane as it fell. Two days later, John and the Eager Beavers' ball turret gunner and right waist gunner were loaded into a German Ju-52 Trimotor and flown to Saloniki, Greece for interrogation. After thirty days they were loaded on a German troop train for the long trip to Germany. It was February 1944.

The prisoners were loaded into boxcars for the trip. On the third day John became very sick. "As a humanitarian gesture, the Germans unloaded me at Thorne, Poland and put me in a German military hospital, where I had an emergency appendectomy." The suture used to sew him shut had not been sterile, and his wound became infected. "The doctor opened me back up again, clamped the skin back, with no anesthetics, and put a drain in. It was incredibly painful," says John. He shows me the scar on his lower abdomen. It is about five to six inches long and deep enough to put a finger inside.

Two weeks later, he was released from the hospital and taken to Stalag 20-A. Most of those in the camp were British soldiers captured at Dunkirk. He was well treated in the camp. In May or June, he was shipped to Stalag Luft VI at Hydekrug, a camp for American noncommissioned fliers. Conditions at Hydekrug were not nearly as good as they'd been at the British camp. While in the camp, John kept being approached by fellow kriegies saying "Wing Ding, when did you get shot down?"

He found out that brother Gene, now nicknamed "Wing Ding", was becoming something of a legend in the 8th as the flying baker. Back in the States and assigned to duty as a baker, Gene hung around the flight line bumming rides from pilots. His luck ran out when one ride ended with the crash of the AT-6 trainer in which he had illegally hitched a ride. Though he and the pilot both managed to bail out safely, he became known as "Wing Ding" for his apparent craziness and utter disregard for rules and regulations.

John also found out at Stalag Luft VI that witnesses of the explosion and crash of Eager Beaver had reported the plane breaking up and falling to earth with no chutes. All on board had been reported killed in action.

To keep their mother from worrying, Gene told her that he was a cook and that John was flying easy missions out of North Africa. Esther might have needed some smelling salts had she known what her two sons were really up to. On October 13, Gene flew on one of the roughest missions of the war, Schweinfurt. What's more, it wasn't until the plane was over the English Channel that he realized he had left his parachute sitting on the hardstand back at Knettishall. Not wanting to cause an abort, he suffered in silence as flaming Forts fell like flies around him. "I just forgot the damn thing," Gene says. "We had no spares. I had a little more religion that day."

In February 1944, both men were making journeys. John was being freighted across Europe as a POW, and Gene had returned home after surviving his 25th mission with the 388th Bomb Group. Shortly after his arrival in New York, Gene and a group of other returning airmen were feted at the Wings Club at the Waldorf Astoria Hotel. "Somewhat of an overwhelming experience for a young staff sergeant barely twenty years old," observes Gene.

During the evening, Gene called Esther back in Pennsylvania. She dropped a bombshell on him. John had been reported shot down and killed in action. "I knew in my heart the probable accuracy of the report," remembers Gene. "Never the less, I assured mother that such reports were not necessarily correct and I promised her I would find my brother. I kept the news to myself that evening. The next morning I was in the orderly room looking for orders to return me to the 8th Air Force".

Gene wrangled orders to Lincoln, Nebraska, where he hoped to hook up with a bomb group and make it back to combat. On a thirty-day delay-in-route, he stopped by Hershey and then took the train to the town where his mother lived. But he was unable to get off the train. "I continued to sit and stare out the window. I was three miles from home. I spoke to no one. When the train pulled out of the station I continued to sit and stare out the window at the passing countryside. I could not bring myself to go home without my brother."

John tried to adjust to life in the prison camp. The main thought on the minds of almost every prisoner of war was the same, and it wasn't on sex. "Sex doesn't seem very important when you're being slowly starved to death," he explains. "All we thought about was food. The average ration for a day came to about six hundred calories per man."

In July, the Russian advance forced the Germans to evacuate Stalag Luft VI. Twenty-five hundred POW's were jammed into the holds of two dilapidated coastal coal tramp steamers. "We spent five days on the Baltic en route to the German port of Swinemunde," says John. "Looking into the hold of the ship reminded me of fishworms in a can. Men that were ill or suffering from wounds were stacked in there with no thought of comfort or survival. Rather than go into the hold, I stopped on the ladder halfway down and took a seat on the prop shaft. I sat clinging to the ladder for the entire trip."

"This trip was a horror of horrors. No water to speak of, no means of relieving the body. There were no sanitary facilities at all. The Germans allowed only one man at a time to go topside to relieve himself, one man of the roughly 1,250 in the hold. I think I made one trip up but it is one of the periods that are no longer vivid in my mind. One of our group went topside and jumped overboard. He was immediately machine-gunned."

Survivors of the five-day trip were off-loaded at Swinemunde into boxcars. "Our shoes and our home-made knapsacks were taken from us and placed in the other end of the car. We were then handcuffed in pairs. Many of the group were ill or wounded. In my case my appendectomy was still draining. We spent an uncomfortable night in the box cars as the train traveled to our unknown destination."

The next morning, the disoriented and suffering kriegies were taken out of the boxcars, given back their belongings, but left cuffed in pairs and told to fall out alongside the tracks. The prisoners were then forced to run a gauntlet between two rows of young German Marines "who had been whipped into a frenzy by a German captain. As we double-timed between the cordon of guards, they liberally used blows to keep us moving. To lag behind meant jabs with a bayonet or a blow from a rifle butt, to fall meant dog bites as well. It was not a pretty scene."

"I was handcuffed to a New Yorker, a Jewish man named Adler, and he was of course concerned. I told him we'd move into the middle of the pack. This way we were protected from the beatings. We ran the one or two miles to Stalag Luft IV, our new camp."

"The worst thing about the camps was the lack of heat," John remembers. "To avoid getting bored, we walked around the compound, made plans for the future, and talked about food. There were some books to read. Somehow we had some boxing gloves. Some guys played softball."

Since there were no officers in the camp, the process of selecting a camp commander was done differently than in the officers' camp, where rank determined everything. "We called our commander a 'man of confidence'. He was just another noncom. We had an election and he won." Once the men were settled into life at Stalag Luft IV, a level of "reasonable survival" was reached. Hungry, dirty, often sick, the men of Stalag Luft IV did their best to keep sane. Their meager food rations were supplemented with the occasional Red Cross parcel. Mail trickled in sporadically. John didn't get any.

The Russians continued to roll back the German front. On February 6, 1945, the German guards ordered all the prisoners to evacuate the camp. The men set off on foot in the middle of one of the coldest winters Europe had experienced in a hundred years.

John had taken two wool blankets and laced them together with shoestring to make a sleeping bag. He'd also managed to get an overcoat and a new pair of shoes, as well as some lightweight food items such as Jell-O. Cold, hungry, lice-infested, sick, the prisoners began a long march away from the advancing Russians. "I'm not sure how many men started out on the march," says John. "And I'm not sure how many finished."

"It was just as bad for the Germans. They didn't have anything, either. We weren't mistreated, really. They were cognizant of the fact that the Russians were coming and they weren't the 'bad-asses' that they could have been." Never the less, the weakened prisoners marched all day long each day, on a diet of 700 calories a day, in sub-freezing temperatures.

"You didn't stop marching. I didn't dare take my shoes off. I wore my shoes for fifty-seven straight days. We slept outside some of the time, but mostly we slept in barns. The Germans were humane people most of the time. Men died, though. Most died of pneumonia or frostbite." John flexes his hand. "Every time the temperature falls below forty degrees, I'm still in pain."

"The days were long and arduous," writes John, "with snow storms, slush and snow on the roads in this mindless trek to nowhere. Constant companions were the body lice and dysentery. I kept going thinking about my young wife, having a home and raising a family. Had I known what the future held in that regard I am uncertain how I would have handled it."

The men trudged onward, uncertain of their destination, and uncertain what fate awaited them there. "As we marched spring approached and life was a bit better, except for the lice and constant hunger," John wrote later. "We kept it going one step at a time." He tried to push the pain and hunger from his mind as he walked. However, "to this day", he admits, "hunger or the thought of it is difficult to deal with."

"We were still marching when Liberation came on April 27, 1945, at Bitterfeld, Germany on the Moldau River." The prisoners were liberated by Gen. Patton's 104th Timberwolves. "As we marched through the front lines at Bitterfeld a pair of P-51 fighters flew over us, canopies open and wings wagging. I am sure I was not the only man that choked back sobs of joy. Our incredible journey was coming to a happy ending. German soldiers were also in the front line of marchers coming in to surrender rather than to stay and face the oncoming Russians."

"As to the march we'd just completed, it had lasted 86 days and covered approximately 600 miles. Although it ended in freedom for myself and the other survivors, many others were not so lucky. Over the course of the forced march, the lives of about 1,500 POW's were lost to disease or starvation or at the hands of German guards while attempting to escape."

At last, John Carson was free.

In the meantime, Gene was back flying combat, this time with the 92nd bomb Group, based in Podington, England. On January 15, 1945, he had taken a piece of exploding flak in the groin while manning the top turret on a mission. "I thought I had lost my pecker," Gene wrote me. "Not so, just my right gonad. It was as you may well imagine momentarily stressful." This incident earned Gene his second Purple Heart.

Gene spent February and early March in the hospital. Though he had everything he needed, he pestered the medical staff to release him so that he could return to duty. After a corpsman told him he'd soon be shipping home to the States, Gene went directly to the commanding officer. "The prospect of leaving without finding my brother pushed my button at the wrong time," he writes in his book. "I told (the CO) that I was not going to fly any more but had to wait for my brother. My persuasiveness prevailed and I was on my way back to Podington."

March saw Gene back in combat. On several missions, the crew barely escaped with their lives. The crew's copilot had to be removed from the crew after panicking and almost killing the entire crew in a mid-air collision.

"Somewhere near the end of that second tour I had lost count of the number of missions I had flown," Gene writes, "The mission count was not important. I was not flying with a goal of going home. I was waiting for my brother who, unbeknownst to me, was marching across Germany in one of Europe's worst winters in nearly a hundred years. I had no idea he was slowly starving and getting weaker with each passing day. In my ignorance I continued to be thankful he was no longer flying and was safe in a prisoner of war facility."

"After we were liberated," remembers John, "we hitchhiked to Halle and got hold of the U.S. military". "We got our rations. A C-47 flew in and a colonel was flying it. We conned the colonel into taking us to Rheims." They were deloused, given clean clothing, and fed. "After that, we went to Camp Lucky Strike. From there, we managed a boat ride from the British back to England."

Now John began the search for his twin brother. Someone recommended he get hold of the Red Cross at the Rainbow Corners USO in Picadilly Circus, the Times Square of London and a favorite hang-out of American airmen. When John arrived at the Rainbow Corners, he started asking around about his brother.

"A kind woman named Adele Astaire, who was Fred Astaire's sister, knew my brother and managed to contact him. We met on the evening of VE day and London was absolutely wild. It was one of the happiest and greatest moments of my life," John wrote later.

"I can still see my brother coming down the left side of the hall to greet me," he remembers. "We hugged each other for the first time since I had last seen him in Rapid City, South Dakota." They celebrated by taking in a show at the Windmill Theater, a burlesque house. "It was a reunion to remember, and the lights were on in my heart as they were all over London."

All that was left now was to get home.

After John missed a scheduled plane ride back to the States after the Captain in charge of his group left without him, he hung around London for nearly a month, attending the theaters. Gene, stationed nearby, introduced John to his circle of friends, mostly ladies. Finally, John and five of his friends went to Southhampton and contacted the Navy about a return trip to the States. It turned out the Navy needed a gun crew for a high-octane tanker that was waiting to depart for Bayonne, New Jersey. After the ten-to-twelve-day trip, the men made their way to Fort Dix. In the mess hall, John was shocked to find German POW's working the KP of the serving line in the mess hall.

John's next stop was Chicago, to reunite with his young bride whom he had married sixteen months ago. When he pulled into the Van Buren Station, Dorothy Carson and her mother were waiting to pick him up. "We got in the car and she kept sobbing," John wrote later. "I told her, 'Don't cry. I am fine. Just skinny.' She announced that she had something to tell me. I had been reported killed in action for over a month and in the meantime she had married an old high school sweetheart. What a shock. I was nearly speechless and her mother thought she had done the right thing."

"I was already so beat up," John told me, "that I said 'get me a suitcase for my clothes and a Pullman compartment and I'm gone.'" Suitcase and ticket in hand, the divorced former POW boarded the train for Fort Meyers, Florida, where he was reunited with his mother.

When he arrived in Fort Meyers, Esther did all she could to buck up her son and to put some meat back on his bones. "I weighed 115 pounds when I showed up," John says, "and she nursed me back to health." He got his separation orders from the military and bought a Harley-Davidson motorcycle. "When I rode that bike into Fort Meyers my mother nearly died on the spot. All she said was, 'Oh, no, John, not that.' Here I'd been flying missions and been a POW and she was worried about me riding a motorcycle."

A year and a half after leaving the military, John enlisted in the Air Force in April of 1947. He applied for OCS, Officers' Candidate School, and was accepted. In July of 1949, the former Sergeant became a 2nd Lieutenant. Brother Gene enlisted in the Army. Gene also became a commissioned officer and served time in the 82nd Airborne as a paratrooper in the fifties.

John married and had three children. He rose through the ranks in the Air Force to become a Lieutenant Colonel. His most satisfying duty was at Ton Sun Nut Air Base in Saigon, Vietnam, commanding the 1876th Comm Squadron.

Gene also ended up in Vietnam, and there is a picture of the twins meeting at Saigon airport in 1969. Gene, a good deal taller than John, has just gotten off the plane from the States. John has his arm around his brother. He is wearing his fatigue uniform and a fatigue cap, and looks a good deal wearier than his brother. A painting of the photograph hangs in the family room, done in Vietnam by a Vietnamese artist. "It had been a bad year," he remembers. His oldest son, John H. Carson, had joined the Marines and became a first lieutenant. He was sent to Vietnam. On June 5, 1968, John H. Carson was killed in combat.

Despite the hard lessons of Vietnam, "I'd go back to war in a heartbeat." Why? I ask him. He gestures at the world around him, his arms wide. "Because this is worth fighting for."

Despite all the challenges and tragedies life has thrown at John Carson, he refuses to let it get him down for long. "I still have bad dreams from time to time. Sometimes it can be very emotional. But it's nothing I can't handle. It's important to keep a positive attitude," he says. In addition to losing his oldest son John in Vietnam, both of John's other children also died young. He and his second wife divorced after a rocky marriage. He then met his soul mate, Wanda. Wanda has been riding motorcycles herself for nearly sixty years, though she hardly looks like she could be that old. They have been married for eighteen years, and it is clear that they are in love and very happy together. Her kids call John 'Dad'. They have ten motorcycles between them, not including several that they are in the process of restoring. They have traveled together all over the United States. When they travel, they take the world's only motorcycling marsupial sugar-glider with them. Pockets, who is about the size of a large mouse but more closely resembles a raccoon or an tiny possum, travels with John and Wanda inside a leather fanny pack Wanda wears around her waist. "He's a great ice-breaker," laughs John. As we talk, Pockets skitters around the family room.

John spends time on the Internet, where he has a large circle of friends with whom he regularly corresponds. He counsels some of these. There are Vietnam veterans and children of veterans. Some have problems with alcohol. "That must be why I got out of that plane all those years ago," he muses, "To help others."

Esther, John and Gene's mother, died in her eighties in 1987. Having outlived his own three children, John's closest relative remains his twin brother. Gene lives in Kaneohe, Hawaii, after retiring from successful careers in the military and in the private sector. He recently wrote a book about his experiences in the war called *Wing Ding: Memories of a Tailgunner*. One of its main themes is the search for his twin brother, of how Gene volunteered to fly another tour of combat at a time when chances of surviving a tour were one in three, in the hopes that he could find John. When asked what he would tell a young person today about what he learned in the war, Gene's response was short and sweet: "War is one of the greatest obscenities in the history of the world".

As the twins approach eighty, they have both found happiness and peace despite the difficult and at times painful journey.

The story of John and Gene Carson is just one story, but it exemplifies the extraordinary courage to which otherwise ordinary men can aspire to in times of crisis and the bond of love that exists between brothers. It also attests to the ability of the human spirit to recover from all sorts of adversity and heartbreak and find the courage to go on living. On any given weekend, you will be able to find John and Wanda Carson on the roads of America on their powder blue Harleys, heading not towards the last sunset, but towards the next sunrise.[1]

Notes

[1]   All quotes with Gene Carson are taken from a series of email interviews with the author in 2001. All quotes from John Carson are taken from an author interview in Spokane, Washington in June, 2001. Some background material is from *Wing Ding: Memories of a Tail Gunner*, by Gene Carson, published by Xlibris Corporation in 2000. Used with permission of the author.

Chapter Eight

Gus Mencow: Survivor

It's a long way from the bloody skies over Europe in 1943 to the classrooms of Worcester State College—about fifty-nine years, to be exact. Most men would live life the other way around, starting with the college life, the marching band, and the late-night term papers, and would eventually move on to the more serious aspects of life—jobs, families, and the responsibilities of adulthood.

Such was not the case for Nathaniel 'Gus' Mencow. In his early twenties, he was in the vanguard of the US Eighth Air Force's aerial assault on Hitler's 'Fortress Europe'. At a time when the odds of finishing the required twenty-five missions were all but nil, Gus felt the awesome responsibility of personally guiding as many as 45 bombers, filled with 450 men, to and from Europe's most heavily-defended targets. At this point in the war, the big, slow bombers, leaving their telltale four white contrails in the cold, blue sky, flew the most dangerous parts of their missions with little or no fighter escort. The early models of the Boeing B-17 had not been modified to reflect the dangers of aerial combat or of extreme cold at high altitudes. German fighters screamed in from the front, guns blazing, trying to kill the lead pilots and crews, for the B-17 didn't yet have the remote chin turret. Oxygen masks froze up, clogged with ice. Men's hands froze to their fifty caliber guns in seconds. Herman Goering's Luftwaffe was still mighty, its best pilots still alive. Gus lived each day as if it were his last. After each mission, empty bunks testified to the loss of friends. Bomber crews shared an almost sacred bond. They came to love each other as brothers. So much so that sixty years later, many men admit that their brief but deadly tours are the touchstone of their lives, and that the friendships they made in those times will never be extinguished, even as the friends themselves, one by one, fall to a new adversary—old age.

Now, a full lifetime later, Gus Mencow is back in school, working on his Master's Degree in History, taking advantage of the State of Massachusetts' generous law of free tuition for senior citizens. He is a teacher in every sense of the word as well. He frequently substitutes in Worcester classrooms. He is a guest lecturer on a variety of topics, from the Civil War to the Armenian Genocide. And he runs a World War II Museum in one of Worcester's middle schools. In 1990, when a documentary producer wanted to make a film about air combat, Gus and his fellow crewmen of the 390th Bomb Group's famed "Betty Boop-The Pistol Packin' Mama" were selected. The film continues to be shown to classes at the U.S. Air Force Academy, sells well in video, and appears on educational television.[1]

Not one to miss out on the joys missed over the flak-filled skies of Europe, Gus spent time as the water boy for the Worcester State College football team, and played in the college pep band. His days are full, and they have to be. It is the time alone, in the large house he has lived in since 1946, that forces him to reflect on the many losses he's experienced, both in the air over Europe and in his family.

Gus was born April 24, 1918 in Worcester, Massachusetts, about three miles from where he now lives, the sixth of seven children. His father, David Louis Mencow, and his mother, Ida Sugerman Mencow, were from the small Russian village of Barisov, near the border with Poland and Lithuania. Ida was a seamstress, known for her beautiful bridal gowns. David was a businessman. As Orthodox Jews, they were subject to the frequent pogroms of the Tsarist regime. "Life in Russia was harsh," says Gus, "The only thing they could depend on was God, and the only person they could complain to was God." David was conscripted into the Tsar's army and became a second lieutenant, one of the few Jewish officers. "He was just a little guy, smaller than me," says Gus, who is small of stature. Gus's father emigrated to the United States in 1901, and passed through Ellis Island. At Ellis Island, the family name was changed from Minkove to Mencow. [2]

Ida came the following year. She fell ill on the trip to the U.S. In Berlin, doctors removed parts of her stomach and gall bladder. Doctors told her she would never be able to have children. Gus's father married her in Worcester, spent a year working for another tailor, then opened his own shop, which soon became a big success. Even at the height of the Depression, the shop kept busy. Gus's father spoke Russian, Polish, French, English and Yiddish. Though he and his wife sometimes spoke Yiddish or Russian between themselves in the home, they always spoke to the children in English. "They were brilliant people," says Gus. "They had brilliant kids and grandkids." One brother, Abe, graduated from Harvard magna cum laude. Another, Sam, became an electrical engineer. A sister, Dorothy, became a nurse.

Gus was raised as an Orthodox Jew, but later became a Conservative.

Gus attended Classical High School in Worcester. When the war broke out, Gus entered the Army Air Corps pilot training program, but didn't do well. He ended up at Navigation School at Mather Field in Sacramento, and found he was a natural navigator. "I cottoned to it," he says, "I could picture it—azimuths, east and west of the horizon, and so forth." He finished sixth in a class of six hundred. The Air Corps wanted to make him an instructor, but he refused. "I said I was there to fight the war, not to be an instructor," says Gus. "Little did I know what was ahead of me."

In Boise, Idaho, he met his new flight crew—men with whom he would form lifelong bonds. The crew was assigned to the newly formed 390th Bomb Group, 570th Squadron in late March, 1943. The crew consisted of Pilot James Geary, Copilot Dick Perry, Bombardier Hugh McCarthy, Navigator Mencow, Engineeer/Top

Turret Gunner Shirl Hoffman, Ball Turret Gunner Clifford Puckett, Waist Gunners Leonard Baumgartner and Paul Morris, and tail gunner Donald May. The pilot, James Geary, was a tall, rangy fellow who had gone to sea at the age of sixteen and had already seen the world. Copilot Perry, from Detroit, was younger, serious, impressionable. McCarthy was a rowdy Irishman who loved practical jokes. Hoffman was a farm boy from Pennsylvania who had joined the Air Corps because "it was better than sleeping in the mud". Clifford Puckett, the baby of the crew, was a Choctaw Indian from Muskogee, Okalahoma. They were a typical crew, men and boys from all over the United States. Geary ran a tough ship. He expected a lot from his crew, and he got it. In the process, he molded the men into one of the finest crews in the Eighth Air Force.

In Walla Walla, Washington, Pilot Geary walked out of the hangar with a slip giving him proprietorship over "1 B-17F Airplane". "It still had that new-plane smell", Gus remembers. This plane would become a dear friend to the crew. They would name it "Betty Boop/The Pistol Packing Mama", the first after Geary's wife, the second after a popular song of the day. After further training in Spokane, Washington; and Lewistown, Montana, the crew flew to Bangor, Maine; Gander, Newfoundland, and then across the wide reaches of the Atlantic Ocean. Gus plotted their course across the Atlantic, using the B-17's Plexiglas astrodome to shoot fixes on the stars. The crew arrived in Scotland, where McCarthy went around in the bars introducing his Jewish navigator as Angus MacIntosh. "The drunker he got the funnier he got," says Gus. "I used to ply him with liquor just to get him going." Like Gus, McCarthy was from Massachusetts. He was from Millis, about a forty-minute drive from Worcester. Though the Jewish Mencow and the Irish Catholic McCarthy were from different worlds, they became close friends.

The green crew settled into their new base at Framlingham, England. Framlingham was sixty miles from London and thirty miles from the North Sea. The day after they arrived at Framlingham, a bomber from another group, crippled and returning from a mission, crash-landed at Framlingham, plowing in with no landing gear, and blew up, killing the crew. "It was our baptism into fire," remembers Gus.

They were selected as the lead crew of the squadron by their commander, Joe Gemmill and flew their first mission in July 1943. The crew flew its twenty-fifth mission in February of 1944. As a lead crew, they did not fly as often, alternating with lead crews in the other three squadrons, thus prolonging the agony of the tour. At the time, odds were only one in three that a bomber crew would live to see its twenty-fifth mission.

"We pretty much made up our minds we were dead people," says Gus. "Our crew, our whole squadron . . . was a pretty wild bunch. None of us expected to live very long." Each mission lasted for many hours. The danger began as hundreds of planes began assembling in the cloudy skies over England. It continued as the slow bombers entered enemy territory and were harassed by German fighter planes all the way to and from the target. Often the fighters were from the famed "Abbeville Kids", the yellow-nosed German group stationed in Abbeville, France. These superb German pilots would scream directly through the formation, executing a slow roll as they passed through. The Germans concentrated their attack on the lead aircraft, as it held the lead crew, so the Pistol Packing Mama took a lot of abuse. The temperature outside the aircraft often reached fifty to sixty degrees below zero. Going to the bathroom was next to impossible. The crew had to stay on oxygen for hours at a time, and often the hoses became clogged with ice. "Somehow," remembers Gus, "I still found myself sweating." During the bomb run, the entire formation flew straight and level, regardless of fighters and flak. The moment of bombs-away brought some relief, as the planes could then make a run back home to England.

On August 17, 1943, the crew went on its second mission as part of one of the greatest air battles of World War II. It was a deep penetration. Part of the attack would concentrate on Schweinfurt, the other part on Regensburg. Pistol Packing Mama flew lead in the high squadron. Waist gunner Baumgartner took a bullet in his

head and was killed instantly. In the flak over Regensburg, Gus
struggled to pick out the correct target through the German smoke
screens. After bombs-away, the formation headed south, towards
Africa, where they would land and refuel. "So many aircraft were
hit that as we went across the Mediterranean, every fifteen or twenty
miles there was a B-17," says Gus. Finally, after nearly thirteen
hours in the air, and with the dead body of their friend and crewman
Baumgartner on board, the crew landed at Cape Bon. They slept
under the wing of the aircraft that night. McCarthy managed to
buy or steal a donkey, which he smuggled onto the aircraft for the
return trip to England. The donkey weighed about four hundred
pounds, according to Gus. The crew hid it in the tail of the plane,
and gave it a spare oxygen mask so that it would not pass out.
Geary fumed up front, confused that he could not trim the plane,
unaware of the extra crewman. The Egyptian beast ended its days
behind a plow on the farm of Percy Kindred, who owned the
farmland around the Framlingham base.

   Of the 315 planes sent to bomb Schweinfurt and Regensburg,
sixty were shot down. Seventeen more were so badly damaged they
were scrapped.

   Another rough mission came on October 10, 1943, when the
crew of Pistol Packing Mama led the entire Eighth Air Force on a
bombing mission to Munster, Germany. 180 aircraft flew on this
mission. The fighting was fierce. The entire aircraft shuddered from
flak hits and fighter bullets. Cordite hung in the freezing air.
Gus shot down a German fighter, an Me-109. The fighter attack
became so bad that in a matter of about eight to ten minutes,
planes everywhere began to get shot up and go down. The
Germans would barrel roll through the formation, strafing the
lead plane and trying to break up the formation. In the 100th
Group, flying low squadron, twenty-one planes just disappeared.
The Pistol Packing Mama had a gaping hole in the wing. Gus
thought to himself over and over: "Gus, you're not gonna make it
through this." He looked over at McCarthy and saw the resignation
in his friend's eyes as well. "It was as if to say 'Goodbye, old buddy'",
remembers Gus.

What was left of the bomber group straggled back to England only to find that the island was socked in by heavy cloud cover. Geary managed to land the plane at Thorpe's Abbott, the base of the 100th Bomb Group. "When we got there, the Hundredth was in a shambles," says Gus. "They'd sent out fifteen planes and only one came back." Back in their own barracks the next evening, the enlisted men of the Pistol Packing Mama noticed that they were the only remaining crew in the entire barracks.

The crew frequently used humor on rough missions to lighten the terror. McCarthy was the resident wag. On the Schweinfurt mission, McCarthy got on the interphone and asked Pilot Geary: "Geary, is there any way you can back this crate up?" When the flak got bad, he would ask "is your head up and locked?" When the flak got particularly bad, he would reassure the rest of the crew that "it's the flak you don't see that kills you".

"It was a real strange kind of war," says Gus. "You could be up in the air one day risking your life, getting shot at and watching your friends get killed and that night be in the middle of London at a bar drinking and looking at the girls and having a hell of a time."

"Life at the base between missions was pretty wild. The only booze to drink was Irish whiskey and Scotch. There was an endless card game going on all the time at the Officers' Club". Back in the barracks, the men played 'snap' or 'Red Dog'. Sometimes girls came to the base. McCarthy would look at the more homely specimens, turn and say to Gus, "Let's have a few drinks, and they'll look prettier".

They also occasionally went into the tiny hamlet of Framlingham to drink in the pub.

The best times of all were the trips into wartime London. The men of the Army Air Corps had the run of the town. As Americans, they made much more money than their British counterparts. And they were flyboys, which added to their attraction for women. Many Americans congregated at Picadilly Circus, where you could buy condoms from the paper vendor. London was in blackout. Everyone carried a flashlight. Gus remembers the Reindeer Club and the Regent Palace Hotel.

On their trips to London, McCarthy entertained Gus with stories about his youth. He told of selling tickets as a teenager to boys who wanted to go out with his beautiful older cousins and then spending the money. Occasionally, they were accompanied by the Catholic chaplain. Perry came along, though he was convinced that the practical joker McCarthy was out to get him.

Only four days after the Munster mission, the men of the Pistol Packing Mama went up again, this time as the lead of the high squadron on a mission to Schweinfurt. Schweinfurt was another deep penetration without fighter escort, and the Eighth was still smarting from the many losses on the Munster mission. The fighters and flak were thick. Red and orange bursts of flak surrounded the plane. "Every so often out of that black flak I could see sheets of flame as a B-17 was hit and a plane went down," Gus remembers. Up in the cockpit, Geary and Perry wrestled with the giant aircraft, trying to hold a tight formation. Geary demanded that the pilots in the squadron fly extremely close. It kept the losses down considerably. The men of the Pistol Packing Mama were becoming a formidable team. Gus had full faith in the tall pilot, and Geary had a deep respect for his navigator.

"Gus Mencow, he is probably one of the finest navigators you could find," he remembered years later. "When he said he was someplace, he was there. You could count on him." On the Schweinfurt Mission, Gus kept the wing right on the planned flight path. The First Air Division was less lucky. After deviating from the plan, the First lost six hundred men on the Schweinfurt mission.

After the crew made it safely back to Framlingham, it was apparent to them from the losses at Munster and Schweinfurt that they would not survive the war. There were too many empty beds in the barracks. Within hours of a mission, men would come through and remove all the personal belongings of the missing. It was as if the men had never existed.

The next day, Gus sat down and wrote a letter to his mother.

"Dear Mom: I am leaving this letter in my uniform jacket because I know it will be the one item of clothing that will be sent back to you in case anything happens to me. I hope that day never comes. If the worst happens, and you get this letter, do not mourn, do not bow your head. Out of all of this madness there will come righteousness and peace and all hatred will vanish. Remember this above all that I died for the right of all of us to live in dignity and peace and to enjoy what is our birthright. I love you and the family so much. Gus."

Being a Jew and flying over Germany was fraught with many extra dangers. Although some Jewish air crewmen hammered out the "H" on their dogtags (the 'H' denoting Hebrew), Gus refused to do so. Though he rarely went to religious services while in England, "I prayed to myself a lot," says Gus.

He encountered no anti-Semitism in the 390th. The wing commander, Wittan, was Jewish, and there were a few other Jews in the wing.

Like most Americans, Gus was unaware of the Jewish genocide taking place below in Germany. "I wasn't aware of the Holocaust until after the war. We knew terrible things were going on, though." On October 9, 1943, the crew flew a Yom Kippur mission to Marienberg, East Prussia, to bomb a Focke-Wolfe factory. They passed over Poland, and McCarthy came on the interphone. "I wonder how those people are doing down there?" "We knew Jews were dying," says Gus.

Gus flew knowing full well that each mission could be his last. The crew set their sights on number twenty-five, the magic number, the mission that would allow them to go home. The stress affected different members of the crew differently. Gus swears that Geary was affected least of all. "The man had ice water in his veins," he says. "War is a funny thing. Some people like it. Geary turned into a war lover." Gus insists that Geary was the model for John Hershey's character in his book, *The War Lover*. Hershey had met and talked with Geary in England. Geary was mad that he didn't have a gun to shoot when the plane was under attack. He brought a tommy gun into the cockpit with him, and would hang out the tiny side window of the B-17 and shoot at the German fighters. Gus would yell at him over the interphone: "Put that God-damned gun down! You'll shoot the propeller off the plane!" "I lived in mortal fear of that," Gus admits. "That this crazy bastard was going to shoot his own aircraft down!"

As the twenty-fifth mission approached, the men were sent to a 'flak house' for some rest. The stay was supposed to last a week, but after two days, they went back to the base to get it over with.

"As you approached that twenty-fifth mission," says Gus, "you got very apprehensive, very fearful that you weren't going to get through it."

Mission twenty-five took the crew over Emden. Ralph Hansel was Gus's good friend. They'd flown together on the Munster mission. On the Emden mission, Hansel was flying with another lead crew in the next plane when it took a direct flak hit. "I looked over at Ralph. He was flying in the right hand seat. There's a little window, maybe a foot and a half square. Ralph had his chest pack on and was trying to get out of that little window and he just couldn't make it. And I'm looking over, and the plane just exploded," remembers Gus, and weeps. Pistol Packing Mama took over the lead, finished the bomb run, and headed back to England.

"Coming back, and seeing those white chalk cliffs of Dover, was about the friendliest sight you could ever see."

The crew of Betty Boop/Pistol Packing Mama, with the exception of Leonard Baumgartner, had beaten the odds and survived its tour. The enlisted men finished out their tours in safe duty and went home. The officers were also transferred to safer jobs. Gus went to Wing Headquarters where he became the wing bombardier. He planned all the rendezvous points on future missions. McCarthy came back to the States and sold War Bonds. Geary, the war lover, signed up to fly a new tour of duty over Europe, was shot down, became a POW, escaped, and eventually made it back to the United States after the war.

Gus's brother William followed him into the Air Corps, and was shot down and killed. The blow to Gus and the Mencow family was severe. To this day Gus feels a certain amount of responsibility for the death of his little brother.

When Gus returned from England to his native Worcester, he had lived more in three years than many men live in a lifetime. It was time to put the war behind him, get on with his life.

While on thirty-day leave in August of 1943, he'd met his future wife Anne on a blind date. After the war, he looked her up again. She didn't see Gus in civilian clothes till 1945, and when she did, she didn't recognize him. Gus's mother was concerned with the amount of alcohol Gus consumed after he returned from the war, and she asked his future wife to talk to him about it.

Gus's oldest, Ruthie, was born in 1948, ten months after the wedding. Ruthie was followed by Barbara, in 1951, and William, named for Gus's brother, in 1954. Bringing up kids is "seventy-five percent luck, and twenty-five percent parenting" he says now. All three of his children are happy and successful. He also has eight grandkids.

He spent his working years in the wholesale furniture business.

Gus returned to school the late 1960's. He began taking classes at Worcester State College, working towards his Bachelors. While there, he caught up on all the things he'd missed as a young airman. He played in the college pep band, primarily trumpet but also "crashing the cymbals for touchdowns". At one game, Gus's granddaughter turned to his daughter and said "My grandfather's crazy!" He wanted to be the waterboy for the football team, but the coach said that with his bad knees, "you can't even run to the middle of the field with the water". He also sang in the chorus and was president of the Elder Advocates. He got his BA in 1988 at the age of 70.

In 1993, Gus met another crisis head-on when he found out that his beloved wife Anne was ill with Alzheimer's Disease. Gus visited her every day for the last three years of her illness[3]. She didn't know him most of the time. She died in 2001.

His large house, on a peaceful cul-de-sac on a hill in a working-class neighborhood in Worcester, seems too big for one man. The rooms are filled with reminders that this was once a busy place. The room I stayed in was filled with Bruins hockey pictures and other sports items from Gus's son. Gus keeps a kosher kitchen, using separate dishes for various foods. The house is neat and orderly, and very large for one man in his eighties. Gus spends his days as a substitute teacher, researcher, guest lecturer, museum curator and student.

Over the years, the men of Betty Boop/The Pistol Packing Mama have been overcome by age. Gus's close friend McCarthy died in 1967. Dick Perry died shortly after the completion of the film about the crew of Pistol Packing Mama. James Geary, Gus's beloved pilot, died less than two years ago. Those lucky few from the early years of the war that the flak and fighters failed to get, are now succumbing to the more insidious effects of old age. Each year, Gus finds himself more and more alone.

"If I sit down I start to brood," says Gus. "I keep working as a defense mechanism."

And work he does. Gus is a frequent substitute teacher at the high school in Worcester. He is a guest speaker on a variety of subjects, from World War II to the Armenian genocide to the Civil War. In 1995, Gus went to the Principal of the Arthur J. Sullivan Middle School and asked if he could turn an unused assembly room into a museum. The principal wasn't so sure, but the Superintendent jumped at the chance and the district agreed to kick in thirteen hundred dollars a year for upkeep. Gus found "surprising support from the community". Everyone, it seemed, wanted to donate service-related items to the museum. One wall is filled with photos of men killed in World War II. "If someone brings one in, I never refuse to put it up," says Gus. One of the first photos to go up was of Gus's brother Billy. It reads "1st Lt. William Mencow, KIA 2 Nov. 1944, 401st Bomb Gp".

Gus procured grants for display cases, trolled for donations, and watched the museum take shape. The unveiling ceremony took place November 9, 1995, in time for Veterans Day.

"This is the nerve center for what I do," said Gus as we looked around. The room is filled with foam-mounted posters, old magazines, books, displays, papers, pictures. Models of airplanes hang from the ceiling. Gus is rightly proud of it. "As far as I can determine, this is the only public school in Massachusetts that has a room dedicated to World War II."

During the school year, Gus lectures every Monday and Friday at high schools in Worcester. Tuesdays through Thursdays, he shows up at the museum about eight, signs in, and leaves about nine. Most days, he heads out to give lectures at various schools on a variety of topics. "I won't speak to more than thirty kids at a time," he says, preferring to keep his talks personal and informal. He has lectures on George Washington ("more for the elementary kids"), the Armenian Genocide, the Holocaust, and a variety of other history topics. He brings in guest speakers. He encourages kids to email World War II veterans and learn about the war first-hand. "Storage is the biggest problem," he admits. "I have enough stuff to fill four more rooms."

Gus has numerous awards for his service to the community. One news article is headlined: "City's Oldest Teacher Keeps War Years Alive". He has also been awarded the key to the city of Worcester.

Despite the busy schedule, Gus works towards his Master's Degree in History from Worcester State College. While I was visiting, he was applying the finishing touches on a paper about General Sherman's Civil War March to the Sea.

Gus also spends time doing research at several of the fine research libraries in the area, where he is well known. He is a member of the American Antiquarian Society, a stately old building with thousands of rare books and "five running miles of newspapers." He does research at Clark University's Center for Holocaust Studies. He follows all the Boston sports teams. He drives a small economical Toyota Echo. He keeps in touch with his friends.

Gus attends the conservative synagogue every other week. Religion is an important part of his life. His maternal grandfather Nathaniel Zuckerman, "fought his way from the shtetl in Russia all the way to Israel", and is buried on the Mount of Olives. His grave faces the sealed gate into the Old City of Jerusalem, out of which the Messiah will come. In 1972, Palestinians desecrated the grave. The family put up a new stone.

As for the fine old Betty Boop/Pistol Packing Mama—the plane that the crew admits to having a personal affection for, kind of like the family dog? Her biography is summed up in the archives of the 390th Bomb Group Museum.

She was officially aircraft 230434, a B-17F, and one of the original aircraft of the 390th Bomb Group. She was accepted by the Army Air Corps on May 29, 1943, was modified in Cheyenne, Wyoming on May 31. By June 19, she flew training missions out of Rapid City, South Dakota, and by the 22nd, she was at Geiger

Field in Spokane. In July, she became part of the U.S. Eighth Air Force and flew to Europe and Framlingham air base. She saw the loss of Leonard Baumgartner, Waist Gunner, KIA on August 17 at Regensburg. She watched as the rest of her original crew defied the odds and finished their twenty-fifth mission. But she was not done. The B-17s flew as long as they were able. She got a new crew. On February 25, 1944, her thirty-first mission, she was shot down by fighters over Regensburg, and crashed near Laon. Two of her crew, Bowman and Phillips, were KIA. The rest became POW until the end of the war.

Gus Mencow tries hard to keep busy. But the days are long. He thinks of his wife. The big house is quiet. The kids are gone. He finds himself inexorably drawn back to those days sixty years ago, the days that defined him as a human being. "I fight the war every day," he says. "I think about it every day."

"I'll wake up in the middle of the night, and I'll hear the roar of the engines, and I cry to myself. Where are those guys?"

Notes

[1]   Some quotes are from the video "Betty Boop/Pistol Packin' Mama: The Missions of a B-17" released in 1991 by Kenwood Productions, Directed by Tom Lenz and Produced by Bill Semans and Jeff Hohman.

[2]   All quotes from Gus Mencow are from author interviews in Worcester, Massachusetts in the summer of 2002.

Chapter Nine

Goering Bombs Germany

The name 'Goering' is intricately tied to the history of the air war over Europe, but when most students of aviation history hear the name, they do not think of a B-17 pilot. Instead, they think of Herman Goering, the German Reichsmarschall entrusted by Adolph Hitler to build and oversee the mighty German Air Force, or Luftwaffe. Under Herman Goering, the Luftwaffe was a formidable foe for the Allied airmen, sending up highly skilled adversaries in technically advanced aircraft. Early in the war, as American and British bombers struggled with minimal success against what seemed at the time to be an unbeatable Luftwaffe over an impregnable Germany, Goering boasted that no American or British aircraft would even darken the sky over Berlin. What would Herman Goering have thought, or what did he think, if he knew, that his own nephew, son of German immigrants, would end up flying an American heavy bomber into the heart of the Third Reich and over Berlin itself? In another proof to the adage that truth is stranger than fiction, Herman Goering's nephew Werner was a B-17 bomber pilot who flew missions over Germany as part of the Eighth Air Force's 303rd Bomb Group.

Herman Goering, one of Germany's great heroes of the First World War, had been an ace fighter pilot with 22 kills. After the death of Baron Manfred von Richthofen, the 'Red Baron', Goering took over command of Richthofen's squadron, the famous "Flying

Circus", and led it with distinction. Had he been content to rest on his laurels after the First War, he might have gone down in history as a great fighter pilot and fearless warrior. However, after the war he hitched his star to a young Austrian corporal and failed watercolorist named Adolph Hitler. Goering joined the Nazi party in 1922 and became a leader of the Strumabteilung (SA) also known as the Brownshirts. A member of the aristocracy, his social contacts were very valuable in selling Hitler's upstart National Socialist German Worker's Party to conservatives as the salvation of a post-World War I Germany in economic ruins.

Injured in the Beer Hall Putsch, he became addicted to morphine, a problem that would plague him the rest of his life. Goering lived to see the short-lived triumphs and eventual destruction of Hitler's barbaric Third Reich. Tried as a war criminal at Nuremberg, he escaped the hangman's noose only by killing himself with a cyanide capsule.

A chance encounter with Mormon missionaries set one of Herman Goering's brothers on a different road in life. Goering and his wife moved from Germany to the Mormon Zion of Salt Lake City, Utah. One of their sons was Werner G. Goering.

When World War II began, young Werner enlisted in the Army Air Corps. The government, for obvious reasons, took an interest in the fact that the nephew of the General of the German Luftwaffe wanted flight training and the FBI started an investigation. There were serious concerns that young Werner Goering might be a security risk. The FBI began an intensive background check on Goering, holding up his training for several months. Concurrently, they began to search for a man to fly with Goering, a man uniquely qualified to do whatever it took to ensure Goering's loyalty or to deal with any act of betrayal.

Jack Rencher grew up in rural northern Arizona. "I grew up with a gun in my hand," he remembers. "We lived up in the mountains. We ate deer and turkeys and whatever else we shot." From an early age, Jack became a crack shot with a pistol and rifle. When the United States entered World War II, Jack enlisted in the Army Air Corps. "I wanted to be a fighter pilot. In cadets, I trained as a fighter pilot." However, he caught the attention of his instructors on the shooting range. "At classification, we took a small arms course. They had three levels—marksman, sharpshooter and expert. I qualified expert on the first try." Jack put all ten of his .45 slugs through the 'X' in the center circle of the target.[1]

When it was time to go to Advanced pilot training, Jack asked for twin-engine fighters, hoping for a P-38 Lightning. He was assigned to P-38 school. After graduation, they kept him as an instructor. "I didn't like that. I demanded to be assigned to fighters and combat," he says. His superiors instead sent him to Yuma, Arizona, to fly the slower B-17 Flying Fortress bomber at the Yuma Air Force Base Gunnery School. In Yuma, Jack's job was to fly eight hours a day in two shifts, flying aerial gunnery students as they learned to fire the .50 caliber guns. "We'd do air-to-air for four hours. Then we'd do air-to-ground for four hours," he recalls. In air-to-ground we'd fly a hundred fifty feet over the ground. In air-to-air the gunners would shoot at a tow target behind a B-26. We'd take up 22 gunners a shift, eight hours a day, six days a week." This was not exactly the adventure that young Rencher had been thinking of when he'd enlisted in the Army Air Corps, but he eventually learned to love the B-17. After he'd accumulated about 1,000 hours in B-17s, he was transferred to Salt Lake City to become part of a B-17 combat crew.

A short time after arriving in Salt Lake, Jack got a letter from his aunt back in northern Arizona. She said, "Jack, I'm afraid you're in some kind of trouble. There are two FBI agents going door-to-door asking questions about you". Jack wasn't too concerned. He didn't particularly believe her. But a week later he got a letter from his high school principal. "Two FBI agents have been here," he wrote. "They spent most of one afternoon in my office, asking questions about you. I didn't know what to tell them, so I just told them the truth. I hope you're not in trouble."

A week later, Jack was ordered to report to the CO's office at 1300. This was unusual. Usually, when one got orders to ship out, they were told to report to Operations. When Jack arrived, he found two civilians in the office. The CO introduced them and then excused himself from the room. The civilians showed Jack their identification badges. They were FBI agents.

"We want to ask you to volunteer for an assignment," they told him. "It's strictly voluntary. If you don't want to do it, it will be no blemish on your record. We have a pilot whom we have investigated thoroughly. We can't find anything wrong with him, but we just don't trust him. He is a nephew of Herman Goering. We are afraid he will land his B-17 in Germany, and we want you to sign on as his co-pilot".

Jack explains now, somewhat cryptically, "Now keep in mind that our job and training is to kill and destroy. I was physically and mentally prepared to do both. When I flew combat, I carried three fully-loaded .45s and knew how to use them—one in a shoulder holster and two in my flight suit pockets." He told them he'd accept the assignment.

The next day the Goering Crew was formed, and Jack first met Werner Goering.

"We were just a bunch of kids fresh out of high school," Jack remembers now. "Some of us maybe had two years of college. But due to the pressure of the war, we were rushed through training."

"Goering was tall, about six feet or six-one, and cut a trim figure. He was also an immaculate dresser. He didn't smoke, drink, cuss or go out with the boys. He wasn't a social guy at all. He preferred to stay to himself." Jack found that the two had things in common. "I wanted to be strong, independent and healthy, and I didn't drink or smoke, either." The two men seemed a pretty good match.

"Goering was a much better-than-average pilot, but due to inadequate training, he had trouble with instrument take-offs and cross-wind landings. We usually took turns with the takeoffs and landings, but I had to help him the first few feet with every instrument takeoff he made to keep him on course and out of the ground."

"Goering later told me that he, too, had been held up for two or three months during which he was investigated."

Both were qualified first pilots. Normally, a B-17 first pilot had about a hundred hours in B-17s, while the copilot might well have none. Jack had over 1,000 hours of B-17 time, thanks to his forty-eight hour flying weeks in Yuma. Goering had about a hundred. Despite this, Goering was officially the first pilot and Jack the copilot. "I was a better pilot that he was," says Jack, never one to pull punches. "When I trained, I was practicing, not just boring holes in the sky. I studied every position on the crew."

The crew was assigned on August 7, 1944 to the 358th Bomb Squadron of the 303rd Bomb Group, and began stateside training in preparation for overseas combat duty. While in training, Jack and Werner developed a good friendship. "We made a good team," Jack remembers. "We flew all day together. We double-dated a bit, roomed together, slept in the same hut."

While in Savannah, Georgia, Werner told Jack that he was Herman Goering's nephew, not realizing that Jack already knew. Goering believed his relationship to the top Nazi was a well-kept secret, but many of the men on base somehow knew about it anyway. Though he had no accent and was thoroughly Americanized, it didn't escape the men on the crew that Goering, in order to be funny, often launched into fluent German when calling a stateside control tower.

Jack also learned that the Air Corps was taking no chances with Herman Goering's nephew. There was another plant on the crew. The radio operator, a Polish-American named Chester "Chad" Brodzinski, spoke fluent German and could spend time during missions monitoring all the plane's radio channels. Jack is not positive Brodzinski was a plant, but he feels it is certainly possible that he was put on the crew to listen to all of Goering's conversations on other frequencies, especially any transmitting in German.

One night, the enlisted crewmen showed up to talk to Jack. Telling him they wanted to go for a walk, they then told him they knew that Goering was Herman Goering's nephew, despite the fact that he'd told everybody he was simply a very, very distant cousin. They were concerned about going overseas and flying with

Goering and wanted to know what Jack thought. "I said, 'We're the best crew in the squadron. Good crews have a better chance of survival than bad crews. I don't think you have anything to worry about, but it is your call.'" Remembers Jack. "They all stayed."

Another event changed Jack's attitude towards flying shortly before going overseas. While attending one of his enlisted crewman's wedding in Florida, he was talking to the crewman's mother. She asked him to take care of her son. "At first, I thought, he can take care of himself. But then it hit me. It is my responsibility, as a pilot, to get him back alive. I changed. I quit taking unnecessary chances. I quit flying under bridges." It was a promise he would keep.

The crew was assigned to the 303rd Bomb Group out of Molesworth, England. The loss rate for flight crews was still very high, and there was no guarantee any of them would complete their tours. Each mission carried with it its own dangers. Sometimes the reason was German flak or fighters. Sometimes it was inadequate training. "We were expendable," remembers Jack.

"On one trip, not a mission, I was back in the tail section when all of a sudden the aircraft went into a dive, pulling two or three G's. I rushed to the cockpit. When I got there, we were going 360 miles per hour in a screeching, turning dive. 305 miles per hour is the redline on a B-17, and Goering was sitting there laughing. I jumped into the empty seat and pulled the plane out of the dive. I chewed him out and said 'if you ever do that again it will be the last damn thing you ever do!'"

Goering insisted that he was just having some fun, but he had terrified the crew, and putting such stress on the aircraft could have caused damage that would have showed up later on a mission, possibly leading to the crew's death.

Goering's loyalty was never an issue with Jack. Goering never gave any indication other than that he was simply a patriotic American man doing his duty to his nation.

"I'm sure the Germans knew he was up there," says Jack of Goering. "Herman Goering probably knew, too. If he'd been shot down and KIA, that's one thing, but if he'd become a POW, who knows what would have happened."

When the crew had finished about half its missions, the CO called Frank into his office. "What do you think of Goering?" he asked. "I said I thought he was a good pilot, but that he had one or two habits that will kill him one of these days, but I'm not going to let him do them."

"No, I don't mean his flying ability," the CO shot back. "I mean his loyalty."

To be humorous, Jack replied, "If the Germans offered him a major's leaf, he'd switch right over. And if the U.S. offered him a major's leaf, he'd come right back. I trust his loyalty," Jack finished, "but he is rank-happy."

This apparently satisfied the CO. His next comment was "I'm short of crews. We can't afford to have two first pilots on one crew. I have enough spare people to make up a crew except for a first pilot. Would you object if we split your crew?"

"It's fine with me, sir," Jack replied, "As long as I can have the enlisted men".

"You've got them, then," said the CO, and he split the crew.

Jack left the Goering crew in November of 1944. On February 15, 1945, Goering plowed his B-17 into the ground during a blind takeoff. Conditions at Molesworth that day were described as "visibility 70 yards, obscured sky requiring instrument takeoff". Goering's bomb-loaded plane plowed into the ground three hundred yards from the end of the runway.[2] "He went back into the ground and after the crew got out it exploded and blew a hole in the ground you could put a three-bedroom house into. Everybody survived. He said it was because he lost an engine and blamed mechanical failure."

Jack finished his thirty-five-mission tour and went home. He flew over ten missions as a first pilot or as an instructor pilot with new crews, in November and December 1944. He completed his tour on Christmas Eve, 1944.

Goering signed up for a second tour and flew well past his thirty-five missions. He became a Captain when he became a lead crew pilot. He stayed in the military for another twenty years and retired as a Lieutenant Colonel. After the war, he moved back to

Salt Lake, married a girl named Jean, and had second thoughts about his Mormon faith. Eventually, he moved to Arizona, where he managed large absentee ranches. Still alive and well at age eighty, time has mellowed Werner Goering, and Jack has seen him a few times since their war days. "I like him all right," says Jack. "Jean straightened him out, and he became quite a nice guy. When my wife was alive, we'd go visit him in Tucson. Still, we were never real, old buddy-buddies. He wasn't a social person at all. He only came to one reunion."

Werner Goering himself has no interest in rehashing his war experiences or his ties to infamous Germans. "I didn't do anything that a lot of other guys didn't do," he told me in our only short phone conversation. When I mentioned that nobody else had an uncle who was head of the German Luftwaffe, Goering dismissed the fact out-of-hand. "He wasn't my uncle. He was a second cousin, and so far removed he might as well have been on the moon."[3]

Polite, friendly, and encouraging, Goering wished me luck on my book as well as wishing me a Merry Christmas, but he was insistent that he had nothing more to say to me. "It was sixty-odd years ago," he said before the call ended, "and I'd just as soon not rehash ancient history."

The fact remains that Werner Goering did not have to enlist or train to fly in the dangerous heavy bombers over Europe in the Second World War. He was undoubtedly a patriotic American, ashamed of his link to such an infamous Nazi character. He endured background checks into his loyalty. The FBI personally recruited a fellow pilot to watch him and kill him should he turn out to be a traitor or a spy, and possibly recruited a radio operator to monitor his radio transmissions. Despite all this, Goering flew thirty-five missions and then re-enlisted and flew more dangerous missions over Germany. He gave his country twenty additional years of military service, and his family includes a successful lawyer. Despite his quirks and imperfections, Werner Goering did his duty. Given a strange assignment, Jack Rencher did his as well. One can only wonder what Herman Goering thought about the whole situation, if he knew about it. That story is forever lost to history.

Notes

1   This and all subsequent quotes from Jack Rencher come from an Author
     Interview in December 2003.
2   303rd Bomb Group Website.
3   Author Phone Conversation with Werner Goering, December 23, 2003.

Chapter Ten

Ball Turret Gunner

"It's hard to imagine a worse place to go to war in then the ball turret position of the B-17 Flying Fortress," begins one history. "Isolated from the rest of the ten-man crew, the ball turret was extremely cramped quarters and required a man with a slight build. In almost every case, there was not enough room for the ball turret gunner to wear a parachute." Colonel Budd J. Peaslee, a noted Group commander, remarked, "It is a hellish, stinking position in battle. The gunner must hunch his body, draw up his knees, and work into a half ball to meet the curving lines of the turret. The guns are to each side of his head, and they stab from the turret eyeball like two long splinters."

The Sperry ball turret was designed not for comfort, but for the defense of the underside of an aircraft. It hung from the bottom of the belly of the B-17, a tiny, self-contained, womb-like aluminum ball, bristling with two .50-caliber machine guns. On most missions, the ball turret gunner remained cramped in the fetal position for as many as nine hours. Functions as simple as eating, drinking or going to the bathroom became impossible. Temperatures plunged to more than fifty degrees below zero. If the plane were hit, the gunner was completely dependent on someone up in the main fuselage to open the ball and help him out. If those above were too busy or incapacitated, he rode the ball to his death.

What type of man did it take to go down into the ball turret, mission after mission? How did a man end up in the ball turret in the first place? What did he see, feel, and hear? And how did he maintain his mental equilibrium under such trying and often violent circumstances? The biggest obstacle to finding the answer is that most ball turret gunners don't feel that what they did was terribly out of the ordinary. Like most air war veterans, they go out of their way to minimize their courage and accomplishments. The fact remains, however, that the ball turret gunner was a breed apart. His story is often ignored. Most of the existing air war literature was written by and about officer crew. In addition, he was a citizen soldier, an enlisted man, less likely to make the Air Corps a career, and less likely to be trying to make a military mark for himself. After his foray in the sky, he usually returned to civilian life and moved onwards. He didn't talk much. He seldom recorded his experiences. No movies were made about him. He is, in effect, the B-17's forgotten man. To change that, at least a little, I enlisted the help of two old ball turret gunners, Frank Coleman and Bob Capen. They flew a combined total of 71 missions in the ball, and they are right proud of the fact, too. Frank and Bob pitched in to provide hours of taped answers, and it is their stories that form the backbone of this chapter.

The Boeing B-17 Flying Fortress was manned by ten men. Four were officers, six were enlisted men, usually sergeants. The officer crew was made up of a pilot and copilot, a navigator and a bombardier. The noncom crew was made up of a Flight Engineer, who also manned the top turret, a radio operator, two waist gunners, a tail gunner, and the ball turret gunner. The Fortress was designed to provide maximum defensive firepower forward, sideways, aft and to the bottom to defend the slow-moving heavy bomber from fighter attack. This crew configuration remained fairly constant throughout the war, despite some weaponry reconfigurations. Simply put, the ball turret gunner existed to defend the aircraft against attacks from below. The Sperry Corporation, designer of the ball turret, was charged with building a device that could rotate in such a way as to defend the entire underside of the ship. To do so, the device would have to be suspended below the structure of the ship itself. Sperry also had to design a system that could deliver firepower quickly and efficiently and at the same time defend its user from enemy fire. It was a formidable task.

According to one technical history, the Sperry Ball Turret, officially named Model 645473E, was "located in the bottom of the fuselage just aft of the radio compartment. The electrically powered turret on the B-17 could not be retracted into the fuselage. It had to be rotated manually using a hand crank to allow entry and exit. The whole unit was suspended on a gimbal that was attached to the ceiling of the fuselage. To control elevational pitch, the ball hinged on a frame on each side of the guns. The yoke of the gimbal pivoted giving the turret free movement in azimuth. On the backside was an entry hatch that also contained armor plating to protect the gunner from aircraft fire from the rear. Inside the ball was a small radio, a K-4 type computing gunsight, a breathing oxygen regulator, interior lighting, a first aid kit and the gun turret controls."

"Because of the severe cold in the unheated ball, the turret also had a plug-in point for an electrically heated flight suit. Once inside the ball, the gunner sat curled up in the fetal position, swiveling the entire turret as he aimed the two guns. The turret had a full 360 degrees of horizontal motion and 90 degrees of vertical motion. The gunner could be in any attitude from lying on his back to standing on his feet. The gunner sat between the guns with his feet in stirrups positioned on either side of the 13" diameter window in front. An optical gunsight hung in front of his face. His knees were up around his ears and his flight suit was his only padding. A pedal under the gunner's left foot adjusted a reticule on the gunsight glass. When the target was framed therein, the gunner knew the range was correct. Two post handles, pointing rearward above the sight, worked valves in the self-contained electro-hydraulic system to control the movement of the ball. A firing button located at the end of each handle would fire both guns. Empty shell casings were ejected through a port just below the gun barrel."[1]

It is hard to imagine a more unnatural position. Cold, cramped, often under fire, without a parachute, unable to eat or drink, the ball turret gunner sweated out his twenty-five, thirty or thirty-five missions suspended beneath an aircraft he knew could be brought down at any time by flak or fighters.

Frank Coleman was born in 1921 into a large Mormon family in Snake Creek, Utah, where his father Henry worked for Utah Power. At any early age, Henry Coleman moved the family to the mining town of Pioche, Nevada, where he installed the power lines to the Bristol Silver Mine. Frank grew up in the high mountain country of Nevada, "a good but tough place to grow up", he remembers. After graduation, he went on to Utah State University, majoring in Business Administration and minoring in Political Science. Bitten early by the flying bug after a barnstormer passed through, Frank also got his pilot's license.

"I enlisted in the military my junior year in college. The war started Dec. 7 1941 and I enlisted on January 19, 1942," Frank remembers. "I wanted to be a hot-shot fighter pilot, but I guess it wasn't meant to be. I had a disagreement with the flight instructor. He tried to get me to do a maneuver that I hadn't learned yet. I couldn't talk to him from where I was sitting, and he got angry and washed me out. That was it." Terribly disappointed, but wanting desperately to do something for the war effort, Frank then enlisted as an Army private.

Thus began a series of adventures and misadventures during which it seemed that the harder Frank tried to get into combat, the harder the Army tried to keep him out. He shuttled from one assignment to another, even giving up a chance at an officer's commission when he found out that he would be a "ground gripper". Along the way, he cajoled, talked back to superiors, was threatened with a court-martial, threatened his superiors right back, and had more disappointments than some men have in a lifetime.

"I asked for a transfer where I could get some training where I could get into a combat organization," he remembers. "I ended up at Buckley Field, Colorado. The training there was for fighter airplane armament and I went through that training. And then they said they needed more people for bombardment armament and I transferred. I finished that and I went down to Lowry Field in Denver and went through bombardment armament and was waiting for assignment to a group. They called us all together and said 'anybody that's interested in being an aerial gunner we'd be very happy to send you to aerial gunnery school'. About three-fourths of us raised our hands and I ended up a few days later on a troop train heading for Kingman, Arizona."[2]

Frank was the last man assigned to his crew. He showed up at a small fifteen by fifteen-foot shack at Kingman only to find out that all the crew positions but one had been taken.

"The next morning we went down and met the pilot and the bombardier and navigator and copilot and went off on a training flight. I got on board and as we stepped on the plane the pilot showed me the ball turret and said, 'Okay, that's your position'. In training I'd gotten in the ball turret a couple of times and I said, 'Do I have any choice?' and he says, "Well, you're the last man, and that's the only choice you have'. So that's why I became a ball turret gunner."

Like Frank, Missourian Robert "Bob" Capen enlisted in 1942 shortly after the U.S. entered the war. He requested the Air Corps because he'd always wanted to fly. "I was given the ball turret according to my size. I was the shortest guy on my crew and it took a small person to get in a ball turret. I was also qualified for the top turret but we already had a top turret, so I got the ball turret. I didn't have much of a reaction when I found out. I'd learned my gunnery in a T-6, and I'd never even seen a ball turret in gunnery school. I never saw a ball turret till I joined up with my crew."[3]

Fighting men from all branches looked on the ball turret gunner with respect and many thought he must be just a little bit crazy. After all, the position combined three of man's greatest fears—small enclosed spaces, heights, and death. It had all the tightness and claustrophobia of a submarine, it dangled under a piece of slow-moving aluminum 25,000 feet above the earth, and the Air

Corps had the highest casualty percentage of any service, including the Marines. Bob remembers that his pilot wanted to experience every position on his ship, and that on one occasion he went down into the ball turret. "He came right back out and said, "I wouldn't fly in that thing if they court-martialed me!" chuckles Bob.

While in England, Frank was in a restaurant in London when a soldier got into an argument with him about wanting to switch jobs because the Air Corps had it so easy. Frank told him he'd be happy to switch. "What do you do?" the soldier asked. "I'm a ball turret gunner," Frank replied. "Forget that!" said the soldier, and that ended the argument.

Though both men were, so to speak, victims of fate when it came to ending up in the ball turret, both quickly adjusted. "I was a miner," says Frank. "I'm not claustrophobic, so that was never a problem." "I never thought about it," says Bob. "I was always too busy looking for this or looking for that. I never felt claustrophobic."

Both men went through extensive crew training in the States before heading overseas to fly with the 95th Bomb Group out of Horham, England. Each had a particularly memorable training incident. Frank was nearly blown out of his turret when his improperly installed fifty-caliber machine gun bucked during a low-level training mission. He woke up hanging halfway out of the tiny trap door. The only thing keeping him and the haystacks twenty-five feet below from a quick meeting was his safety harness. Bob's crew flew into restricted airspace over Washington, DC after a navigational error and was almost shot down by two bursts of flak fired by gunners protecting the nation's capital from air attack.

Once in England, both men were quickly indoctrinated into the horrors of air combat over Europe. Bob's first mission was to Berlin, so "we got introduced to combat real nice". His plane also took "a direct hit over Warsaw, Poland and an .88 went right smack through the wing just behind the fuel tank. (Though) they're supposed to go off on contact or they have a proximity fuse, this one went through the wing and didn't go off. It left a hole big enough to stick your head through and then exploded after it went through. That was close." Frank had many close calls in combat, including a screaming dive where he ended up on the top of the ship with the sun in his eyes for a change, and his plane was shot up on numerous occasions. Both also had damage to their ball turret. On one occasion, a round penetrated Frank's small circular window, but somehow missed his head. "When we got back down, the ground crew took a pencil and stuck it through the hole to try to see how that round could have possibly missed my head," he says. "They couldn't figure it out. But I know. There was another guy in that turret with me that day." On two occasions, Bob had flak damage the glass on his small turret window, but neither penetrated the one and a half-inch thick tempered window. "My plane was shot up a lot, but not my ball turret," he remembers.

Before missions, the ball turret gunner had a practiced routine. First, he went and checked out his weapons. Steve Perri, who flew his missions starting in 1942 with the 91st Bomb Group, remembers, "We cleaned and oiled our guns the day after each mission and covered the breech mechanism with an athletic sock. When alerted for a mission, we stopped by the armament shop and thoroughly removed the oil lest it freeze at altitude and cause the gun to jam."

"After briefing, the gunners drew their guns and were transported to their aircraft. From outside the turret, I removed a small cover on each side of the entrance door and inserted the guns into their rigid mounts. After pre-flighting the turret, I helped the pilot and flight engineer pre-flight the aircraft."[4]

Because of the extreme cold in the unheated ball, the ball turret gunners wore many layers of clothing.

"We started with two pairs of heavy socks," remembers Frank. "We also had wired electrically heated socks. Over those three pairs of socks we wore fleece-lined leather flight boots. We wore longjohns and our regular GI clothes, and over that we wore a heated flying suit. This was heavy felt or wool with wiring through it. The suits kept you reasonably warm, but they did burn out. Over these we wore leather shearling flight pants."

"We each had a fleece lined leather flying jacket. Some guy at the base charged us twenty-five dollars to paint our plane on the back and a bomb for each mission."

"We had a fleece-lined leather helmet with a headset in it. I wore two pairs of gloves. The outer gloves were fleece-lined leather gloves. But sometimes your guns jammed and you had to take these off to fix them. So most guys also wore other gloves underneath. I used a lady's opera gloves. Some lady in London had turned in her dark brown silk evening opera gloves and I got 'em. That way I could make repairs at 80 below zero without losing skin off my hands."

The ball turret gunner wore a throat mike so he could talk to the rest of the crew. He wore his oxygen mask at all times above ten thousand feet. The ball turret had its own oxygen setup. Often gunners wore goggles.

Once the ball turret gunner had picked up his guns and gotten on all his gear, he entered the aircraft through the waist. Since the ball hung down beneath the plane, the gunner would never get into the turret until the plane was airborne. The clearance between the ground and the turret was only fifteen inches. Had the gunner been in the turret during takeoff or landing, any accident would have certainly crushed him to death under the ship.

"If we were taking off and forming over the North Sea," remembers Bob Capen, "we'd get in when we were safely airborne. But if we were circling over the field, we didn't get in till ten thousand feet, which is when we'd go on oxygen. Before that, we'd sit in the waist or stretch out on the floor in the radio room and take a little nap." Frank spent his time after takeoff in the radio compartment. "I slept. I didn't get into the turret halfway across the channel. The radio operator would kick me and motion me down into the turret."

"Once you were up, you could get into the turret," remembers Bob. "It had an outside crank inside the plane. You had to unlock the turret, put your hand on the crank, and turn the crank. This would run the turret down till the guns were facing down. You held the crank, opened the door, and reached inside to engage the clutch. Then you could let go of the crank. The clutch engaged the inside mechanism to the gear rings."

"It wasn't really that hard to get situated. You'd crank it down, step on either side of the round glass on the front, and lower yourself into your seat. Then you'd buckle your seat belt and that was it."

Steve Perri writes, "Once inside, I connected my throat mike, earphones and oxygen hose and fastened my safety belt. I was curled up with my back resting against the armored door, my legs bent and my feet resting on each side of the 13-inch diameter armored glass panel which was my main window on the world."[5]

Bob remembers the inside of the compartment well. "There was an oxygen regulator, a heat control for your electric suit. There was a computer sight and the two control handles with the triggers on them. Also, you had two places where you put your feet beside the glass. One controlled your mike switch and the other controlled the light reticules in the computer. Your left foot controlled the sight and your right foot controlled the mike switch. You also had one machine gun within four to five inches of either side of your head."

Perri remembers, "The two .50s were just inches away from your head with the ammo boxes above them. Your face was about 30 inches from the armored glass panel and suspended in between was the optical display glass for the computing gun sight. With your left foot you could adjust the lighted reticules projected onto this glass. When they framed a target, the range was correct. Two post handles projected rearward above the sight and flexing then moved the turret in azimuth and elevation. The firing buttons for the guns were in the ends of these handles, hence, to move the turret and fire the guns, your arms were bent with your hands above your head. As cramped as it sounds, it was actually quite comfortable. If I was firing straight out, it was like an easy chair".[6]

The predominant noise in flight was the droning of the four huge engines just outside. Other than that, remembers Bob Capen, "I couldn't hear much from inside the compartment. I had a helmet and earphones on. I could just hear a little motor whine, but mostly just the engines".

As for the smell, "all military aircraft had their own odors," says Bob. "It was 100-octane fuel, ozone, the smell of hydraulic fluid, and oil. In the plane we were allowed to smoke, as long as we weren't on oxygen, and when anyone in the plane smoked, I could smell it in the ball. It must have been the slipstream or something."

Bob remembers a definite feeling of suspension as he rode beneath the plane. "I felt that all the time. All I could see were the two wheels hanging down, and the engine nacelles down there and the ship's radio antenna."

Encased in his little pot-metal office, the gunner now settled down to wait for hours on end. Flight crews were given a diet suitable to men who had to fly many hours at high altitude in an unpressurized aircraft. For example, Frank remembers that they never ate foods that could cause gas, as the gas would expand at high altitude and cause incredible pain. However, the flight crews did drink coffee or other fluids before a mission, and this could cause problems for a ball turret gunner.

With so much cumbersome clothing to keep warm, relieving oneself was a major undertaking. Frank rarely bothered. "I call it the ball turret blues. You just couldn't pee. My kidneys have been weak ever since from holding it." There was a relief tube in the plane, but it didn't work, as the urine would freeze in the tube and cause a backup. Plus, remembers Frank, wincing, "when drops of urine turn to ice on the tip of your penis, it hurts. The ball turret gunner was sometimes a little damp in the groin region."

Bob never used the relief tube either, as it would kink, freeze or both and come right back at you. "I used a hydraulic can. The relief tube was useless. I'd roll the turret up, ask for the hydraulic can, and go that way."

Crewmembers inside the ship did use the relief tube, a long hollow rubber tube with a funnel on the pissing end. This tube emptied out the bottom of the ship. Both Frank and Bob relate how high-level usage by their fellow crewmen occasionally coated the ball turret with a glaze of yellow ice. "I got mad and yelled over the intercom," says Bob. "They heard me, they knew what I was talking about, but nobody answered me. It wasn't funny at the time, because I was done for the mission until we could go down in altitude and the ice could melt. But it got funnier later when they told the story."

The British Royal Air Force had suggested, early in the war, after evaluating the B-17 that it was impossible for a man to remain in the ball turret for an entire mission. However, Eighth Air Force ball turret gunners often spent ten to twelve hours in the ball while over enemy territory. "I never cramped up," remembers Bob. "And on the Russia mission, I was in the ball turret for nine hours."

Eating and drinking while in the ball turret were also an impossibility. "You couldn't eat or drink, really," says Bob. "Liquids would freeze. I know some guys took candy bars but I don't know how they ate them unless they stuck them under their armpits. It was anywhere from forty-five to fifty-five below zero. They did give us two little boxes of malted milk tablets and some high dextrose candy to munch on, but that was about it."

Defending the Fortress during aerial combat required great cooperation and communication among the crew. Ensconced in his tiny ball, the ball turret gunner's visibility was poor. He listened for cues as to enemy fighter position over the interphone. By doing so, he had to learn to predict when an enemy aircraft would enter his field of fire. Trying to shoot down an enemy fighter when both planes were going in different directions and different speeds was extremely difficult. On one mission, Frank shot and killed a German fighter pilot at close range. The German plane passed right under him. "The pilot was no further than twenty to thirty feet below me. He was shot. The pilot was already dead. His head was rolled back. You don't forget stuff like that. It was very sad."

It was important to keep the ball moving at all times, to remind the German fighters that the turret was manned. Frank found that by spinning the turret, he could deflect some of the bullets fired at him by fighters. Bob didn't think spinning would work. His only trick was "to have a sharp eye and keep the turret moving".

Both men participated in the ill-fated long-range shuttle

missions to Russia in 1944. On these missions, the 95th flew a deep penetration bombing mission in Germany, then landed in Russia for rest and refueling. On one of these missions, the Germans wiped out 47 B-17s on the ground at one base at Poltova. The group then flew to Italy, bombed oil installations in Romania, and flew back to England. Frank flew his thirty missions in only three months and seventeen days, second fastest in the history of the bomb group. "We were accelerated because of Normandy and D-Day and the bombing before and after, in preparation and so forth. Sometimes we were flying as many as five days in a row. That got pretty tough." On D-Day, Frank's crew flew two missions, landing in England only long enough to refuel, rearm, and grab a bite to eat. By the time the crew was finished, "we were pretty flakked up", he remembers.

Once safe over the North Sea or the Channel, the B-17s would descend to allow the men to remove their oxygen masks. The ball turret gunners would emerge from their turrets once there was no chance of enemy attack. "I'd get out of the ball turret after the plane was over the base," says Bob. Frank did the same. The sound of the bomber's rubber tires screeching against the paved runway on English soil was a sound savored by all air crews.

Once a mission was over, and the ball turret gunners had gone through debriefing and stowed their gear, it was time to reflect. "I'd thank God," says Bob. "'It's over,' I'd think. 'One more down.' You felt very tired. Mentally exhausted. Especially after a long flight."

"When we got back", remembers Frank, "we took out our guns and gave them to the ground crew. We'd go to our quarters, take a shower, get something to eat. We were in a farming area, in the countryside, and our Quonset hut was away from the rest of the base. I'd walk up a farming road, with rolling hills around me, about a half a mile. I'd come to a fence. There'd be cows, trees. I'd climb over the fence, go by a clump of trees, look around, and thank the Lord I was back."

"I'd talk with the Lord. I did a lot of apologizing. We did some serious damage to people who didn't deserve it. I felt badly. I still do."

Frank remembers one mission shortly after D-Day. "We were bombing not too far in front of our troops. They still had a bunch of Germans up in that area and they were trying to get out and we were trying to block their exit and destroy their equipment. We broke up into three-plane formations, went down to about 9,000 feet and bombed targets of opportunity. After the war, I saw some moving film taken by Germans at ground level and it showed the carnage and the death, face to face. It made me sick. I cried. It was a terrible thing to see that we did that kind of stuff. When you're at 25,000 feet it doesn't bother you, but when you're at nine thousand feet, you saw too much of it. And when you saw it at ground level, on camera, it was devastating to us. But, it was necessary."

During the course of his missions, Bob remembers, "we didn't talk about death. We just took 'em (the missions) as they came. We had no choice, really." But death was a daily occurrence, and all the men who flew the heavy bombers knew it. Bob remembers one mission where six of the sixteen bombers in his squadron went down in a matter of minutes during a fighter attack. This constant knowledge of death made surviving one's tour all the sweeter. The men had a club complete with certificate for those who managed to complete their missions without getting killed or becoming a POW—"The Lucky Bastard Club".

"When we finished," remembers Bob, "I was greatly relieved. A ton of weight went off my shoulders. We celebrated. Our last mission was the September 18, 1944 Shuttle Raid. We dropped supplies to the Poles in Warsaw, stayed one night in Russia, bombed a refinery in Hungary, and went on to Italy. While in Italy, we each bought two bottles of wine, the kind that's made, bottled and sold all the same day—real good stuff—and had a good vino party. We came back on September 19 and got credit. We were done."

Frank also survived his tour and returned to the States. However, he found himself reliving the horrors of combat on a daily basis for almost six months. He was recruited to be a guest speaker on a tour of the United States to encourage American workers to stay on the job in defense plants and keep productivity up. As part of the "Shot From the Sky" tour, he traveled from city to city, speaking to as many as five thousand people a day about the war effort. "I was reliving the war every day and every night and I was sort of going downhill the last couple of months. So they sent me to a convalescent hospital for a couple of months. Then after my thirty-day furlough, I was discharged in September of 1945."

Both men went on to have successful civilian careers, raise families, and enjoy old age. Frank appeared on a History Channel documentary "Suicide Mission: Ball Turret Gunners" and also returned to Europe on three occasions. Both men are rightly proud of serving their country in the ball turret of a B-17 Flying Fortress. They both attend 95th Bomb Group Reunions when possible.

"You can pick out the ball turret gunners at a reunion," says Frank. "There was no heat in those ball turrets. All the ball turret guys walk stooped. I've had back pains ever since the war, and I got disability after the war." In addition, he is now plagued with arthritis and uses a cane. Plus, he claims that ball turret gunners have weak bladders from all the long missions.

Do ball turret gunners see themselves as a breed apart? "I always thought we were just a shade different," says Bob. "But it was what we were assigned. It was our job. That's all it was. We had a job and we did it."

"You can't explain the flak and the fighters and the other planes going down and seeing people dying," says Frank. "That kind of stuff, those are the things I think should be known. It becomes difficult for me to talk about it. I get a little weepy at times. But I think it's good for people to know, and to understand, that WWII was a critical era in the history of our country and the world. By the grace of God and good luck we won, and it was just that—by the grace of God and good luck. We had to go fight a terrible war, and then we come home and went back to school, and turned out, for the most part, to be pretty reasonable and successful people."

The story of the Sperry Ball Turret and the men who manned it is one of the more obscure stories of the air war, but it is a story about men who, while many were short in stature, were long on courage. No men in modern aviation warfare have to fight in such exposed, frozen, cramped and dangerous positions. Few men in the history of warfare have had to. As Bob Capen says, "it was just a job", but it was a job that needed doing, and the Fortresses would never have survived without the man in the ball turret.

Notes

1   http://freepages.military.rootsweb.com/~josephkennedy/sperry_ball_turret.htm

2   This and all subsequent quotes by Frank Coleman are the result of extensive author interviews in 2001 and 2003, taped, over the telephone, and in-person in Salt Lake City, Utah in May, 2003. Some biographical date about the Coleman family also comes from *Franklyn Robey Coleman: A Life History*, by Jerod Bybee, Frank's nephew, self-published by Mr. Bybee in 2001.

3   This and all subsequent quotes by Bob Capen are the result of extensive taped author interviews done in 2001 with the help of Bob's son-in-law.

4   Steve Perri, Ball Turret Gunner, website http://www.geocities.com/milbios/perrisbio.html

5   Perri

6   Perri

Chapter Eleven

No Purple Heart, Died Serving Country: Training Accidents in the Air Corps in World War II

"Rifle fire shattered the winter afternoon and Taps reverberated over snow covered hills. A mother received a letter of condolence from the office of Henry "Hap" Arnold, Commanding General of the Army Air Forces. It stated, in part, that her son had 'lived up to the promise of his training period and developed into a conscientious, trustworthy pilot.'"[1] Slowly, the small group of mourners dispersed into the thin winter sunlight, leaving the white stone marker to bear its own witness. It was a scene repeated, with variations, many times over the course of the war. Another young life was gone. The difference, however, was that these young men had been killed in training. Some had seen combat. Many never saw a shot fired in anger. None received a posthumous Purple Heart, and their names sometimes do not even appear on the rolls of the dead from the twentieth century's greatest conflagration. Funerals just like this one were repeated over 60,000 times in the course of the war.

At the onset of World War II, less than forty years had passed since Wilbur and Orville Wright had coaxed the first rickety flying machine off the ground. Aircraft had come a long way, but were still dangerous machines that required great skill and physical strength to fly. Human error, especially in the early stages of training, was common. But not all crashes were the result of human error. Early in the war, combat aircraft were works in progress, and many contained serious flaws that were only detected through trial and error. The bottom line was, flying continued to be a glamorous but deadly occupation.

U.S. Army Air Force casualties in World War II totaled over 120,000, the highest casualty percentage of any armed service, including the Marine Corps. Forty thousand men died in actual aerial combat. In addition to the 15,000 Stateside deaths, as many as sixty-five thousand were killed overseas in training accidents or non-combat accidents. Aircraft losses during the war came to 65,200. One third of these aircraft were destroyed in crashes in the States.[2]

Early in the war, crews were killed by a combination of untested equipment and human error. Later in the war, the machines improved. However, "as the daylight bombing campaign in Europe reached its height, casualties mounted and replacement crews were needed. This resulted in shortened training schedules, a large number of training-related aircraft crashes, and crew fatalities. The cost of a conflict is often tallied in battle casualties. But the enormity of mobilization for WWII can also be seen in the observation that four years of war claimed the lives of 14,900 airmen in 6,000 fatal crashes of military aircraft within the continental United States . . . These stateside fatalities represent 12.5% of the approximately 120,000 U.S. Army Air Forces casualties during the war."[3]

And it wasn't just men who died. Women pilots served with the United States Army Air Corps from September 12, 1942 until December 20, 1944. They flew all the same equipment as their male counterparts, tallying 60 million miles through the continental United States, Canada and the Caribbean on ferrying and utility flight missions. These women, directed by Nancy Harkness Love, became known as the WAFS (Women's Auxiliary Ferrying Squadron) and the Wasps. These pilots all held commercial pilots' licenses and had logged over 500 hours of flight time. As a group, they were the most highly qualified women aviators in the nation. They were considered Civil Service employees but subject to military discipline under military orders. Thirty-nine WASPs were killed on active duty and three women were killed on termination leave in December, 1944, but their families received no survivors' benefits."[4] And it wasn't until June, 2002, that any WASP received full military honors.[5]

All told, the deaths of so many of America's best and brightest deserve a chapter in the history of the air war. In one day at Douglas Army Air Field, six young men died in the crashes of four training planes. A historian calls the event "a microcosm of the larger sacrifice"[6]. Each man or woman died serving his or her nation. Each deserves a nation's gratitude. Each truly is "a microcosm of that larger sacrifice".

Alamogordo Army Air Field—now Holloman Air Force Base—in New Mexico was just one base that trained heavy bomber crews throughout World War II. Here, crews completed final flight training in B-17s, B-24s, and B-29s before receiving overseas assignments for the war in Europe and the Pacific. The base saw its share of tragedies. In one month in 1943 over 100 airmen died in training-related accidents. As many as 117 accidents occurred during "routine training flights" that involved Alamogordo-based aircraft between 1942 and 1946. "To give the reader an impression of the risks inherent to the aircrew before they even faced the enemy, in 78 crashes alone, 540 crewmembers were involved and 171 were fatally injured".[7]

Central High School in Omaha, Nebraska, lost 79 young men in World War II. Of these, seven were killed in training. Second Lt. Gerald Beem, Class of '37, "crashed in his Flying Fortress over Musselshell, Montana, December 8, 1942." Second Lt. Victor Boker, Class of '41, was "killed October 8, 1944, in a training accident near Nadzab, New Guinea". First Lt. William Brookman, Class of '34 and a "member of advanced flying school, Bradley Field, CT, was killed on a training flight on June 25, 1944". Ensign Lloyd Dworak, Class of '41, was "killed in a crash of his Navy fighter during a training flight at Vero Beach, Florida, on January 6, 1945". Richard Forcade, Class of '40 and a Pilot Instructor, was "killed in a crash at Thunderbird Field, Arizona, on December 30, 1943". Second Lt. James Milliken, Class of '36, and an Air Corps bombardier, "was lost in an over-water flight from Langley Field, Virginia, on April 24, 1943". Ensign Charles Nestor, Class of '38, was "lost in a Navy training flight over Puget Sound, Washington, in September 1943".[8]

During stress-filled flight training "washing out and getting killed were always on every cadet's mind, though it could probably be safely said that most gung-ho young cadets preferred the latter. To most, "washing out was a fate worse than death".[9]

Mozart Kaufman is, fortunately, a living example of how equipment could kill an airman in training. Mozart entered advanced fighter pilot training at Hamilton Field, California in 1942, where he was assigned to master the Airacobra P-39 D-1 Warbird fighter plane. "The plane was small," he remembers, "but it was a compact power house, built with not only .50 caliber guns but also a .37-milimeter cannon in the nose. The cockpit was entered by a door on the wing into the smallest possible space. Flying this plane was like being in a powerful hornet[10]," he remembers. With a maximum speed of 386 miles per hour, the plane seemed like a dream come true for young Mozart. "I had a love for this P-39. It was the first fighter plane that I flew after graduation from flying school, but this plane was a killer. I had a feeling of love/hate filled with respect for what it could do to me[11]," he remembers.

However, the pilots soon became concerned with "the troubles being experienced with the P-39. Some of the pilots talked about the plane 'tumbling' when it was in aerobatics and spins, but no one could pin down what was wrong. Since I had arrived at Hamilton Field, we had lost four pilots in P-39s. On October 27, we lost our fifth pilot, my friend Lt. John Nioso. We had no answer as to the cause. There was no radio communication from John to give us any hint that he had been in trouble—just another crash without warning."

"On the evening of October 30, my wife and I had a buddy pilot over for a visit and we discussed the troubles we were having with our planes. I told him I was scheduled to fly the next morning and to do spins and stalls for the first time. I said, 'There is no way I'm going to go into the ground with that damn plane.'"[12]

The next morning, Mozart took off into a cloudless blue sky, the San Francisco Bay twinkling below him. "The beauty was not on my mind this morning. I had before me the most serious mission of my life."

Sure enough, while practicing a power-on spin at 15,000 feet, the P-39 went suddenly and completely out of control. No matter what Mozart did, the plane continued to spin, and the waters of the Bay were getting closer by the second. It was time to bail out. He pulled the release handle on the right-hand door and gave it a firm yank. Nothing happened. He slammed against the door with as much force as he could muster in the confined cockpit. It wouldn't budge. He tried the left-hand door with the same results. Neither door would open. He turned back to the right hand door, adrenaline surging through his body, and gave it a superhuman shove. Finally, he felt it give and fly off into space. He jumped clear and parachuted into the Bay, where a sport fisherman picked him up.

A few days later, Mozart was called before a hearing board to report what had happened on the flight. The group commander, Major Frederick Gambo, tried to pick every corner of his brain, to find out why the plane had gone into an unrecoverable spin. Finally, "I was asked if I had pulled the throttle when I went into the power-on spin. I told them that there were no instructions anywhere about pulling the throttle in a spin."

The next day, the group commander took a P-39 up to 17,000 feet and attempted the same maneuver. Anxious pilots stood on the ground and watched.

"When Major Gambo landed, we all gathered around him to hear his report. He said he had gone into a power-on spin . . . and that this was the most violent flight he'd ever been in. There was no way he could have recovered from the spin with the power on. But when he pulled the throttle all the way back, the plane slowed to a normal spin and he was able to recover without any problem."

Forty-five years later Mozart wrote to the Air Force for a microfilm copy of the test and found that, because of this test, the instruction to cut throttle in a spin had been added to the operations instructions for the P-39. He also wrote to a friend who had gone to Hamilton ahead of him, and who had practiced the same maneuver. This man informed Mozart that he and a partner had been practicing the spin over the Bay and that both had lost control. Though his friend had managed to recover, the partner had crashed into the Bay and been killed.

Another great improvement, partly as the result of Mozart's difficulty in bailing out, was that future models of the P-39 were equipped with a large emergency release handle on the right-hand door. "It took the loss of many lives to solve the problems with this plane after it was first produced," he says. In Mozart's case, he had not only managed to save his own life, but to save the lives of many pilots who would follow him in the P-39.[13]

Many more Air Corps crewmen met their fates in training once overseas. The official bomb group records are filled with references to the dangers faced by crews in training. For example, during its stay at Rougham Air Base in England, the 94th Bomb Group lost 153 aircraft. Twenty-seven of these were lost through operational accidents. From 1943 to 1945, the 100th Bomb Group lost 177 aircraft missing in action. It also lost 52 in operational accidents.

Herman Fieber lives in Bakersfield, California today. He is one of only two survivors of a training accident that occurred while he was serving as a Tail Gunner in the 34th Bomb Group, Mendlesham, England.

Born in Bakersfield, California in 1925, young Fieber entered the service in 1943, and he and his crew survived all the Stateside training before being shipped to England as a B-24 bomber crew. The thin, baby-faced Fieber and the rest of the crew arrived in Mendlesham on Christmas Eve, 1944, only to find that the 34th was being transitioned into B-17s. This would require the crew to retrain on the new equipment. Herman was unconcerned. Pilot John Steffen and Copilot Frank Reinecke were excellent flyers as well as good friends. The entire crew was very close, and had built a high level of trust and camaraderie over the many weeks of training in the States.

On January 17, they were scheduled to make six touch-and-go night landings. Herman was in his usual position in the tail of the aircraft. "On the sixth touch-and-go, our plane exploded and crashed[14]," he remembers. "My memory is that we had just turned onto the downwind leg, because I just flashed a light which I would flash so that the B-17 following us would know our position. One thing I do remember was that when we were flying I could not buckle my seat belt because it was tangled. Of course when we crashed I was thrown clear, sparing my life."

"Either unconscious or in shock, the next thing I remember is lying in a field groaning and Sgt. Joe Baker, the waist gunner, who was semi-conscious, crawling over to me to put mud on my clothes because they were on fire." Herman had been thrown fifteen feet from the wreckage of the severed tail section, which had fallen separately from the rest of the ship. "As I drifted in and out of consciousness, I remember hearing voices as the medics arrived to assist. Joe Baker, Joseph Longtine, the ball gunner, and myself were taken to the hospital at Bury St. Edmunds. Joseph Longtine was riding in the nose section and when we crashed he was thrown against a tree and was unconscious, dying shortly after arriving at the hospital. All other crewmembers were killed instantly.

When I regained consciousness, about twenty-four hours later, I was not told of the fate of my fellow crewmembers, although I suspected they were gone. Whenever I inquired, I was told that they were okay, but I knew that none had been taken to the hospital".

In a letter to me in 2001, Herman continued his story. "I was treated (at Bury St. Edmunds) for excessive burns to my body and face. I also had a broken right wrist. Due to the severity of the burns I was wrapped in Vaseline gauze from head to toe like a mummy. I was also given a lot of blood plasma to keep me alive. I remained in this position with my eyes bandaged for approximately two months."

"When changing my dressings they discovered that my eyelids were completely burned off so they decided to graft new eyelids. This was accomplished by removing some skin from inside my left upper arm and sewing it on where my eyelids were supposed to be. They used a new drug called sodium pentothal to put me to sleep. The operation was successful. Today few scars remain."

"About a week before I left England I was able to get out of bed and some of my bandages were removed, especially the ones covering my eyes and I was able to start to see and do things.[15] "He returned to the States on a hospital ship, docking in Boston, spent some time at a hospital there before being put on a hospital train to Menlo Park, California. This hospital specialized in plastic surgery and was called Dibble General Hospital. "There I was given a skin graft to my left hand which was severely burned. I was discharged from the hospital on October 11, 1945, nine months after the crash. I then returned home and attended Bakersfield Junior College."

"I had nightmares for at least twenty years, and have a constant fear of fire and still think about the crash today and the loss of seven of my best friends." For his wartime service, including nine months of extensive rehabilitation, Herman received the European Medal, the Good Conduct Medal, and the Victory Medal, but because his painful wound had happened in training, Herman received no Purple Heart, which is reserved for those injured by the enemy.

"The seven crewmen who were killed in the crash were buried at the American cemetery in Cambridge, England. Later the Army gave the families the option of returning the bodies home to be buried and five of the families brought them home. Three remain buried in their original graves in Cambridge, as the families decided to leave them there."

"Not much has been reported on service personnel killed in training," writes Herman. "The spotlight has been on those killed in action. A book such as yours highlighting these deaths is one way to bring attention to these deaths. During the war they sometimes tried to minimize the accidents for reasons of morale."

Still, he isn't bitter and doesn't feel slighted. "The treatment given to me after the accident was the same as that accorded to anyone wounded in combat. We were all treated as special for having served our country."

Surviving such a catastrophic crash was nothing short of a miracle, and the event reaffirmed Herman's belief in God. He is rightfully proud of his service to his country during World War II, and "it pleases me that today's generation seems to be rediscovering and embracing our participation in World War II. This was an important time for our country and for all the soldiers who served. We must never forget our fallen friends. Everyone must remember the sacrifices we all have made".[16]

This advice of an aging veteran to a nation nearly sixty years after World War II bears heeding. It is fitting that we take some time, in our remembrances of the sacrifices of those past, to remember the staggering number of brave young men—and women—who died training to serve. Their deaths are no less noble because they were not felled by an enemy. No small white stone, whether it rests in Arizona or England, deserves to be walked past without at least a quick word of thanks and a prayer. Never forget them.

Notes

1   George R. Herman, "A Bad Day at Douglas Army Air Field" *The Journal of Arizona History* 36 (4), 1995, 379.

2   http://personal.trxinc.com/dpixler/

3   Herman, 379.

4   Major Natalie J. Stewart-Smith, New Mexico Military Institute, http://home.earthlink.net/~reyesd99/stewartsmith/introduction.html

5   Pamela Feltus, http://www.centennialofflight.gov/essay/Air_Power/Women/AP31.htm

6   Herman, 379.

7   "Routine Training Flight:" The Legacy of World War II Aircraft Training Accidents at Alamogordo Army Air Field, New Mexico. Holloman Air

Force Base *Cultural Resources Publication* 7 (October 2000, Matthew Vandiver and William B. Boehm)

8   Ben Sylvester, Omaha Central High School Class of '42, Researcher, http://www.ops.org/central/WorldWarII.html

9   John R. Lester. *Frontline Airline: Troop Carrier Pilot in World War II*, Sunflower University Press, Manhattan, Kansas, 1994.

10   Mozart Kaufman, *Fighter Pilot: Aleutians to Normandy to Stalag Luft I*, M.& A. Kaufman Publishers, San Anselmo, CA, 1993, p. 17.

11   Kaufman, *Fighter Pilot*, p. 21.

12   Kaufman, *Fighter Pilot*, p. 20.

13   Mozart Kaufman, Phone Conversation with Author, December 2003.

14   Herman Fieber's story is on his website, at http://www.34thbombgroup.homestead.com

15   Herman Fieber, Letter to Author, August 30, 2001.

16   Herman Fieber, Letter to Author, August 30, 2001.

Chapter Twelve

Shot down by the Swiss

In 1943 and early 1944, the chance that an aircrew of a heavy bomber would complete its obligatory twenty-five missions was roughly one in three. After each mission, combat crews would return their base to find the bunks of those who had not returned stripped and their possessions already packed and gone. They would go to sleep with visions of exploding bombers and men, remembering how they'd prayed to see chutes billow. It didn't take a genius to look around the briefing room and realize that most of these young men were destined for death or imprisonment. There was a way out, though. You could set a course for Switzerland and spend the rest of the war in the neutral country, hiking and skiing and learning to yodel. Life would be good, and— better yet—it would continue.

Unfortunately, many popular historians have perpetuated this myth. In so doing, they have done a great disservice to the many American aircrews that ended up interned in Switzerland or Sweden during the war. At best, internment in Switzerland was life deferred, freedom taken away, and severe rationing. At worst, it meant serious injury or death at the hands of the Swiss.

In Gerald Astor's popular history *The Mighty Eighth*, there are only two references in roughly five hundred pages to Swiss internment. They are both negative. In the first, Astor makes his own comment that "aside from Sweden, Eighth Air Force planes with mechanical trouble or battle damage could also resort to the other neutral turf, Switzerland. Whether or not it was necessary to take refuge rather than to try to make it home to fight another day was a matter of some controversy." He then goes on to record the thoughts of group commander Archie Old. "Archie Old growled about seeing aircraft head for the two countries. 'It happened a small amount of times. I sat in the cockpit and cussed those sons of bitches when I would see them leaving. I didn't really know whether they were crippled or not'."[1]

In Astor's only other reference in what is otherwise a respectful overview of the Eighth Air Force, he draws his thoughts from the same man who earlier in the book so maligns the internees. "What so disgusted Archie Old when he spied B-17's headed for the safety of Switzerland is the failure to support those who shared the life and danger."[2]

In all, sixty American airmen lost their lives in Switzerland during the war. Two committed suicide during internment. Twenty-seven were killed by Swiss fighters or anti-aircraft fire or by parachute failure after such attacks. They are some of the war's forgotten dead. Originally, these men were buried at a cemetery in Munsingen, Switzerland. In 1948, the State Department and Defense Department decided Munsingen would no longer be an American cemetery. The men were disinterred and reburied either in Epinal, France, or returned to the United States for burial. The only evidence that Munsingen had been the burial place of sixty American airmen was a plaque placed in 1946 by the American ambassador on the front wall of the Munsingen cemetery. Over the years, the plaque deteriorated badly. Finally, a retired Swiss Air Force colonel sought to have the U.S. Embassy remove, clean and remount the plaque. The Embassy did nothing. The Swiss colonel then paid to have the work done out of his own pocket, thereby earning the eternal gratitude of the Swiss internees.

Modern histories, such as Stephen Ambrose's *The Wild Blue: The Men and Boys Who Flew the B-24s Over Germany*, have been more fair to the Swiss internees. Ambrose writes that despite widespread rumors of crews hightailing it to Switzerland, "investigation revealed that such reports were almost wholly inaccurate. The bombers that landed in neutral countries had indeed been so shot up that the pilots had no choice."[3]

In his book *Shots at the Liberators*, Swiss historian Peter Kamber writes about the strange circumstances which resulted in the Swiss military firing at Allied aircraft. He begins his book by recounting the events of the night of July 12-13, 1943, when a British air fleet strayed into the corner of Swiss air space on its way to upper Italy. Fired upon by Swiss air defenses, two aircraft crashed and all the crews burned to death. "Even when many units put up passive resistance and shot with skill to miss the bombers, fifteen Allied airplanes were shot out of the sky by the war's end and thirty-six (or if questioned cases are included, forty-eight) (Allied) crew members were killed in these attacks."[4]

Once interned, and under direct orders to escape and return to their units, young American airmen were shocked to be told by the American Air Attaché in Bern, Barnwell Legge, that they were not to attempt escape under any circumstances. Those who attempted escape anyway were severely punished. Several ended up in a Swiss maximum-security prison and nearly died.

In preparing this chapter I talked with many airmen, both those who were interned and those who escaped such a fate. Many of those who did not end up in Switzerland have memories of watching other crews diverting. One, Maurice Rockett, recalls radioing a crew that was turning towards Switzerland and telling them "learn how to yodel for me!" Others candidly admit that they discussed the possibility with their crews of diverting to Switzerland. In some cases, they had wounded comrades aboard who would die without immediate medical attention. In others, they were struggling to keep a dying aircraft airborne. Some went as far as to put the idea to a vote. None of the airmen I talked to and corresponded with has ever had anything negative to say. In fact, most admit they have little idea what happened to their colleagues once they got to Switzerland.

During the war, a total of 166 U.S. aircraft sought refuge in Switzerland. Eighty-two were B-24s, 74 were B-17s, and the remaining were a variety of makes. Forty-one were destroyed in crashes, thirty-nine landed badly damaged, and eighty-six landed in repairable condition. Ninety-six were salvaged as junk. Of these, seventy were repaired after more than 19,000 hours of repairs.[5] All aircraft were impounded by the Swiss for the remainder of the war. Nearly 1,500 American airmen were held for the duration. Aircrews became 'internees', as opposed to 'Prisoners of War'. The distinction arose from the fact that the Swiss were a neutral power. There were two classes of interned airmen in Switzerland. The largest was made up of those who had made it to Switzerland with their aircraft. A smaller contingent, called 'evadees', did not land in Switzerland but walked in from other parts of Europe. According to Swiss law dating back to the Middle Ages, evadees were given sanctuary and were free to move about the country like tourists. They were kept separately from the internees, who were kept under guard at fixed locations.

The first U.S. aircraft landed in Switzerland on August 13, 1943. 'Death Dealer' was a B-24 Liberator from the 93rd Bomb Group. Its crew managed to set fire to the plane near the city of Wil. The last aircraft to land in Switzerland was a B-17 named Princess O'Rourke, from the 30th Bomb Group, that landed April 20, 1945. The record number of arrivals in one day during the war was sixteen, on March 18, 1944.

Almost all landings were made at the Swiss air base at Dubendorf.

At least one of these landings was, indeed, questionable. One B-24 from the 93rd Bomb Group landed at Dubendorf on March 16, 1944. The Swiss who examined it noted that the aircraft was "undamaged with enough fuel (1,058 gallons) for a return to England". But this was by far the exception.

At war's end, forty-one B-24s, thirty B-17s, and one P-51 were flown from Switzerland to Burtonwood, England, for repatriation. The rest were scrapped in Switzerland. The planes that flew to England arrived too late to return to the States and they, too, were scrapped at Burtonwood. Miscellaneous equipment from the aircraft were loaded into six trucks, each carrying twenty tons, and was hauled out of Switzerland to Munich-Erding, Germany where most was burned and destroyed. The Swiss government also presented the US Army Air Corps with a bill for $104,000 for the food and lodging of the interned airmen during the war.[6]

Bob Long is a former B-24 pilot and president of the American Swiss Internees Association. He looks like a tough military man who even today could hold his own if he had to. And he won't mince words. Bob Long will go ballistic if you try and tell him that American airmen used Switzerland as an easy way out of the air war. And Bob knows what he's talking about. He was a Swiss internee himself, and has spent the better part of his life fighting for the recognition and respect that interned airmen earned during their incarceration in Switzerland.

During the war, aircrews were told that if for some reason they were unable to make it back to a friendly airfield that they had the option of landing in Switzerland. The advantage to this was that the planes, along with their secret equipment, would not fall into the hands of the Nazis. Another advantage was that the crewmen would not be classified as Prisoners of War, since Switzerland was a neutral country. The U.S. did not recognize internees as POW's and there was no provision under the Geneva Convention to protect the internees from abuse. In fact, it wasn't until 1949 that the Geneva Convention changed wording to read "Combatants who are in neutral countries have the same rights as prisoners of war in a combating country".

An internee was not a Prisoner of War. He was a guest of the neutral nation. His own government paid his expenses. After the war, he would be ineligible for POW benefits or the POW medal, no matter how traumatic his circumstances. Worst of all, he would have to listen to a small minority of his fellow airmen, at reunions and in day-to-day encounters, insinuate that he was a coward who had turned tail and ran instead of staying and fighting like the rest.

"Damn lies," Bob Long will tell you. He will hotly refute any charge that American aircrews used Switzerland as a way out. He points out that in some cases, the incarceration and hardships endured by the American airmen in supposedly neutral Switzerland were as bad—or worse—than those suffered by their fellow airmen in German Stalag Lufts.[7]

Bob Long asserts that the Swiss were neutral in name only. They had a small but capable Air Force, made up of German aircraft painted with Swiss markings, as well as batteries of anti-aircraft guns. They used them to shoot down American bombers with German-made fighters, killing American crewmen. They kept American airmen under armed guard in areas from which escape was impossible. If the American internees tried to escape, then the Swiss sent them to federal prisons. On the other hand, the Swiss repatriated German internees on a regular basis. In fact, fully 783 German airmen refused repatriation offered them by the Swiss. Not a single American airman was repatriated. German internees were free to wander the country. Americans were not. German internees were free to travel back and forth across the border between Switzerland and Germany.

Swiss factories produced items for the Nazi war machine while at the same time, due to a treaty signed on July 18, 1941, they refused to trade with the Allies. At the time, Switzerland held worldwide dominance in specialized industrial machinery and precision micro-bearings. The Allies needed these components for aircraft and scientific instruments, and had to scramble to find new producers. In the end, the Allies smuggled millions of the minute jeweled bearings out of Switzerland to meet the demand in an operation called "Operation Viking". Meanwhile, the Swiss continued shipping arms to Germany until October of 1944.

The Swiss also provided electric power and a countrywide rail system for transporting German rail supplies. The Allies, respecting Swiss neutrality, never attempted to bomb rail lines, even when Nazis were shipping supplies by rail from Germany to the Italian campaign.[8]

In one instance, the Swiss destroyed a Nazi aircraft containing a new top secret radar so that the Allies could not get hold of it, and in return were given twelve German Me109s. And, as has been conclusively shown in recent years, Swiss banks willingly profited by guarding Nazi plunder-much of it stolen from the Jews. Many high-ranking Swiss were enthusiastic members of the Swiss Nazi Party and very bit as zealous as their German counterparts. In a report by Alan Morris Schom, Ph.D., entitled "A Survey of Nazi and Pro-Nazi Groups in Switzerland: 1930-1945" published by the Simon Wiesenthal Center, Schom states "pro-Nazi, fascistic, and super-patriotic associations . . . thoroughly saturated every one of the country's twenty-one cantons and the core of Swiss society—from the working classes to the ruling elite".[9]

Granted, the Swiss were caught between a rock and a hard place. They shared a common border with Europe's biggest bully, Hitler's Germany. They depended on trade with neighboring nations for their livelihood. Many individual Swiss did all they could to help the American airmen, including, in many cases, aiding in their escape. Some did it for the money, some did it out of goodness, and others took the Americans' money and then turned them over to the Nazis for an additional payment, earning from both sides in the bargain. Swiss civilians who were caught trying to help American internees escape from Switzerland were arrested, prosecuted, jailed and exiled as traitors up to a year after the war ended.

Being an interned airmen in Switzerland was anything but a leisurely existence of skiing, drinking beer with the locals, and picking edelweiss in the Alps waiting for the war to end.

To make matters worse, the American military attaché in Switzerland, General Barnwell Rhett Legge, turned his back on his own servicemen and on the instructions they had been given throughout their training. They had been taught not to cooperate: name, rank and serial number only. General Legge pressed them to provide more. General Legge, in a meeting with Swiss military officials, stated that he had a directive from Washington that American internees were not to escape. Repeated searches of the National Archives and other military repositories of historical records by former internees and the internee association have failed to find any such order or directive from the War Department.

Legge's orders said that any interned airman captured trying to escape would be turned over to the Swiss government for imprisonment in a Swiss prison. There were three Swiss concentration camps, Wauwilermoos, Hunnenberg, and Diablerets. Wauwilermoos is considered by far the worst. The commandant of Wauwilermoos was a Swiss Nazi named Hauptman (Captain) André Beguin, who spent funds meant for the running of the prison on himself and his four mistresses and who was a cruel and sadistic man. American airmen unfortunate enough to be caught trying to escape from Switzerland were sent to these federal prisons, which held mostly rapists, murderers, and other violent criminals. Legge refused to inspect the prison camp at Wauwilermoos or look after any of the American airmen held there. In fact, he insisted that there was no such place. And for many years after the war ended, the United States government would not admit to its existence, either.

Food at Wauwilermoos was served once a day in slop cans, there were no sanitary facilities, raw sewage ran through the camp, and prisoners were often beaten or placed in solitary confinement. The horrific true story of one man who spent time in Wauwilermoos, Sgt. Dan Culler, is told elsewhere in this book.

Long has his theories as to why many had and continue to have misconceptions about the Swiss internees. During the war, an American diplomat in Sweden wrote to the U.S. Army Air Corps High Command, suggesting that many escapees and internees in Sweden and Switzerland were simply fleeing the war. The commander of the Eighth Air Force at the time of the report, General Spaatz, ordered a USAAF maintenance supervisor with a ground crew of five to fly to Switzerland and inspect the impounded American bombers at Dubendorf. This supervisor, according to Long, remained in Switzerland until the end of the war. In a November 7, 1944 report, the supervisor reported that there were no USAAF aircraft in Switzerland without just cause.

A British TV company, years later, produced a film with the basic premise that the aircraft that flew to Sweden and Switzerland were undamaged and that the crews were deserters and cowards.

The TV show also reported that American fighter pilots had been commanded to shoot down any American bomber seen heading towards a neutral country. In fact, according to Long, the show misinterpreted a command given to fighter pilots to shoot down "rogue" USAAF aircraft. These "rogue" aircraft were usually American planes that had been forced down behind enemy lines and then flown by the Luftwaffe with the intention of infiltrating American formations and sending detailed information to the Luftwaffe for the purpose of interception.

"Since the end of the war," Long writes, "there have been numerous references in books and articles written to defame Swiss internees. These stories are misrepresentations and many are absolute lies."

Once a U.S. airman had been interned, he was not allowed to leave Switzerland and in many cases not even allowed to leave the immediate vicinity of his lodging. Many were initially sent to town or city jails. After processing, most were taken to several small villages high in the Swiss Alps. The three main villages were Abelboden, Wengen, and Davos.

Abelboden lies in a deep valley surrounded on three sides by steep mountains and on the fourth by a steep ravine with only one narrow road providing access to the outside world, the village of Fruitigen. Wengen sits on a jutting ledge below the Jungfrau, its only access a cog railway from Lauterbrunnen. Davos is in a valley with a road and railroad running through town, but at the time the internees were there, a Swiss report estimated there were 400 guards watching the 350 Americans.

"We were placed in stripped-down hotels," says Long. "Some of the hotels were all right; others had been condemned as unfit for human habitation and scheduled for destruction. The hotels were unheated. We dressed in winter as if outside even when in the hotel. The wash bowl water would freeze and that was what one had to wash with. When the toilets froze a bucket was placed beside the toilet."

Switzerland had a severe food shortage during much of the war, and struggled to feed its own people. The internees were no exception. Long writes that after the 1944 food embargo, "There were five meatless days a week. All portion sizes were small . . . the worst—one potato, one beet, one onion for dinner, every day for months. A meat serving was a slice of Braunschweiger, a blood sausage or what we said was a piece of ibex (Alpine Mountain Goat). It was cold in the dining areas and gloves often were worn while eating."

"Upon arrival at one of the three villages internees were not permitted to be out of the hotel for two weeks. Thereafter, they could roam the streets within limits. If you were beyond the posted limits, the guards could shoot you. After D-Day . . . the guards were tripled and the machine gun emplacements doubled at the camps. There was supposed to be a command of 'Halt' given three times before firing. However, those who were wounded contend that 'Halt' and the firing were simultaneous. There were two or three bed checks a night, depending on where you were assigned."

The following stories of individual American airmen who were themselves interned in Switzerland in World War II testify to the fact that many of the planes landing there was severely damaged or had seriously wounded crew on board. They also testify to the fact that the Swiss were far from neutral when it came to welcoming American flyers to their airspace and their nation.

It was early in the war, on October 1, 1943, when a B-17 named 'Sugarfoot' lumbered into the air from the isolated Oudna Air Base twenty miles from Tunis, Tunisia, in North Africa a little after eight in the morning. The base was home to the 99th Bomb Group of the 15th Air Force. On board 'Sugarfoot' was young waist gunner Norris King. Though he didn't realize it as the plane labored into the blue North African sky, Norris was beginning what would prove to be the longest of his 26 missions. There were ten young crewmen on board that morning. Seven would be dead by day's end, killed by Swiss bullets.

As 'Sugarfoot' climbed to altitude, each man busied himself preparing his workstation for the mission. It was their first mission over German soil. The target was the Messerschmitt factory in Augsburg. It was to be a long mission, over 1,800 miles round trip, and only those planes outfitted with Tokyo Tanks, capable of carrying extra fuel, would be making the trip.

Nineteen-year-old Norris manned the right waist gun in the midsection of the B-17. It was his responsibility to track and shoot down attacking German fighters with his 50-caliber machine gun. He'd enlisted in the Air Corps in August of 1942 at the age of eighteen. Originally wanting to be a pilot, he'd transferred into gunnery school because he thought it would be a quicker way to get into combat. "How little I knew what I was in for," he admits today. He ended up an armorer/right waist gunner on the crew of baby-faced pilot Burton C. English—"a fun-loving compatible crew of officers and enlisted men who trained together and played together". [10]

Sugarfoot was a B-17F, known to the U.S. Army Air Corps simply as #42-30126. She was not the crew's original plane. That plane, "Rodger the Lodger", which the crew had flown for about fifteen missions, had been seriously damaged and grounded, and the crew had inherited 'Sugarfoot' from a different crew. After adopting her, they had commissioned one of their ground crew to paint a naked woman on the side. Little did they realize that this painting would end up in the garage of a Swiss Army Colonel's home as a war trophy.

As the formation droned on over the continent, it became wrapped in a dense mass of clouds that enshrouded the Alps and socked in all of Southern Germany. When the navigators were finally able to get a fix on the ground after several hours, they found that the formation was way off course. Instead of being over Augsburg, they were close to Munich. The formation quickly made a left turn. Shortly thereafter, crews were told to drop their bomb loads on targets of opportunity. Unknown to the formations, some of the planes in the front of the formation dropped bombs through the overcast that landed in neutral Switzerland; luckily, there were few casualties and the bombs did not cause serious damage.

German Me-109 fighters scrambled to intercept and shoot down the formation. As sharp-eyed crewmen on the American ships detected the first specks of German fighters, the bombers quickly tightened their formation, maximizing their firepower and protecting the individual planes from attack. Once out of formation, a plane could expect no mercy from the battle-wise German fighter pilots.

As the formation tightened up to defend against fighter attack, it also neared the Swiss/German border.

Moments later, air raid sirens sounded in Switzerland as the American planes, off course, violated Swiss airspace.

Flak Detachment 21, on the ground at Ragaz-Beul, only three miles from the Swiss/German border, was placed on alert. This flak battery had 75-mm Vickers anti-aircraft guns and was the first heavy anti aircraft unit established in the Swiss Army. On several occasions in the past, its guns had fired on foreign planes violating Swiss airspace.

Col. C.F. Ruegg commanded flak Detachment 21. Ruegg watched as the planes of the 99th Bomb Group crossed into Switzerland, pursued by German fighters.

"The group was flying in three moderately open wedges a little over the Sargans basin," Col. Ruegg recalled later. "There, the group was once again attacked by German fighters . . . The group did not change formation during the aerial fighting and flew, with some loss of altitude, directly towards our anti-aircraft position. I could see that the second or third plane had a contrail behind one of the engines on the left wing, yet there was no fire."

The plane was 'Sugarfoot'.

Marion Pratt, the waist gunner opposite Norris King in 'Sugarfoot', remembers the attack by the German fighters. "We were flying on the extreme left of the formation and enemy fighters singled out our plane for concentrated attacks. On the first attack, our ship was hit by cannon and machine gun fire that caused a lot of damage to the front of the plane. A minute or so later, the fighters attacked again, with one diving at us from above. This time we were hit by everything they had. The front, waist and tail were filled with bullets and exploding cannon shells."

At this point, as 'Sugarfoot' struggled to fight off a fierce German fighter attack, Col. Ruegg, on the ground, made his

decision. "I decided to fire at the group as it passed overhead." The
AA battery sited in on the lead plane in the formation as well as on
the smoking 'Sugarfoot'.

"We opened fire about thirty seconds after the flight passed
directly overhead . . . The second aircraft of the left unit was shot
down by our AA fire and plunged towards the earth with long
flames trailing from the engines."

Pratt remembers, "Suddenly, the plane gave a buck and I was
thrown to the floor. This may have saved my life for just as I went
down a burst of fire went through the waist and back towards the
tail. During this attack, I believe most, if not all, of the five men in
the front of the aircraft were killed. I am also convinced that this
burst killed Elmer Wheadon, our tail gunner."

"Just as I was trying to get to my feet again, the plane exploded.
When the Fort exploded, it nosed forward and started towards the
ground at an enormous rate of speed. The plane was going down
so fast that Norris King and I were floating against the top of the
plane. I was quite sure . . . that it was all over for us."

Col. Ruegg recalls that a few seconds after his men had shot
Sugarfoot down, "the Flying Fortress exploded. Two men bailed
out of the plane, their parachutes opening immediately."

According to Norris King 57 years later, it was 12:25 p.m.

Actually, of the ten men on Sugarfoot that day, three managed
to struggle against the centrifugal force and somehow get out of
the plummeting plane. The other seven perished, killed by the
accurate bursts of anti-aircraft fire from Col. Ruegg's guns.

The lead plane in the formation, also hit by Flak Battery 21's
anti-aircraft fire, managed to limp along in the formation for several
minutes before it, too, crashed near the Swiss town of Alvaneu.
Only the men in the nose section managed to bail out. The other
six went down with the plane.

Norris floated down beneath his parachute and landed in a
tree. "I wasn't able to evade at all," he recounts. "A soldier was on
top of me in a matter of minutes. He may have seen my chute in
the top of a tree, or burning parts of the wreckage. His uniform

looked German and I think I put my hands up in surrender. I couldn't even stand up, I had a concussion. I was taken to a hospital called Villa Flora in Bad Ragaz, Switzerland where I received excellent care for the next three weeks."

Today, Norris King is coming to terms with the fact that 'Sugarfoot' was shot down, not by the enemy Germans, but by the neutral Swiss, as his plane struggled to stay aloft after the devastating fighter and flak attacks. "I had always thought we were shot down by German fighters," he says. "Even after I did hear we were shot down by Swiss ack ack I think I was in denial."

Four days after Swiss Flak Detachment 21 shot down two American planes, killing 13 American airmen, the Swiss tried to make amends. It buried the thirteen men, along with another American who had died in the crash of another plane, at the cemetery in Bad Ragaz with full military honors. Each of the fourteen coffins was draped with an American flag. Among the guests were U.S. Military Attaché General Legge and military attaché's from Poland and England.

A photograph taken at the funeral shows Norris's two surviving crewmates talking with Hauptman Ruegg at the funeral.

The wreckage of the B-17 known as Sugarfoot was taken to Dubendorf, Switzerland, where it was reassembled so that the Swiss could study the aircraft.

Norris was now a captive 'guest' of the Swiss, officially known as an interned airman. He was sent to the Swiss resort town of Abelboden, where he was "well treated by guards and civilians and had no fear of serious harm". His family was notified in a letter from Jimmy Doolittle that he "had made a successful parachute jump from the plane over enemy territory on October 1 and is reported interned." Norris received his first letter from home almost seven months after being shot down, on March 27, 1944. Interestingly, the note had been read and cleared by a German censor. Eventually, Norris escaped into France.

When asked about his feelings on Swiss neutrality today, Norris says: "I think it would be fair to say that Switzerland was pro-German.

Also that they were, as the saying goes, 'between a rock and a hard place'. The reason we were fired on is that we were still in formation and over Swiss airspace."

After the war, Norris attended the University of Colorado on the GI Bill, dropping out after the first year. He married but had no children. He lost contact with the other two Sugarfoot survivors, but re-established it a few years after the war. One has since died. He has also attended all the Swiss internee reunions since 1993, including two in Switzerland, where he was warmly welcomed by the Swiss and even filmed for Swiss television at the spot where his parachute landed in 1943.

Over fifty years later, Norris King returned to Switzerland with other Swiss internees. "I met Col. Ruegg, commander of the anti-aircraft detachment, on one of our reunions to Switzerland. He was around ninety years old and showed some remorse, but never apologized. I couldn't make myself shake his hand, but I did give him a B-17 belt buckle. I convinced myself that it was just his job." Later, Norris received a photo of the naked lady 'nose art' from Sugarfoot. Colonel Ruegg had displayed the grisly trophy in his garage since the war. On a later visit to Switzerland, Norris was actually given a small piece of his former aircraft. "After fifty some years, that was quite a gift," he admits.

On April 24, 1944, the U.S. 8th Air Force launched a massive 754-bomber raid against southern Germany and Bavaria. German fighters attacked a B-17 of the 384th Bomb Group named 'Little Chub' over Stuttgart, Germany. Two cannon shells burst in the nose of the aircraft, seriously wounding the bombardier and wounding the left waist gunner. Fearing for the life of the dying bombardier, who had been hit in the face, the plane's pilots were forced to leave the security of the formation and try to make it to neutral Switzerland and safety.

As 'Little Chub' entered Swiss air space, it was intercepted by a Swiss Air Force Me109 and escorted to the Swiss airfield at Dubendorf, where it could make a safe landing. However, the crew discovered that one of the landing gear would not go down. This meant that they needed to get rid of the ball turret because it was difficult to land wheels-up with the ball turret extended beneath the plane. Instead of proceeding to land at Dubendorf, the pilots flew over the Lake of Zurich and circled while the crew attempted to free the ball turret.

On the ground, a Swiss officer ordered Swiss fighters to intercept and shoot down the American plane. He said later that he was afraid the plane was trying to escape back to England. Three Swiss 109's attacked the crippled bomber over the lake. The attack killed the gravely wounded bombardier and the left waist gunner. The B-17's crew had already thrown out its guns and ammunition and was unable to return fire. The pilot ordered the crew to bail out of the plane. Four men were able to do so. One crewman's parachute failed to open and he plunged to his death. The plane quickly lost altitude and crashed into the lake. Rescuers found the bodies of three men floating in the lake. The body of the copilot was recovered from the cockpit at the bottom of the lake some years after the war.

Bob Long's own story, told to me more than fifty years later, shows how desperate the situation was for many flight crews, deep over enemy territory and flying damaged aircraft, often with dead or injured men aboard. In some cases, the closest Allied landing strip was over a thousand miles away. Switzerland was the only choice.

Long was a young bomber pilot on his 19th mission when his plane was crippled and forced to limp to Switzerland. It was late in the war—March 24, 1945—and the 459th Bomb Group was taking part in a bombing mission of a Me-262 jet fighter assembly plant at Rheims Aerodrome in Munich, Germany.

"We didn't know if we'd been hit or not," he wrote me in August of 2001, "However, the #3 engine ran away and could not be feathered. It began spewing oil and then the #4 engine began to surge and drop Rpm's in ups and downs . . . In order to keep the #3 from turning red and throwing the prop God-knows-where the power was reduced. The aircraft began to sink at 750 feet per minute. We were at 22,000 feet and in ten minutes we would be below the 15,000 feet required to cross the Alps. I broke radio silence and gave the call 'Sungold A for Able Fir Tree-Call for Little Joe' (translation: 459th Bomb Group, 756th Squadron, A-box in trouble will seek Switzerland. Any fighter welcome for escort)."

Long asked the navigator if he thought it was possible to navigate through the Alps to the Adriatic Sea. The navigator's response was "Hell, no! I might get us in a box canyon where you could not make a turn." In addition, he nixed an escape route taking them over Innsbruck and the Brenner Pass because of heavy flak batteries. The pilots then told the navigator to set a heading for Switzerland that would take the plane over the southern part of Lake Constance. When they arrived at the lake, Bob told the crew they had made it to Switzerland and told them any could bail out if they wanted to. All chose to stay with the plane and hope the pilots could land safely.

During the descent, flak batteries fired on the plane. Swiss fighters approached and the American and Swiss planes signaled back and forth. Long then descended down to the "postage stamp runway" at Dubendorf Airfield. "After landing, we were followed by an armored vehicle with machine guns and bayonets protruding. The waist gunner told us there was a civilian motioning us to open the bomb bay doors and many soldiers with guns with bayonets, and machine guns. We opened the doors and up comes a civilian" accompanied by machine-gun toting soldiers. "'Welcome to Switzerland, gentlemen,' said the civilian. 'Do you have wounded aboard?'" After Long answered in the negative, the civilian asked what the plane's problem was; all four engines were running. "I told him we had two doing the work of four." The civilian then ordered them out of the plane, had each surrender his .45-caliber pistol, and trucked them away for processing. The crew was shortly thereafter shipped off to Abelboden, where most of the interned American airmen spent the war.

In an intriguing contrast, Long tells of a German plane that was forced to land at Dubendorf during the war. A German Me-210 landed at Dubendorf after exchanging mortal fire with a British Lancaster bomber. The Me-210 had the latest Nazi radar, capable of detecting a Lancaster at 6,000 yards. It also had the latest vertical firing cannon. "The Nazis did not want the ship and equipment to be examined by the Allies," Long told me. "The Me-210 was blown up by the Swiss under the eyes of the Nazis and the Swiss received 12 Me109s in exchange for the destruction of the Me-210 . . . The German crew was taken over by the Nazi Embassy and outfitted as dapper Swiss and placed in a Bern hotel. They were allowed to roam all over and just check in with the Embassy daily. They did this for two weeks and then were repatriated."[11]

Charles Cassidy lives in Scobey, Montana. His memories of internment are quite a bit more pleasant than those of Bob Long, Norris King, Dan Culler, or the crew of 'Little Chub'. On the thirteenth of July 1944, he was a young bombardier on his 13th mission to Munich, Germany. His B-17 was badly shot up when a flak shell crashed upwards through the left wing, exploding mere seconds after tearing a six-foot by three-foot hole. Cassidy surmises that the gasoline in the wing tanks evaporated and the fumes dissipated thus preventing a catastrophic explosion. He commented on his good fortune, noting "the gasoline carried in the wings of each B-17 would be enough to drive my car over 100,000 miles".[12]

The pilot put the plane on a heading for England and they flew across the hostile sky alone. Shortly, two P-51 Mustang fighters drew up alongside and motioned for the plane to turn and head to Switzerland. The P-51's accompanied the plane to the Swiss border, where it was met by two German-built ME-109's from the Swiss Air Force. Charles was busy tearing up and tossing his bombing tables so that they could not fall into enemy hands.

The plane was escorted to Dubendorf. It landed "on a seemingly very short runway, without flaps, (possibly on only two engines), ran over a ditch at the end of the runway and into a small grain field" where they were immediately met by Swiss military. A Swiss captain told them later he'd counted over a thousand holes in the plane.

Upon capture, "our crew was treated very well," according to Charles. "We were fed and allowed to take showers, albeit in cold water. From Zurich, the pilot, co-pilot, navigator and I, with one

Swiss summer soldier as guard, entrained for Chaumont, above Neuchatel, on the French border, where we spent three weeks in quarantine." They were the only crew at that location. The enlisted men on the crew were sent to the enlisted camp at Abelboden.

The officers ended up at Davos. "We were quartered in hotels with kitchens from which we received our meals. Conditions were excellent—far better than a prison camp." For recreation, Charles did lots of hiking around Davos. There were tours available to any airmen who would give a parole, which was an agreement not to try to escape. Charles refused to sign a parole, so he stayed in the immediate area. However, "at Davos we had all the freedom that could be desired. We were told we had to be in our rooms at bed check. I didn't see any guards, although there was a contingent of Swiss Army stationed at Davos."

Charles escaped from Davos in late October and early November of 1944. He had never heard of Wauwilermoos until seven or eight years before I wrote to him in 2001. He says, "we were treated well by the Swiss. At that time Switzerland had no tourists but lots of penniless displaced people—the Americans there had money to spend."

Though his experience was better than some other airmen, Charles has never bothered to go back to Switzerland. He also detests reunions. He sent me a photo of his plane on the ground in Dubendorf. It is a close-up of the left wing, which is a twisted mess of bent aluminum and tangled wires and cables. Here is a good example of a plane that never would have made it back to England.

Cyril Braund is another Montanan—from Great Falls. Today, he is suffering from Alzheimer's, and his wife Kitty shared his story. He was first pilot of the B-17 'Champagne Lady' starting in June of 1944. Cyril saw his share of brutal missions. On one mission, he was leading the group of eleven planes and lost eight of those planes and eighty men.[13]

On his thirteenth mission, the group took off and headed for Lechfeld, Germany. Near the target, another plane in the formation was hit, lost control, and came up underneath his right wing, hitting the #3 and #4 engines and the right aileron. They went into a spin at 28,000 feet, and terrifying moments later, somehow pulled out at 11,000 feet. The plane continued to lose altitude and Cyril ordered the crew to throw out everything they could to lighten the load. Flying with only the two engines on the left side of the plane, the navigator plotted a course to Switzerland.

Finally, flying near the Swiss border, the plane weaving through mountains, Cyril saw an unwelcome sight. The plane was surrounded by mountains to the front and both sides, and did not have sufficient altitude to climb over any of them. He ordered the crew to bail out, and he and the copilot put the plane on autopilot and bailed out seconds before the bomber smashed into the mountainside.

The officers aboard the plane were interrogated (Cyril's interrogator was a former Penn State student) and then sent by train across Switzerland to Davos-Platz. The enlisted men were sent to Abelboden.

"We were treated very fairly and like guests of the Swiss military," Cyril writes. "However, after a few weeks of cheese and bread for breakfast, I started thinking about getting out of there . . . We were paid our regular salary through the Embassy, so we had money we could use . . . I will not go into all the details of my internment . . . All I can say is it was not unpleasant. However, due to the fact that you are not really free and thinking a little more dangerous adventure might be in the offing, I began to plan an escape—just to see if I could do it, I guess!"

With the help of a barmaid, Cyril was able to buy train tickets to the French border, and, dressed in civilian clothes, he and the girl managed to make it to the border, where he crawled through some barbed wire and later hooked up with the French underground.

Fifty years later, Cyril and his wife Kitty returned to the mountainside where his plane crashed. A video shows Cyril sitting in a steep, lush mountain meadow, telling of how he got stuck in the escape hatch momentarily as the jagged peaks loomed before him, and how he bailed out just before impact. In the video he finds bits and pieces of the plane lying about the meadow, all that is left to prove that the event ever took place.

Many of the young men who spent part of their lives as Swiss internees have already passed away. The rest are in their eighties. Sixty years later, despite the revelations about the Swiss and Nazi gold and other dubious dealings between the Swiss government and Nazi Germany during the war, most Americans believe the Swiss were staunchly neutral. Some popular historians continue to perpetuate the myth that American airmen who flew to Switzerland did so to get out of the war. Others have the misconception that being interned in Switzerland was a fairly enjoyable experience. Bob Long has spent years countering such claims. He has fought to get internees POW status. But when all is said and done, all Bob Long wants people to know is the truth, so that the many Americans who were interned in Switzerland during the war will be accorded the respect they deserve and that the historical record accurately reflects their experiences.

Notes

[1]   Gerald Astor, The Mighty Eighth, p. 301.
[2]   Astor, p. 494.
[3]   Stephen Ambrose, *The Wild Blue: The Men and Boys Who Flew the B-24s over Germany*. Simon and Schuster, 2001. Page 123-4.
[4]   Jakob Tanner, Review of *Shots at the Liberators* by Peter Kamber. *Basler Magazine*, #10, March, 1994. Review translated from German by Dr. Joseph Howard.
[5]   Bob Long, statistics on downed US Aircraft.
[6]   Adolph Scolavino, "Switzerland-An Escape to Neutrality", Minnesota 8AF Newsletter.
[7]   This an all other quotes from Bob Long were obtained in author interviews during 2001 and 2002.
[8]   Don Waters, *Hitler's Secret Ally*, Switzerland, Pertinent Publications.

9   Alan Morris Schom, Ph.D., "A Survey of Pro-Nazi Groups in Switzerland: 1930-1945", published by the Simon Wiesenthal Center, June 1998. Web page http;//www.wiesenthal.com/swiss/survey/

10   This an all quotes from Norris King were obtained in author interviews with Mr. King in 2001.

11   Bob Long, Author Interview, 9/11/2001.

12   Charles Cassidy, Author Interview, June 19, 2001.

13   Cyril Brand's story courtesy of his wife, Kitty Braund, sent to the author April 19, 2001.

Chapter Thirteen

Swedish Internees

Switzerland was not the only neutral nation that became a final destination for flight crews. A sizable number of men from both sides ended up in Sweden, which, like Switzerland, had found itself in a highly vulnerable position at the outset of hostilities. Germany occupied Norway and Denmark, and Sweden had legitimate fears that it, too, might become an occupied nation.

It was with much alarm that the Swedes noticed that their airspace was regularly filled with foreign aircraft, both German and Allied. The Allies flew many bombing missions that took them through Swedish airspace. They had two main attack routes to Germany; one went over Holland; the other passed north of Denmark, down the west coast of Sweden, and into Germany.

Sweden instituted a policy early on that "upon arrival in Swedish airspace military planes of a belligerent power were to be fired upon for effect (except ambulance planes) in an attempt to repulse them. In practice, however, these regulations proved to be impracticable and were changed to: 'All foreign aircraft were to be repulsed by being fired upon for effect only after the firing of warning shots'. In addition, when it appeared that the pilot wished to land on Swedish soil and there was no sign of hostile intent the plane was allowed to land without being fired upon."[1]

"Later on, when alien aircraft flew over Swedish territory, they were met with antiaircraft fire. After they had given distress signals, they were escorted by Swedish fighters to a nearby airfield. The bases were Bulltofa (near Malmoe), Torslanda (Gothenburg) and Bromms (Stockholm). From 1940 to 1945 Swedish records show that there were 4,667 airspace violations. Of these, 610 aircraft were fired upon. Involved were many different aircraft of which 20 were shot down by Swedish military units."[2]

One hundred and forty-one American military aircraft crashed or made forced landings in Sweden during WWII. 69 were B-17s, 61 were B-24s, and 9 were P-51s. Rounding out the list were a single C-87, Mosquito, and P-38. During 1939-1945, 64 English, 125 German and 20 Polish, Finnish, Soviet and Norwegian aircraft also landed in Sweden.[3] All told, 1,128 American airmen ended up in Sweden after either flying in or evading capture in nearby nations after their planes had crashed.[4]

The first German aircraft to land in Sweden, a Heinkel He 160 seaplane, arrived September 22, 1940. According to one Swedish report, compared to Allied airplanes, which often suffered from battle damage, most German aircraft landed in Sweden because of navigational errors or/and lack of fuel.[5]

The first American aircraft arrived on July 24, 1943, when a lone bomber named "Georgia Rebel" limped into Sweden with heavy damage sustained on a bombing mission over Norway.

A Swedish story about the 'Georgia Rebel' reports how this first interned aircraft and its crew were received. "The forward hatch is towards the ground, so exit is made through the waist-door. The summer of '43 had been relatively dry, and the bog is quite easy to walk on, although wet and soggy. The crewmembers file out of the plane, relieved the landing has gone well. Soon they are joined by a young man from a nearby farm. He speaks English, and they learn that they are in Sweden."

"They are so close to the Norwegian border that these parts are literary crowded with border-troops. Very soon military personnel reach the crash-site and seal it off from the interested civilians that have gathered. The Swedes are informed that live ammunition is in the guns, but that there are no bombs on board. The military tries to confiscate film rolls from the civilians, but some manage to hide their film. Curious Värmlanders mingle with the military personnel and the ten Americans who proudly show their big aircraft."

"The crew is taken by car to a courthouse in nearby Långelanda, where they are given coffee and sandwiches. Soon they will be joined by Swedish Air Force Officers from the base F7 at Såtenäs."

"A day later they are interviewed by Captain Löwkrantz from F7. Later they will be taken to the town of Falun for internment."[6]

In the days and weeks that followed, the "number of aircrews that came down in Sweden grew rapidly and it thus was necessary to establish special camps to house these flyers. Four main camps were used: Granna, Rattvik, Korsnas and Loka Brunn. The German and Allied crews were kept apart. In the camps every possible effort was made to keep avoid mixing American internees with their British and Polish counterparts after when it became evident that American internees' salaries were far higher than those of the other internees." This even led to fistfights in some cases. "The Americans had tremendous amounts of money to spend. They scattered money all around buying bicycles, kick sleds, skis and clothes. They were able to move about the towns freely." They fraternized with the young Swedish girls.

"For the Swedish Air Force, taking custody of the belligerents' aircraft became increasingly burdensome. To ease the workload and also to make the use of available expertise Sweden began to use interned American and British crews to maintain and repair aircraft belonging to those countries. Interned pilots were allowed to fly the planes in order to maintain their airworthiness. An armed Swedish control officer was always to accompany these flights and the planes were fueled only for short runs."

"Most of the planes were justified in diverting to Sweden. Some were not. Such were the fortunes of war."[7]

Sam Mastrogiacomo lives today in New Jersey, but during the war, he had several other addresses. The first was at the 445th Bomb Group's air base at Tibenham, England. The rest were in various locales in the lovely Nordic country of Sweden, where he was interned after a mission that epitomizes the term SNAFU. He has a sharp sense of humor and a heavy South Philly accent.

His parents came from Italy as youngsters, and Sam was working at the Philadelphia Naval Shipyard, building battleships, including the U.S.S. New Jersey, when the war began. "When I was nineteen, I started to bug my mother and father about going into the military. My mom said, 'When they need you, they'll call you'. I didn't want to wait, so a friend and I went to the recruiting station. We wanted to become paratroopers. They took him, but because I was under twenty-one, they gave me the forms to take home to be filled out by my parents. When I got home, I told my mom I had been to the Army to enlist in the Army paratroopers. All I needed from her was her signature."

"What's a paratrooper?" she asked.

"You know, they jump out of planes," I said.

"I raised a crazy son!" she said as she tore up the papers.

A few weeks later, Sam heard on the radio that the Army Air Corps was looking for skilled recruits. "They said that if you have a skill, such as a machinist, that after basic training, they will give you sergeant's stripes and the nearest base of your choice," Sam remembers.

This sounded much better to Mrs. Mastrogiacomo, especially after Sam convinced her that if he waited to be drafted, he'd probably end up slogging around in the mud with the infantry. He ended up after basic working in a machine shop, where he made half as much as the civilians working alongside him.

"I actually wanted to get into the Air Corps to fly. I was reading on the bulletin board that there was an urgent need for gunners, and they gave the qualifications. I said to myself, 'This is for me!' and immediately filled out a form to apply."

Sam had never fired a gun in his life. Worried that he might be part of the one-third of the aerial gunners to wash out, Sam told his mother he had gone for machinist training. However, upon arrival at gunnery school in Laredo, Texas, Sam found that he was a natural aerial gunner. He graduated third in his class. Upon graduation, he sent his gunner's wings to his mom as a surprise and headed off to Lowry Armament School for nine more weeks of armament training. He then spent time in Salt Lake City for advanced training before being assigned to his crew at Gowen Field, Idaho. The crew would become part of the 445th Bomb Group, 702nd Squadron, a B-24 heavy bomber outfit based in Tibenham, England. Sam remembers the 445th's most famous pilot, Jimmy Stewart. When the crew found out that Stewart was aboard their plane one day, giving the pilot a check ride, "we all had an excuse to go up in the cockpit and get a close look at him. Later, he was chosen as one of our commanding officers, and we soon found out that he was one of the regular guys, and wanted to be treated like anyone else."[8]

Before ending up in Sweden, Sam and the rest of the crew of the B-24 'Big Time Operator'—BTO for short—had flown twelve missions over Europe. Sam had convinced a crewmate to trade gun positions. Though the waist allowed Sam much more freedom of movement, the tail was where the action was, and that's where Sam wanted to be in the dogfights. He had to cut out chunks of the gunner's seat to get his feet and long legs into the snug perch at the back of the airplane.

On a mission to Gotha, Germany on February 24, 1944, he'd shot down three Messerschmidt fighters during a dogfight that lasted over two hours. Though thirteen of the twenty-five planes never returned from the Gotha mission, the crew of BTO would fly another day.

Sam remembers that upon landing in England, word quickly got around that he had shot down three enemy aircraft on a single mission. A reporter from LIFE magazine joined the small throng around Sam. As he prepared for his fifteen seconds of fame, another B-24 taxied to a stop a few yards away. This was the real reason the press had shown up. The throng migrated to the new aircraft, which happened to be piloted by the 445th's Jimmy Stewart, leaving Sam "to ponder what might have been."

For the Gotha mission, the 445th received a Presidential citation.

Sam flew his 13th and final mission as a tail gunner on April 9, 1944. It was an ill-fated mission from the start. Sam and the rest of his crew were awakened at 4:30 in the morning and told to dress for a mission to Germany. Within ten minutes, the mission was scrubbed due to fog. Fifteen minutes later, the mission was back on again, and the crew began to get ready. As the men assembled for briefing, they were told that the mission was now off. Before the crews could board the trucks that would take them back to their barracks, a new weather report indicated the fog would burn off—the mission was back on.

Several squadrons of B-24s assembled for the mission. The 445th's 702nd Squadron would fly the lead, with Sam's plane flying Squadron lead. The field, shrouded in fog, reverberated to the sounds of heavy bombers taking off in the thick soup every thirty seconds, and then flying blind into the sky to assemble. Two bombers collided during assembly, killing all on board both planes.

Somewhere over the North Sea, the mission was recalled. Due to the poor atmospherics created by the fog, the message was only picked up by some of the squadrons. The squadrons that heard the message wheeled around and returned to base, leaving only a vulnerable and oblivious twenty-eight bombers flying on to Germany with no fighter escort, Sam's plane among them. Before the little group could drop their bombs, they were jumped by a swarm of 150 German fighters, who probably could not believe their good fortune. In the ensuing dogfight, Sam bagged a German Focke Wulf FW190, his fifth and final kill of the war.

'Big Time Operator' and ten other planes managed to duck into the clouds, scoot across the Baltic and land in Sweden. Only eleven of the 28 planes returned to England from the mission.

Big Time Operator made an emergency landing at a Swedish fighter base, accompanied by one other B-24. Before being escorted off the airfield as prisoners, the crews managed to blow up their navigation/IFF systems. They had already dropped their top-secret Norden bombsights in a Swedish lake before landing. At the sight of the flames, a startled Swedish officer said, "You didn't have to do that. We're Swedes, not Nazis!"

The men from the two crews were first housed in a small artillery camp that also held interned German soldiers. When the Americans marched past the German barracks the Germans sitting on the steps would holler out jeers such as "Amerikana gangsters, schwein!" In anticipation of another razzing one day, Sam suggested that the Americans, who were guarded by only two Swedes, rush the 30-odd Germans and beat them up at the first derogatory comment.

As the initial slur was hurled, the Americans rushed the surprised German contingent with a cry of "Let's get 'em!" Sam, an amateur boxer in South Philly, picked one German up over his head like a log and threw him at three other Germans, knocking them down like nine-pins.

The riot convinced the Swedes to separate the warring parties. The Americans were shipped to a makeshift internment camp housed in a boarding house in Falun. Here, they bunked with captured British fliers.

Life was "far removed from the experiences of prisoners taken by the Germans or the Japanese. Sleeping in clean beds, being provided with ample rations, and given the freedom to walk around town on occasion, as long as you kept your mouth shut, were some of the perks. The only negative Sam remembers is that the diet contained way too much fish. "It wasn't until years after I was discharged from the service that I could eat fish again," Sam says.[9]

Swedish civilians were friendly to the Americans. On one occasion, some Swedes asked a British internee for a proper greeting for the Americans. He told them "Pepsi-Cola" was a good opener. A few days later, the marching Americans were greeted with an enthusiastic cheer of "Pepsi Cola".

At about this time, Sam's long-suffering mother received word that Sam was an internee in Switzerland and that her twin sons, Tony and Peter, had both been wounded in the Battle of the Bulge and were in the hospital in England. "War is toughest on the mothers," Sam says.

As more flyers landed in Sweden, it became necessary to build an official internment camp, complete with barbed wire fences. Sam volunteered, despite a friend's admonishment to stay and enjoy the easy life in the camp, to transfer out of the camp and work for the Swedes rehabilitating shot-up B-24s. He now stayed in a small hotel in a port town on the Baltic Sea, north of Stockholm, where the excellent treatment continued. Officially, the mechanics contingent was listed as "flak-happy fliers" in need of medical rehab. Several visits by German and Japanese diplomatic legations registered their disapproval of the situation, but they could not prove that the men were not being rehabbed.

One evening in late September, the Americans were assembled for their daily two-hour walk, but ended up walking a considerable distance further than usual. As they crossed a railroad track, the group of 35 prisoners was told by the guards to proceed over a small rise. The baffled men curiously walked over the embankment, only to find a B-24 with engines running, waiting and ready for takeoff. An Allied SOE rescue mission, flown by a unit commonly called the Carpetbaggers, was offering a getaway to freedom.

"Before the jubilant POWs took leave of their captors, they were warned that the Swedes would have to shoot at the bomber as it took off, but they were assured that the aim would be poor. True to their warning, the helpful Swedes waved goodbye, then opened fire on the escaping POWs with machine guns and anti-aircraft fire, with accuracy to the point that shells could be heard whistling past the plane. No hits registered, however, and the former Internees were all returned safely to England, where they boarded another plane to come home on October 5."

Happy to have the war over and be on the way back to his South Philadelphia home, Sam returned to his old job at the shipyards. Many years later it occurred to him that he'd never gotten his fifth Air Medal for the FW190 he'd destroyed on his final mission. Squadron rules at the time were an Air Medal for every enemy plane shot down. Five Air Medals got you the Distinguished Flying Cross. Sam had four confirmed kills before being shot down. The fifth had never been confirmed due to the fact that he and the crew had ended up in Sweden.

After his first request was denied, Sam put the request through his congressman. Meanwhile, he had gathered the testimony of other crewmembers authenticating his fifth "kill." That did it. Request approved.

On Oct. 4, 2003 Sam finally got his Distinguished Flying Cross. Brig. Gen. Christopher Joniec, commander of the 514th Air Mobility Wing presented it to him in front of his wife, Joan and 28 family members and friends.

An array of Air Force brass were in attendance. "I felt like Gen. MacArthur," Mastrogiacomo said.

Sam Mastrogiacomo's war has two very distinct chapters. The first is filled with the excitement and fear of combat, and a little bit of Hollywood. "It could get scary at times," he admits. The second is perhaps stranger still. Interned in a friendly neutral country, he had a fist fight with Germans, repaired American planes that were not allowed to go anywhere, ate way too much fish, and was allowed to escape by the same Swedish military that had 'captured' him in the first place. But not before the Swedes shot at the plane that carried him to freedom. He looks back on both chapters with nostalgia and his characteristic humor. If it all seems too strange to be true, so be it. It happened.

Notes

1   Adolf Scolavino, "Internment in Sweden During World War II", *Crosshairs Magazine*, June 1995, pages 15 and 19. Reprinted from New Mexico Chapter of the 8th Air Force Newsletter, December, 1994. Source of Mr. Scolavino's information was Flyghistorisk Revy, a Swedishh Aviation History Society.

2   Scolavino, Swedish Internment

3   Scolavino, Swedish Interment

4   Stragglers Web Page http://user.tninet.se/%7Evwu458u/

5   Stragglers Web Page http://user.tninet.se/%7Evwu458u/

6   Stragglers Web Page http://user.tninet.se/%7Evwu458u/

7   Scolavino, Swedish Internment

8   Sam Mastogiacomo, Author Interview, June 1, 2001.

9   Phil Joyce, *Philadelphia Inquirer*, "After Nearly Sixty Years, Tail Gunner Finally Gets His Due" Sunday, October 26, 2003

Chapter Fourteen

Herb Alf's Journey

"At any moment, man must decide, for better or for
worse, what will be the monument of his existence."
    —Victor Frankl, "Man's Search for Meaning"

"Even the helpless victim of a hopeless situation, facing
fate he cannot change, may rise above himself, may grow
beyond himself, and by doing so change himself."
    —Victor Frankl, "Man's Search for Meaning"

A man in the Hungarian underground once told the young
Herb Alf, "Herb, to suffer is not enough. It is how you
handle the suffering. You can become inhuman or compassionate."
Herb Alf had more than his share of suffering as a POW during
World War II. That, and the many hundreds of hours he had on
his hands while incarcerated, changed everything for the young
boy from Spearfish, South Dakota. It got him thinking about life,
about war, about the very act of thinking and creating. It also
resulted in a lifelong effort—to write an epic novel about the worst
war in the history of mankind. Not just to write about the war,
but try to explore why it happened, what motivated those involved
to act as they did, to explain why some men lived and some men
died under similar circumstances, or why some men, confronted

with evil and suffering, became evil and others, confronted with the same evil, became better.

That work became *Petals of Fire*, a novel of almost 550 pages, originally many times that long but painstakingly edited. The novel's scope is ambitious—to tell the story of the air war over Europe both in terms of the overall strategic effectiveness and from the points-of-view of a cross-section of those who were caught up in it, both American and German. The concept first came to Herb as a young 'Kriegie' or Prisoner, in Stalag Luft III near Sagan, Germany. He had started jotting down notes when he began his combat flying in December 1943 and continued through April 1945 on whatever paper was handy. Much of the early prison sections are written on toilet paper. He kept his writing during a forced march in the winter of 1945: fifty-six miles in thirty-one hours. He continued writing after his release and return to the States, going through draft and revision many times, and it wasn't until 1999 that Herb Alf's life work, *Petals of Fire*, finally made it in print. Not wishing to limit the work to written form, Herb produced a soundtrack to accompany the novel, with period music, sound effects, speeches, and key parts of dialog from the book. And now, in his eighties, Herb and his wife Sylvia get up each day and work on the screenplay for the novel.

One would think that a man who spent fifty years writing a book would be monomaniacal. Such is not the case with Herb Alf. In addition to writing *Petals of Fire*, he has been a bomber pilot, a rocket research administrator, a college professor, a painter, a sculptor, a motion-picture filmmaker, an internationally-known expert on the psychology of creativity, a political activist, a husband and a father. He has written other books, including one on teaching environmentalism. Like most men with questing minds and boundless energy, he moves from one project to the next, always excited, always interested. "I feel sorry for people who have no interests," Herb told me. "Creative people have too many."[1]

I first met Herb Alf in the summer of 2002, when I went to visit him and his wife Sylvia at their home perched high on a pine-covered hill in the small logging town of Roseburg, Oregon.

Traditionally, I try to keep interviews short. Many of those I interview are in their eighties, and the act of recollection is at times painful and arduous. However, Herb and I went at it for most of a day, and though I could tell he was getting tired by the end, his enthusiasm and intellectual energy kept him going.

Herb is a handsome man with muttonchop sideburns. He looks like a cowboy, lean and rangy. He wears cowboy boots and bolo ties, and would make a perfect extra in any Western film. And, in fact, he is a man who spent much of his early life outdoors in the West.

Herb was born in Philadelphia in 1921. His father was a preacher. After spending time in Wisconsin and North Dakota, Herb's mother divorced and moved with her children to the small town of Spearfish, South Dakota. "We lived in poverty there," remembers Herb. Still, the experience was a good one for Herb. "There is a modern truism that delinquency results from parents who don't give attention to their children. My life puts a lie to that. The only thing I ever got from my dad was a bicycle. Paradoxically, I got my independence and individual freedom because of my circumstances as a poor kid in Spearfish, South Dakota. I sold Zanol products door-to-door. I mowed lawns by hand-power. I had a paper route. While other kids were playing ball, I was working."

At the same time, he developed his love for the outdoors. Spearfish is in the heart of the Black Hills, and he spent many hours hiking and camping, eventually getting his Eagle Scout badge despite going to school full time and working. "In Scouts, we went hiking. I was the organizer, the initiator. I organized an off-road bicycle patrol. I got to know the Black Hills and its ghost towns." This passion would eventually earn him his first writing job.

Herb says, "In school, I liked to write but didn't want to be classified as a 'sissy' who liked English. I was a debate team letterman for two years, learning to argue both sides of an issue. This is a very good way to learn the other guy's point of view. Debate training helps one to respect the views of other people. It is a natural progression to writing. To portray human characters that come alive, you have to be able to crawl into each one's skin and see life from his view. If you see a drunk on the strèet, study his circumstance. View life from his perspective. Understand that you are only different by the Grace of God and you will be compassionate."

During Herb's busy school years, he still managed to save up enough money to buy 1/20th interest in an airplane, a small Piper Cub. Little did he know at the time that in a few years he would be an Air Corps combat pilot.

"My first real job was with the Federal Writers' Project in 1938. I was seventeen years old. I was hired to interview pioneers of South Dakota history, find and map ghost towns and research the names of places. What resulted was *The South Dakota Guide*, a 1938 Edition of the Federal Writers' Project. There were about thirty writers who did the field work."

In 1939, Herb enrolled in college at Black Hills Teachers College. He took pre-engineering courses to become an aeronautical engineer. However, when he traveled to California and went through the Sacramento Junior College aircraft technician's shop, "I learned that a picture is worth a thousand words. I took one look and I knew, 'No, Herb, that is not for you. You're interested in humanity more than machinery.'" He studied for a year at Sacramento State and while there earned a private pilot's license in the Citizen's Military Training Program.

Then he hit the road to see America and learn more about humanity. "I rode the rails as a hobo. Kept journals. I wrote a play or two about it. I was protected by being as poor as the other people. I rolled my own cigarettes—no tailor-mades. Smoked Bull Durham. I'd send five dollars ahead of myself to 'Herb Alf, General Delivery' at a certain town, and then I'd pick it up when I got there. I was shot at by the railroad 'bulls' and I lived on meat-ends and day-old rolls. Through this experience, I gained a perspective of life I still value today. I hoboed from California to Missouri to Texas and back to South Dakota."

"Then at nineteen I started to Alaska. On the way up, I stopped at Spokane, Washington, to see my dad; I hadn't seen him since I was twelve. I stayed to work for him as a painter for thirty-five cents an hour. I built a trailer house and decided to become a psychologist. There wasn't much family support; my dad called it 'pissology'."

When he ran out of money and means for getting it, he finally wrote his sister and asked to borrow money. She wrote back that she would lend him the money only if he sent her a written record of how he spent it. That was too much. He turned it down and returned to California to take a job with the Army Air Corps at McClellan Field in Sacramento as a junior aeronautical draftsman.

One Sunday, perched by his drafting table at McClellan Field, Herb learned that the Japanese had bombed Pearl Harbor. "All of a sudden, this little drafting department carried the responsibility of critical duty for a world war." Herb's first crisis job was to draft the air raid evacuation system for a bombing attack, feared imminent. "As upset as I was about what the Japanese had done, I tried to understand what caused them and the Germans to behave as they did. I asked how we could make the world a place where we didn't have such insanity."

The challenge now was to win the war. Herb decided to leave the drafting table. He itched for Air Corps Wings. He took the aviation cadet test. One of the last to finish the test, he got the highest score. This made him wonder about how valid IQ tests are that factor in the speed of thinking. Later, his studies as a psychologist taught him that the most important factor of success was not IQ, but something he called The Factor of Persistence.

Herb obtained his wings and was assigned to the Bloody Hundredth Bomb Group, named for its high losses over Europe. On his nineteenth mission on April 28, 1944, the day after his 23rd birthday, his B-17 was hit and exploded during a mission. He was blown free by the initial concussion, and his parachute was blown open when the ship exploded. Six of the eleven crewmen aboard the B-17 were killed. Herb, severely injured, was captured, hospitalized, and eventually incarcerated at Stalag Luft III near Sagan, Germany.

While a bomber pilot, Herb wrote accounts of missions as they happened. He had hidden his writings behind photos for security reasons. Once he was shot down, he continued to his record on toilet paper. He had an old dime-store billfold with a 'secret compartment' where he stored the early toilet-paper writings. Despite several searches of his billfold by the Germans, they never managed to find the secret compartment. It was a dime well-spent.

On January 27, 1945, the German overseers of Stalag Luft III announced that the kriegies had just thirty minutes to pack their belongings to be force-marched out. The temperature was thirty degrees Fahrenheit below freezing, not counting a blizzard wind chill. Men scrambled to put together what food and belongings they could carry with them with makeshift emergency backpacks and sleds. Twenty-five to fifty thousand Red Cross parcels were left behind in the rush. Thousands of food cans were abandoned. By one account, a million books were left in the camp, and more than two and a half million cigarettes. In addition, as they were forced to run the first mile of the march, many began discarding items that they had with them. The first to go was the food, and when things got desperate, even blankets and clothing to keep warm were sometimes left behind. The roadside was littered with items stacked into piles by civilians busy with a grotesque harvest.[2]

The kriegies and their guards traveled with no destination in mind other than to keep one step ahead of the advancing Russian Army. Soviet Marshal Ivan Konev's Southern Army had already pierced to within twenty kilometers of the camp.[3] No provisions had been made for shelter or food along the march. The German guards were in most cases older men or men who had been wounded in combat and were unfit for other military duty. Their backpacks were carried by horse drawn wagons following for the purported purpose of carrying exhausted marchers.

Herb's West Compound Group was the last to move out. The twenty-three hundred men struggled through snow six inches deep as the icy winds tore through their clothing. At six in the morning, they came to the German town of Muskau and sheltered in a pottery factory where glowing furnaces supplied much-needed warmth.

Article Seven of the Geneva Convention stipulates that prisoners of war can only be marched 12.5 miles per day. The men of West Compound walked fifty-six miles in thirty-one hours, with one four-hour stop. Of the 2,300 who started, only between five and six hundred lasted to the forced march's end in Muskau at 6:00 a.m. after the second night on the road. All who lasted were suffering from exposure and exhaustion.[4]

After a merciful day layover, the men were force-marched again. Eventually, the kriegies of West Compound were put into boxcars and taken to a prison at Nuremberg. They were packed 56 men to a car, so tightly that over half had to stand. The boxcars were locked shut with no provision for human excrement. Prisoners received no food and little water and were allowed little chance to relieve themselves. They lived on what Red Cross food they had with them.

Throughout the march, Herb kept a record on scraps of paper, which he still has. While on the winter march, he began to wonder why it was that some of the most athletic prisoners had collapsed. "It was easy to give up," Herb says of the winter march. "You reach a point where you are about to die. It is your will to live that makes the difference." Some men on the march simply lost the will to live.

A second forced march was ordered from Nuremberg two months later. This march became strange when it was discovered that the German guards wanted their duty as POW guards to save them from SS assignment. The SS wanted to have all soldiers retreat with them into Hitler's "Inner Redoubt" and fight to the death. There were some poignant and ironic encounters on the march— scenes that made it into Herb's novel. One involved a prisoner carrying an exhausted, elderly guard's rifle up a hill. Another involved a guard helping a prisoner push his belongings in a sled bogged down by mud. At times, men on both sides stopped being enemies and started treating one another simply as fellow human beings.

Finally, Patton's Army liberated the kriegies in late April at Moosburg on their way to Hitler's Inner Redoubt. After being liberated, the kriegies were under strict orders not to leave confinement until they had been sent home for sixty days to rehabilitate. Herb made different plans. "When you are a prisoner of war, you develop a mentality of disrespect for the larger authority, the enemy's rules. This idea continued after my liberation." An old friend flew in to Camp Lucky Strike near the English Channel, where the kriegies were being held. The freed POWs were now classified as RAMPs—Repatriated Allied Military Personnel. This friend was on a general's staff in Paris, and the friend flew Herb out of Lucky Strike. Herb spent some quality time in Paris, France, as a guest of the General at Staff Headquarters. As a bomber pilot and former POW, alone out of camp restriction, he was a celebrity. The general's staff served him Scotch, which he poured into the potted plants when nobody was looking. At only a hundred pounds, his health was too poor to drink alcohol. Eventually he went back to Lucky Strike with no problems, thanks to orders from the general's staff.

Herb's series of adventures trying to get back to the States would constitute a chapter all to their own. In the end, he hitchhiked back to the U.S. on a B-17. He jumped out of the plane in the dark in Boston to save the pilot explanation problems and hitchhiked to Camp Kilmer, New Jersey, where he was arrested for illegal entry into the United States. At his trial, a colonel from Washington commented, "You have shown a great deal of initiative but not the kind the Air Force needs". However, he was not penalized.

Herb had managed to hold on to all his scraps of writing throughout his combat and prisoner of war experiences. He had planned to leave the Air Force and write about this war experience and its effect on himself and others. This plan was postponed by an unexpected but exciting assignment to be an Air Force rocket research administrator of German rocket scientists who had been brought to America after the war. He headed the Propulsion Branch of rocket research as a Technical Intelligence Officer. After receiving an official letter of commendation for his work, he was promoted to Captain in the Air Force.

"The scientist I worked with suggested I had talent for a life-long career as a rocket scientist," Herb says, showing a cartoon the six German scientists made of him one Christmas. In fact, while working in the program, Herb came up with a significant innovation in fuel ignition to counter the limits of flame speed. He felt that this fortuitous assignment was clearly the opening for a great career in the new science of rocket propulsion. But after weighing the values acquired from his past, he decided that it was not what he wanted. For him, "the razor of science was sharp enough. Wisdom to control the science was more needed."

He resigned his commission to study humanities and write. His first intent was to write his book as an autobiography, but he soon found that "my personal history was like thousands of others that could be written about the war. Neither my ego or the world needed my private story to be told," he says. "What I wanted to do was to show 'The Big Picture'." In 1947, he decided to write his experience as a novel to bring various perspectives to the history of the air war.

He worked by day, and wrote on his novel by night. He took a biography writing class at Cal-Berkley. He bought two old houses in Berkeley, California, another in Hollywood, and another in Sedona, Arizona, remodeling each and selling it at a profit.

He attended the University of Iowa's famous Writer's Workshop. The first half of *Petals of Fire*, then entitled *Fire From Heaven*, became his thesis for his Master's Degree in Creative Writing in 1961. He learned at the workshop that "you can't send your book off to somebody and find out if it's good or not." Herb worked with five different acclaimed writers at the Workshop. They differed totally in their critical evaluation of his writing, their opinions ranging "from negative to mediocre to glowing".

Next, Herb went to the University of Georgia. He continued to work and rework *Petals*. He sent Herbert Read, a famous philosopher and literary critic living in England, a copy. Read wrote Herb, "Your book is the best intimate account of World War

II I have come across". Herb submitted the manuscript to several agents and publishers without success, then put the manuscript on a shelf and pursued other interests for a number of years.

The novel is a work on two levels. First, it offers profound questions on the policies and politics of the air war over Europe through inquiry at the highest levels. For this, Herb spent years researching official documents and records. The book's finding is that the massive commitment to developing the capability of precision bombing of strategic targets to destroy the enemy's ability to fight was sidetracked. This was a result of two individual decisions. The first was a decision by British Prime Minister Winston Churchill, encouraged by "Bomber" Harris, to resort to "terror bombing of civilian populations, code-named the Key-Point System for de-housing Germans. Beyond reason, this policy was pursued after Churchill had declared that German terror bombing was totally ineffective because it only incited the British to fight harder." The second was the decision by General Dwight Eisenhower to postpone strategic bombing of key targets like the oil industry and instead concentrate on citywide bombing and the bombing of trains and transportation centers to prepare for a ground invasion.

This unfortunate misdirection of air power is primarily dealt with in the discourse of upper-echelon character Colonel Dean Raymond, a disciple of General Billy Mitchell and an advocate of General Carl Spaatz's intentions of victory through precision strategic bombing. It is Raymond who expounds on Herb's own findings of the politics and policies of the Allied air effort in World War II. For example, Herb is convinced that the U.S. high command intended for the Ploesti Raid to fail in order to doom the strategic bombing of oil and change the focus onto ground support bombing, which is what General Eisenhower wanted.

In his research, he found that the U.S. Army ground generals were mysteriously negligent in planning, approving, and helping execute the Ploesti raid. This negligence worked in favor of Eisenhower's intention of diverting bombers from strategic oil targets to ground troop support.

Colonel Raymond says, "This was his (Eisenhower's) World War I tank commander mentality. Air Force failure at Ploesti would get Ike what he wanted—proof that the Air Force could not win the war by trying to knock out Oil—proof that a ground invasion was needed to win the war."[5] Raymond also comes to abhor the 'terror bombing' policies, initiated by Hitler and then copied by Churchill, of using bombing as a means of destroying the opponent's will to fight. Raids on cities such as Dresden, that served no strategic military purpose other than mass killing, especially angered him. "Hundreds of thousands of evacuees, refugees, and prisoners of war were in Dresden at the time of the bombing, because the city had been recognized as a safe haven, a city with no military targets, few air defenses, and no previous bombing attacks.[6] More than a hundred thousand people were killed in the bombings and ensuing fire storm."[7] This terror bombing, following the Nazi model, is seen by Herb's policy mouthpiece in the book, Col. Dean Raymond, as hypocritical, misguided, and downright evil. "We know from the bombing of England that bombing civilians only strengthens a country's will to fight, but that's what we're doing. I'm seeing our promised way to victory twisting into a massacre for vengeance. It's a disgrace."[8] Raymond goes on to say, "What we lived through today (the Nuremberg bombing at Langwasser that Herb lived through) is the stategy of a brain loaded with eighty shots of whiskey (referring to High Command alcoholism). Historians will have to penetrate a mountain of official cover-up to document the warped brain-work ruling our World War Two. You and I have a short cut to the truth through our personal bombing experience—both over and under the bombs."[9]

Herb makes the point convincingly that Ike's policy was misguided. He quotes Leon Woolf's work that "the enemy was at a crossroads in 1943 because of gigantic oil expenditures on the Russian front . . . and fighting in North Africa was also a heavy drain on petroleum resources. Already, Albert Speer was warning Hitler of the increased tightness of oil. America and Britain knew that the German stocks were low, but they did not realize how exceedingly low; therefore, oil was not given priority in the strategic bombing program . . . an error that temporarily saved the day for Germany."[10]

Nazi Air Minister Herman Goering stated after the war "that the greatest effect on the defeat of Germany was caused by . . . precision bombing, because it was decisive. Destroyed cities could be evacuated, but destroyed industries were difficult to replace."[11]

In the novel, the prisoners spend two months in a prison camp called Langwasser, near the rail yards in Nuremberg. The British and Americans bomb the rail yards regularly. On days when clouds obscure the rail yards, the bombers follow orders and area-bomb the city through clouds, which a prisoner names "fertilizing the city free-style". At night, the British area-bomb. The rail yards are missed most of the time. When they are hit, crews of slave laborers quickly repair them. Bombs explode to all sides of the camp the POWs are in.

The POWs must go to their bunks during the raids. There they wait for the one bomb that will blow them to kingdom come. Herb remembers sweating out these freestyle bombings in his bunk at Langwasser. "I shivered uncontrollably in my fright," he says.

In addition to writing a novel that reveals the failures of leadership in the conduct of the Allied air war over Europe, Herb's second thrust is to tell the story of how ordinary individuals from different walks of life deal with the horrors of war. To do this, he carefully chose characters—women as well as men—who cross the entire human spectrum—from the evil SS man to the almost child-like Sam, who is half-Jewish, half-Irish. The reader is brought to witness each character's reaction to the stresses of war, loss, imprisonment, and death.

In his doctoral study of psychology, Herb's learning coincided with that of existential psychologist Victor Frankl, of the famous Third School of Vienna, following Freud and Adler. Frankl was himself a survivor of Auschwitz, where he learned that individual survival correlates with the extent to which a person experiences meaning in his or her life. In the course of Herb's novel, each character must search for meaning, and as it is wartime, they must often try to find meaning in madness. Those who fail to find meaning often die.

The dandelion flower is a reoccurring motif in the novel. It provides the novel with its title, and more importantly, it is a symbol of discovered meaning for several of the book's characters. It is synonymous with the constancy of nature even in time of war—"sunshine fire from heaven that lifted from the ground", "innocence", "beyond the reach of war", "God's heartbeat". In more earthy terms, a character says, " . . . where shit falls, flowers will grow". Buck, the cowboy character says, "When I build my own home, instead of weeding the dandelions, I'm going to let them take over and make me a gold yard".

To research his characters, Herb traveled to such diverse places as Chicago, Illinois and Frankfurt, Germany. To get a feel for the Jewish-Irish character of Sam, he went to the neighborhood in Chicago where the character was from. A chance ride with a Jewish cabby gave him the authentic history he needed. To get a feel for one of the main German characters, Paula, he went to Frankfurt, Germany. "I found it impossible to get anyone to talk about the bombing in 1956," he remembers. "I rented a room in a German house near the Bahnhof to no avail. Finally, I gave up and booked train passage to Luxembourg. I bought the housewife a box of chocolates as a farewell gift. Surprisingly, she responded by talking for two hours about her life in the bombing of Frankfurt. Her account provided the authenticity I needed. I wrote all day as I traveled to Luxembourg."

Herb also had his own experiences for his scenes of Germans being bombed. He survived bombings in London, Paris, Spremberg, and Nuremberg, mostly from his own forces.

Herb's *Petals of Fire* depiction is consistent with Frankl's discoveries. Dr. Frankl went into Auschwitz a firm believer in Freudian psychology, that all behavior derives from sexual energy. He emerged with evidence that behavior is man's search for meaning in life. Frankl quotes Nietzshe in his book *Man's Search For Meaning*, "He who has a WHY to live for can bear almost any HOW".[12] It is, of course, Nietzshe who also wrote, "That which does not kill you makes you stronger".

"The experiences of the camps," Frankl writes, "show that man always has a choice of action, even in the most desperate circumstances . . . Men can preserve a vestige of spiritual freedom . . . even in such terrible conditions of psychic and physical stress. We who lived in the concentration camps can well remember the men who walked through the huts comforting others, giving away their last piece of bread. They may have been few in number, but they offer sufficient proof that everything can be taken from a man but one thing: the last of the human freedoms—to choose one's attitude in any given set of circumstances, to choose one's own way."[13]

Frankl writes, "life in a concentration camp could be called a 'provisional existence of unknown limit'". [14] The lives of the POWs were in similar limbo. Wives, girlfriends, careers, education, everything was out of their reach. In order to survive, each needed to find meaning in something, somewhere. For one character, it is growing a garden. For another character, it is lifting prisoner's spirits through theater. For Buck, one of the main characters, it is his vision of an ideal life after the war in the Big Horn Wilderness, with Randi, a Native American nurse.

Frankl writes of a vision like Buck's: "A man who becomes conscious of the responsibility he bears toward a human being who affectionately waits for him, or to an unfinished work, will never be able to throw away his life. He knows the 'why' for his existence, and will be able to bear almost any 'how'."[15]

The novel carries a cautionary theme as well. Herb Alf is distrustful of a strong government that controls the lives of its people. When we spoke, it was only a few months after 9/11, and the Bush Administration was tightening up on individual freedoms. This worried Herb, who is very much the Western libertarian. "What happened in Germany was not an aberration limited to Germany," says Herb. "It could happen in the United States."

"For me, the strongest scene in the novel is when Hauptman Eiler, the German commandant, says to Dean Raymond, 'Beware of the leader who appeals to your patriotism.'" The novel has a stance that, while not being anti-government per se, is decidedly anti-authoritarian. "Communal authority is what keeps us separated as human beings," says Herb. "In the novel, as the German State begins to collapse, people begin to relate to each other more as human beings, regardless of rank or nationality."

Hauptman Eiler also tells Colonel Raymond near the end of the novel: "What the Nazis got us to do was monstrous brutal. Hitler killed Jewish people with gas; your leaders killed German people with bombs. Guilt has no boundaries."[16]

Herb Alf's novel is, then, an odyssey of one man's life. It lays bare his experiences as a young pilot stripped of his freedom and tells the exciting tale of important historical events, including a 1945 winter death and a spring forced march to Hitler's redoubt. It is also one scholar's verdict on the successes, and failures, of the allied war in the air in Europe in World War II, highly critical of some of the key players, such as Churchill and Eisenhower, highly complimentary of others, such as General Carl Spaatz. It is the embodiment of the philosophy of Victor Frankl which concludes that the primal energy for survival is a meaning for living. And it is a cautionary treatise against the dangers of government becoming too powerful and tyrannical.

Over the years, Herb got married, had three children, continued his university education, and taught at the university level, including a course called 'The Psychology of Creativity'. His students valued the course so highly that he decided to study for doctoral degree in the Psychology of Creativity. He went to the University of Hawaii where he taught English while he studied. He also became active in anti-Vietnam-war politics and did further writing on his war novel. While in Hawaii, Herb managed to finish a 600-page second draft of Petals of Fire. He submitted it to an agent, and the book was "almost published" by MacMillan in 1967. "But," says Herb, "I'm glad it wasn't. The years of further work have made it a better book."

At Christmas time, 1982, Herb met the person who would become his key collaborator and supporter in his quest to publish Petals of Fire—his future wife, Sylvia. Sylvia was director of the Arlington, Virginia campus of Strayor College and had taught

English at Strayor's campus in Washington, D.C. She loved the book the first time she read it. Concerned because Herb's only copy was sitting on a shelf and could be lost in a fire, she had the manuscript moved from Herb's shelf to her fire safe. In all the years since, she never stopped believing in her husband's life work. "There may have been creative differences at times," admits Sylvia, "but my position is that it is his story. I'll argue with him, but the final decision is his."

In 1987, the New Zealand Department of Education asked Herb to develop programs for gifted and talented students. Herb was extended permanent resident status, and they moved to New Zealand and lived there for several years. A huge, beautiful oil painting over the hearth in the Alf's living room in Roseburg shows a wild New Zealand ocean coastline that Herb painted as a vacation from his other creative challenges.

Herb and Sylvia moved to the small town of Roseburg, Oregon several years ago. In early 1999, nearly fifty years after Herb first conceived of his epic novel, they decided to self-publish the novel. They formed a company, the Millennium Memorial Trust, and printed the First Edition of *Petals of Fire* in 2000. This edition was limited to 2,000 numbered, signed, leather-bound copies, complete with a one-hour music CD. Herb designed the book himself, right down to photographing and designing the dust jacket. The front of the book jacket shows B-17 bombers flying in a blue sky, a burning city in ruins below, strands of barbed wire, a swastika in a pile of rubble, and the dandelion. The back shows a peaceful blue sky, a shaft of sunlight filtering out of the clouds and shining on a meadow. In the background are the Big Horn Mountains in Wyoming, home of the fictional Cloud Peak in the novel. In the foreground, standing in a field of dandelions, is a young Herb Alf, trussed up in his sheepskin flight suit, parachute harness, helmet and goggles. Across the peaceful sky, vintage aircraft soar. The first edition of *Petals of Fire* sold out in 2002 and there is no plan to publish a second edition at this time. The book's scarcity, unfortunately, ensures a small reading audience.

The dream to publish *Petals of Fire* and to create a definitive *War and Peace* of the Allied air war over Europe took hold of Herb Alf over sixty years ago. Like the man who wrote it, the novel evolved over the years. The novel, like many other aspects of Herb Alf's life, gives meaning to the man. It is a timeless gift to future generations from a man who knows war, and hates it.

Before I left the Alf's, Herb laid out the old scraps of paper and toilet paper upon which, sixty years earlier, he had scrawled the first lines of *Petals of Fire*. The book had truly been a life journey for him, and these yellowing, tattered remnants of his early efforts are a far cry from the handsome leather-bound final product.

In remarks Victor Frankl often made to his students and audiences, he says the following: "Don't aim at success—the more you aim at it the more you are going to miss it. For success, like happiness, cannot be pursued; it must ensue, and it only does so as the unintended side effect of one's personal dedication to a cause greater than oneself or as the by-product of one's surrender to a person other than oneself. Happiness must happen, and the same holds for success: you have to let it happen by not caring about it. I want you to listen to what your conscience commands you to do and go on to carry it out to the best of your knowledge. Then you will live to see that in the long run—in the long run, I say!—success will follow you precisely because you had forgotten to think of it."[17]

Those old tattered pages are the beginnings of Herb Alf's lifelong dedication to a cause greater than himself, a self-described 'inner force challenging him", a bomber pilot's testament to peace and a better future.

Shortly after we had finished going over the final draft of this chapter, Herb Alf died on January 30, 2004. In a written statement left for his wife, he wrote:

> "I choose to be buried at Arlington National Cemetery where I will be with comrades I honor for their courage and sacrifice in giving their lives in service to others. I separate our service from the politicians who lean on the soldiers to

do what might well have been done a better way. In this
imperfect world, I would be honored to lie in death with
those who were brave with their lives to do what was asked
of them to restore power to our government.

I have no intention of honoring the actions of those
who caused these deaths needlessly. It's the job of the living
to work and fight to be sure that our soldiers are not sent to
die needlessly.

Meanwhile, I would be with the victims of war as my
vote for a world of law and order under a World Court
system with votes rather than bullets to establish
governments, and courts rather than war to decide the right
from the wrong, the weak from the strong."[18]

Notes

[1] This and all subsequent quotes from Herb Alf and Sylvia Alf are from an
     author interview in Roseburg, Oregon, conducted on July 19, 2002, at
     the home of Herb and Sylvia Alf and subsequent emails, phone
     conversations, and an additional visit in Roseberg in the summer of 2003.

[2] Durand, Arthur A., *Stalag Luft III: The Secret Story*. Baton Rouge: Louisiana
     State University Press. 1988. 328-329.

[3] Moosberg Online.

[4] Durand, *Stalag III: Secret Story*, 331-332.

[5] Alf, POF, 223

[6] Recent scholarship, most notably Frederick Taylor's *Dresden: Tuesday, February
     13, 1945*, published by HarperCollins in 2004, has refuted many
     commonly-held beliefs about the Dresden Bombing. Taylor, a bilingual
     historian who researched the Dresden bombing extensively, concludes
     that Dresden was, in fact, a city of great military importance, both as a
     transportation hub and as a major producer of armaments. He further
     concludes that the death toll, commonly held at 100,000, was in fact
     between 25,000 and 40,000 but was inflated by Josef Goebbels for
     propaganda purposes and then never historically refuted. For a full
     discussion of this topic, Mr. Taylor's book is recommended.

7   Alf, *Petals of Fire*. Roseburg, Oregon. Millenium Memorial Trust, 1999, page 360.

8   POF, 185.

9   POF, 368.

10 Woolf, Leon. *Low Level Mission*. New York: Doubleday, 1957, quoted in POF p. 231.

11 Arnold, Henry 'Hap'. *Global Mission*. New York: Harper, 1949, quoted in POW p. 231.

12 Frankl, Victor, *Man's Search for Meaning*. New York: Washington Square Press, 1984, page 97.

13 Frankl, 86-87.

14 Frankl, 91

15 Frankl, 101.

16 Alf, Herb. *Petals of Fire*, p. 487.

17 Frankl, *Man's Search*, p. 17.

18 Alf, Herb. Burial Statement. Courtesy of Herb's wife, Sylvia Alf.

Chapter Fifteen

The Reunion

Lyle Shafer has earned his comfortable retirement. He worked thirty-three years for the NCR Corporation, first as a lawyer, then as the corporate personnel officer when the company had over 100,000 employees worldwide. He now winters in Arizona and summers in Wilson, Wyoming, just a few miles up the road from Jackson. The majestic, jagged Grand Teton Mountains are framed in a floor-to-ceiling picture window in his living room, and aspens shimmer beyond the patio outside. Vice President Dick Cheney lives in a larger house across the way when he's in town. It is an idyllic setting, one he knows he is lucky to see.

It was September 10, 1944, and Lyle was sitting in the copilot's seat of the B-17 known as 'Gung Ho'. This was Lyle's twenty-fifth mission with the 390th Bomb Group, based in Framlingham, England. You needed thirty-five to go home by this stage of the war, now that the German Luftwaffe had been decimated. Still, the group was taking heavy losses from accurate anti-aircraft fire. It struggled to get enough men and machines into the air for missions.

This week had been a bad one. At the Rheinmetall Borsig Arsenal at Dusseldorf, Germany the day before, Lyle's squadron had been engulfed in an inferno of flak one minute before bombs away. Of the eleven planes in the formation, three exploded immediately. Another blew up within minutes, and two others were last seen spiraling downwards through the undercast. Five lone planes limped back to base. Several of these were too shot up to fly again without major repairs. One of these was Lyle's. As he remembers, "flak had heavily punctured the aircraft including holes in the self-sealing gas tanks and the right tire was destroyed, resulting in a hazardous landing."[1]

"I didn't think the mission on the tenth could be any worse than the one the day before," Lyle recalls, shaking his head. He was wrong.

The crew was flying 'Gung Ho' that September 10 because their regular plane flown the day before was not airworthy. Lyle had piloted a total of eight different planes thus far on his tour. Some had been renamed by replacement crews and thus had two names, such as 'Wild Chicken/Lucky Strike' and 'Gloria Ann/Close Crop'. Others, like "Shotzi II", hinted at a lost namesake. He'd also flown planes known simply and impersonally by their registration number.

The crew, known as Crew 30, had come together in the course of the missions. Some men had left and others had taken their places for various reasons. The former first pilot, Stan Wilson, had refused to fly after his near-disastrous third mission. The entire crew narrowly escaped death after the formation was disrupted by heavy flak and the plane nearly collided with another B-17. Wilson, heavily shaken by the incident, said afterward that he just didn't want to be responsible for the lives of the crew any longer. Bill Rosen, the crew's original navigator, had been transferred to a lead crew soon after the crew's arrival in England. For the past few missions, Duward Bare had flown as Crew 30's navigator. Charles Upshaw, the original bombardier, had ended up training with a different crew before assignment overseas and had been killed on a mission. He'd been replaced by Ray Wilson. Frank Stokes was the engineer/top turret gunner. Karl Kolmerer manned the radio operator's position. Roy Demeire, a regular waist gunner, was not flying with the crew this day, a fact that would haunt him in the months to come. Ernest Star manned the other waist gun. Griffith Williams crouched in the ball turret. The original tail gunner,

Morris Smart, had been transferred to ground duty back in the States due to constant airsickness and had been replaced in the tail by Ben Howell. Lyle and all the enlisted men had been with the crew since operational training in the States.

As 'Gung Ho' droned towards today's target at Nuremberg, Germany, Stan Wilson was back on the ground at Framlingham, awaiting his inevitable 'less than honorable' discharge. He'd been replaced by Fred McIntosh. Lyle and Fred were flying their twentieth mission together as a flight crew. Both had skipped transition training back in the States and were shipped to England as copilots. Because of the immediate demand for pilots, the Air Corps had eliminated Lyle and Fred's transition training. Instead, they were expected to learn 'on the job' as copilots. The reason for the rush was the Allied bombing launched in support of the D-Day invasion and its aftermath. Lyle and Fred had both gone straight from cadet training in a twin-engine AT-10 to two months of operational training, flying the massive 60,000-pound, four-engine B-17. Lyle had flown his first mission on June 20. Both had since been certified as first pilots. This was Fred's thirty-fifth—and final-mission. If he could get back in one piece from this one, he had beaten the odds and could go back home to his wife and two-year old son. He was the only married crewmember.

At approximately 11:05, the bomb bay doors opened and the planes of the 390th began their target run. 'Gung Ho' was flying deputy lead, second in the formation, flying off the right wing of the lead aircraft. Anti-aircraft fire began to pepper the sky around them. Lyle already had on his heavy flak vest to protect the front of his body. He also knew he had a steel plate in the seat assembly behind him. However, just to be safe, he bent over to pick up his heavy flak helmet. As he did so, he placed his right arm next to the cockpit's small side window to brace himself as he leaned over. At that moment the plane took a direct hit and almost instantly exploded.

The plane began to tumble wildly and the cockpit boiled with smoke. A body hurtled through the cockpit and slammed into the ceiling. When Lyle looked behind his seat, the rest of the plane was simply gone and he was sure he was going to die. Still, he managed to reach under his seat assembly and grab the cloth handle on the end of his parachute pack. The piece of the plane in which he was trapped was spinning and smoking and he was disoriented, but when the centrifugal forces allowed him, he released his seat belt and fell out of the plane into space.

He did a free-fall from 26,400 feet through clouds, discarding his flak vest and snapping on his parachute pack as he plummeted towards the earth below. He had no sensation of falling. When able to pull his ripcord, he was only about skyscraper's height above the ground. "Another few seconds, and I would have hit the ground," he recounts. Seconds later, he landed in a field in a gritty neighborhood in a suburb of Nuremberg called Schweinau. There was a flak battery firing nearby, and a sailor and an air raid warden ran over and captured him immediately. He watched as a large piece of an aircraft fell out of the sky and landed on the rooftops nearby. It felt like his left leg was broken and he was unable to walk. His captors loaded him into a truck and took him to a police barracks. In addition to the broken leg, he was bloody, shrapnel from the flak burst had shattered right arm, he'd been hit in the face, and one of his jaw teeth had been knocked out.

Lyle Shafer, who only minutes before had been copiloting a bomber at over 26,000 feet, was now a 'Captured Enemy'. The Germans did not consider a captured airman to be a Prisoner of War until after he had been interrogated and they were satisfied he was not a spy. "The Germans used this as an effective psychological whip during interrogation", says Lyle. In the world he'd left behind, he was one of the elite, a bomber pilot on one of the world's most powerful bombers. Now, down on the ground in the red brick suburbs on Nuremberg, he was a "Luftgangster", responsible for raining death and destruction on German civilians. At the police barracks, Lyle was pleasantly shocked to find his tail gunner, Ben Howell, alive. He'd landed safely with no injuries. Once on the ground, German civilians and Home Guard members had beaten him savagely, using fists and a rifle butt.

Of the nine men aboard 'Gung Ho', six had been killed either in the explosion or in 'Gung Ho's' mortal, terrifying plunge to earth. Besides Lyle, navigator Duward Bare had been blown out of the ship by the explosion, and Ben Howell, falling in the severed tail section, had also managed to get out. The plane flying directly behind 'Gung Ho' had also exploded, killing all but two men. Back at Framlingham, the Nissan hut shared by the eight officers of the two crews was now empty. Stan Wilson, Lyle's former pilot, went and collected all Lyle's personal possessions before they could be 'appropriated' by the inevitable scavengers. Within hours of the news back at base, all the men's personal effects would be boxed up and readied to send home. All traces that eight young men had only a day before lived here would be meticulously erased for morale reasons, and soon a new batch of airmen would move in and carry on.

At Nuremberg's Hall of Justice, Lyle was put into solitary confinement. The filthy cell had a wooden table with some straw on it, a tiny window and a heavy door. He was injured and in pain, but received no treatment for his wounds, even after attempting to bribe a curious Luftwaffe pilot by giving him his pilot's wings. The only dressing he had on his arm wound was a dry compress. After three days, Lyle, his tailgunner, and the two surviving crewmen from the plane behind them were loaded onto a train and taken to an interrogation center at Oberursel, for a week to two weeks of interrogation. During this time, Lyle was subjected to the standard psychological questioning of the Nazi interrogators. "They used a very smart psychological approach on some pretty young, scared kids," says Lyle. "But the longer I was a prisoner, the better my defenses became. It doesn't take very long for you to size up the situation and develop your own strategy." Also during this time, a German sergeant froze a spot on his arm about as big as a quarter, and using a knife and a pair of tweezers, took out the piece of flak. He wrapped the arm in dry crepe paper—the only dressing Lyle would get until he arrived at the prisoner of war camp.

From there, the men were sent to Wetzlar, a transit camp, where they were deloused. The tailgunner, a noncom, was then shipped off to another POW camp. Lyle was loaded on a train for the trip to Stalag Luft I in Barth, Germany, just north of Berlin on the Baltic Sea. The train trip took four days and four nights, and there were ten injured men packed into a standard passenger compartment meant for six. Now when the British and American bombers flew over, the POWs had become a target and there was danger of being killed by their own bombs.

The Stalag Luft I camp at Barth was a camp for Allied flight officers. Most of the prisoners were first and second lieutenants. It had been built in sections and had four distinct compounds. The first, built in 1943, housed the Royal Air Force crewmen, some of whom had been captured at Dunkirk in 1940. Later in 1943 North One was added. This compound housed American airmen. In 1944 North Two opened, and housed Americans shot down during 1944. A final compound, North Three was completed in late summer of 1944 and opened in January of 1945. Lyle ended up in North Two.

Life in the camp was strictly regimented, not only by the Germans but also by the ranking American officers. Each compound had a commanding officer, chosen for his rank. Several of the war's top fighter aces had positions of command at Barth. The kriegsgefangen (as the Germans called them), or kriegies, as they called themselves were housed in long barracks. Each barracks had a central hallway, with small rooms on either side. Each also had a crude one-hole latrine at one end, meant only for emergency use, and at the other end, a room that was smaller than the others was reserved for the barracks commander and his adjutant. The rest of the rooms, each containing bunk beds enough for fourteen to sixteen men, had a small stove, a rough table and two benches similar to a picnic table, and a window.

Lyle ended up in Room 9, Barracks 9, Compound Two at Stalag Luft I.

Lyle was a newcomer in his room, which was mostly full by the time he arrived. The only bunk left was the top bunk next to the stove. One of his roommates, Ed Slocum, seeing that Lyle couldn't get in and out of the top bunk with his injuries, agreed to trade and gave Lyle the bottom bunk.

Lyle soon adapted to the monotonous life in Stalag Luft I. At the camp's first aid barrack, doctors soaked his infected arm in a dishpan of disinfectant for several days, and it helped. They then put bandages on each open wound and a cast on the arm, because it appeared to be healing crooked. They ignored Lyle's leg injury, which eventually healed itself.

A big part of kriegie life revolved around food, or the lack of it. The Germans by this time were experiencing food shortages of their own, and this made food scarce. The Germans allocated potatoes, rutabagas and cabbage. All cooking had to be done by the kriegies themselves. Additional food came in the form of Red Cross parcels. When parcels arrived, the German guards cut each metal container of food down the middle with an ax to make certain the contents were as labeled and to prevent hoarding for escape. Each man was supposed to receive one parcel per week. This late in the war, that never happened. "I think the Red Cross parcels found their way into German homes all through the war," says Lyle. "I'm surprised we ever got any at all. If you're willing to kill an American, why not eat his Red Cross parcel? It's certainly easy to rationalize." To ensure fairness and to divide up the duties in each room, men formed 'combines'. The combines divided the food allocations evenly among all members, as well as divided up the domestic duties. In some rooms, arguments resulted in men breaking away and forming their own little combines. The men in Lyle's room trusted each other, and their combine remained unified. "It was a more economical and expedient way of dividing and sharing stuff," Lyle explains now. "Especially in 1945 when food was very short." Early on, Lyle and Ed Slocum became the combine's two cooks. "I could never understand why Ed and I ended up cooking," muses Lyle. "Maybe because our bunk was closest to the stove or because we were the two smallest persons in the room."

The men ate two meals a day, morning and evening. Meals were the high point of the day. "One of the things that was always interesting to me was going through the formal process of having a meal: sitting down at a table and going through the process even if you don't have anything to eat is important," says Lyle. "It makes it seem like you're having something to eat. We had a table and a couple of benches. We all sat down at the table at the same time. We each had our own tin cup and little pan or bowl, and we ate together—even though there wasn't very much."

The rest of the time was spent filling in time between meals. Some men walked the perimeter of the camp. Lyle's injuries prevented him from doing a lot of walking, and he spent a great deal of his time reading or studying. "The Salvation Army had set up a book library for our camp early on," explains Lyle, "I set up a study course, read stuff from *Beowulf* through Robert Louis Stevenson, plus lots of autobiographies and biographies, Dickens and others. I read all of Charles Dickens' works. Others set up their own reading programs. Some learned to play bridge." There was also a ground school set up to keep the men's minds busy. Some of the courses were celestial navigation, math and law. Lyle developed a further interest in law from one of these courses. There were also singing clubs. In his time there, Lyle didn't see any baseball games, though Colonel Zemke, a fighter ace and Camp Commander, appeared in a boxing match one time.

Mail was scarce. Lyle got one or two letters the whole time he was incarcerated. The men got mail from family members, and there was the occasional 'Dear John' letter. One POW received a hand knit sweater. The woman who made it had sewn her name and address in a seam. The kriegie wrote her a thank you letter. In return she wrote him a letter saying she had knitted the sweater for a real soldier, not for a prisoner of war.

One important Red Cross item was powdered milk called 'Klim' (milk spelled backwards) made by the Borden Company. The milk was used in cooking, but it was the Klim can that was the real prize. Kriegies devised ways of turning Klim cans, which were roughly the size and shape of a modern one-pound coffee can, into just about every useful item they could think of. Lyle made cooking pans with them. Because the Germans gave each room only a small amount of pressed coal, the men constructed a forge out of Klim cans to save coal. The various parts of the forge were attached to a base, usually a board taken from the bottom of a bunk. They fashioned a flat sheet of metal from the cans. The sheet of metal was then made into a vertical cylinder about ten inches across. The inside was lined with clay about one inch thick to form a firebox. Air was forced into the bottom of the firebox using a fan with a pulley attached and enclosed in a smaller, horizontal cylinder made from a Klim can and driven by a larger wheel that had a small handle as a crank. The two were connected by a belt made from shoelaces. One lace was threaded into the other providing for a round belt. They cooked their meals on top of the forge, usually in a standard two-and-a-half gallon bucket.

Little was wasted. Potatoes were washed but not peeled and no eyes were cut out—only rotten spots. The potatoes were cut into chunks and boiled in the bucket atop the forge. As the potatoes boiled, a dirty foam rose above the top of the boiling water. It was skimmed off with the swish of a stick. Eventually, after doing this several times, the foam was clean. When the potatoes were removed for the dinner meal, the water was saved in a pan for breakfast (actually more like brunch, as it was later).

Each man now donated a thin slice of his bread ration. One of the roommates, Glen Schlueter, was the designated bread slicer because of his accuracy. The cook then took these thin slices of bread, mixed in a can of Spam, and added the gelatinous glop from the potato bucket. In this way, even the starch from the boiling potatoes could be eaten and provided the all-important calories to the kriegies' meager diets, which averaged only 650 calories per day.

At Christmas, several special Red Cross packages were delivered to each room. The combine held a lottery to see who would win each present because there were more men than presents. One of the presents was a pipe. Another was a bag of tobacco. Lyle won the pipe. "I was an athlete," says Lyle. "I didn't smoke or drink. Actually, I'd had a pipe for a short time in England but I'd never smoked cigarettes. But I won it so I used it." The fact that he hadn't won the tobacco didn't deter him. He went around picking up cigarette butts discarded by other kriegies until cigarettes became scarce, and extracted the tobacco from them. He used his own cigarettes, when he got some in a parcel, as cash.

One of the roommates, Rolland Olson, enjoyed going to the gate and greeting the new arrivals. One such time he picked up lice and brought the lice back to the room. The whole room became infested. As a result, the roommates all had to shave all their body hair except the hair on their heads, and bathe in kerosene. The Germans baked all their clothes in an oven to kill the bugs. "It was painful," says Lyle, of bathing with kerosene. "Especially after using those dull razor blades to shave off all our hair! We walked around sticky and itching for weeks while the hair grew back in." Lyle and each of his roommates had been given one razor blade, which was expected to last 'for the duration'. It was against camp rules to have a beard, so each man kept his blade as sharp as possible by whetting it on shoe leather.

The whole time he was in the camp, Lyle brushed his teeth with Swan soap. "Swan soap was good for everything," he says. Due to his injuries, he never took a shower at the camp, just sponge baths. To wash clothes, "the guys would borrow the bucket we used for the potatoes. We had a broomstick with a Klim can nailed on the end that was used as a plunger. It created a suction and caused the suds like a washing machine action. We didn't have very many clothes; we didn't have a change of clothes. We had to take them off to wash them."

The roommates decided to start a pool to see who could come closest to predicting when the war would end. They wrote their guesses on wrapping paper from a pack of Camel cigarettes. It cost five dollars to get into the pool. The winner would get the pot.

As the end drew near, the Germans began to worry about what would happen to them when the Russians arrived in Barth.

"We could hear the Soviets coming. We also had a radio in the camp constructed from parts obtained by using cigarettes to trade with the guards; it was a secret radio. We got news on the BBC concerning where the various fronts were located. So we knew what was happening. In our case, at Stalag Luft I, we had about 9,000 people there at the time. The internal staff of British and American prisoners had negotiated with the Germans. They said we will permit you to leave before the Russians get here. In return, you will turn over the camp, the town of Barth, the Barth airfield and the flak school to us. On April 30, 1945, at midnight, all the German guards left." Over the previous two weeks, the Germans had systematically blown up all the airplanes at the nearby airfield and also blown up anything of value at the nearby flak school.

The next day, the camp was 'liberated' by a Russian soldier and a girl, both riding horses. More Russians came later, but it was disorganized, chaotic. Many of the Russian troops were drunk. They refused to believe that the Germans had left. If they had, asked one Soviet leader, "why are you people still behind barbed wire"? They even accused poor Zemke of being a German guard and threatened to kill him. Zemke had what must have been a terrifying moment, when, in trying to convince the Russians that he was an American commander, he told them that he would go out to the men and when they cheered, it would prove he was American. When he went out to the men, they were upset and didn't cheer but stood there mute. In frustration, Zemke ordered the barbed wire fences torn down—but ordered all the men to stay in the camp or face charges of desertion later. Most stayed, but two or three thousand left.

After about two weeks, the men were evacuated from Barth via B-17 bombers. A couple of C-46 hospital planes took out the sick and wounded. "One of the nurses on a C-46 hospital plane met her brother when they landed. He was waiting to be airlifted on a B-17 with the other POWs," remembers Lyle. A video that one of Lyle's Stalag Luft I comrades recently unearthed at the National Archives shows masses of gaunt, smiling men lining up along the airstrip, waiting for their turn to board one of the planes. In the background, charred remains of German bombers mar the landscape. Though the prisoners weren't supposed to take anything out of the camp with them, Lyle smuggled out a pair of German flying boots he'd found, notes recording his life in the camp, some cheese, and some pilot's wings he'd made from drops of solder from corned beef cans sometimes included in the Red Cross food parcels.

The POWs were flown to Camp Lucky Strike in France. Most people know that GI is short for Government Issue, and that the men were considered just so much government property by the number crunchers. Still, Lyle is upset that all the POWs, many of whom had previously been listed as Missing in Action or Killed in Action, were classified by the military as 'salvage' when they were processed at the camp. Camp Lucky Strike held as many as 15,000 former POWs in tents as they waited for transport back to the States. "POWs arrived at Camp Lucky Strike in many ways," says Lyle. "In my case, I went first to Rheims, France by B-17. From Rheims to Lucky Strike by train. There were two similar camps elsewhere, Camp Old Gold and Camp Chesterfield". General Eisenhower visited the camp, and Lyle was one of a small group of men who talked to Eisenhower and told him they were willing to double up on the ships returning to the States rather than wait. Eisenhower took their suggestion and passenger lists were doubled.

Lyle Shafer was on his way home.

In June of 1945, Lyle Shafer set out to visit all the families of his dead crewmates to pay his respects. "I did it because they were my friends," he explains. "A lot of crewmen did that if they could". The first families he visited were those he'd met in the New York area before the crew went overseas. Three of the men had lived in the New York area, in Flushing and Brooklyn.

Pilot Fred McIntosh's wife came and stayed with the Shafers in Ohio for a short time. "I told her that my dad had been killed in a highway accident when I was about two, and that if I could ever talk to her son about his father or be of any help to her, I would do that," he explains.

In the summer of 1947, Lyle and a friend took a two-month hitchhiking tour in the western part of the United States to visit the families of the other three men on the crew. This trip took him to Iowa, Oregon and California. "The families were all very appreciative of the fact that I came to see them," says Lyle, "I was the last guy to see their sons alive and had spent the last couple of months with them. I told them I was doing it because I wanted to, but I felt their sons would have done the same thing for me."

Lyle also visited the bombardier, who had survived the explosion and crash, and Stan Wilson, the pilot who had refused to fly after his third mission. Lyle visited Stan several times. He went to Rockford to speak to a flight surgeon about Stan, in hopes of getting Stan's discharge and its stigma erased. This proved unsuccessful. Stan Wilson, the man who had walked away from the Air Corps, died of Hodgkin's Disease a few years later.

Lyle returned to college, eventually becoming a successful corporate lawyer and personnel officer for the NCR Company in Ohio. But he kept thinking about his roommates back in Stalag Luft I. At the end of the war, he'd had each man write down his name and address, telling them that "someday, we'll get this group together again". The kriegies had posed for a final photograph on May 2nd or 3rd, a day or two after their liberation. The photo, taken with a 'liberated' camera, is of poor quality, grainy and overexposed, but it is impossible not to see the relief and happiness on the nineteen haggard faces. Oran Fulton, one of the combine roommates, had his friend take the photo. The friend gave the photo to Fulton, the negative was destroyed, and Fulton eventually sent the photo to Lyle, who made copies and distributed them to the roommates.

"I kept track of a few of the guys after the war," says Lyle. "One, Oran Fulton, was a cop in L.A. I visited him several times while traveling for the company. Don Demmert was from New Jersey. He visited me while I was at Harvard. But over time, I lost contact with most of them." During the eighties, he decided to track down the roommates again. All he had to go on was the piece of paper with the names and addresses the POW's had scribbled down at the end of the war, showing their 1945 addresses, most with just a city and no street address. "The first four or five were pretty easy to find," says Lyle. "They'd never moved or anything." The rest were not that easy. In fact, the stories of Lyle Shafer's sleuthing make one wonder why he never considered becoming a private investigator.

Willis T. Jones had listed his address as Goose Creek, Texas. Lyle first tried to reach Willis on the phone, and receiving no response, followed his normal procedure. He wrote a letter. The letter came back "Return to Sender—No Such Town in Texas". Lyle next wrote the Postmaster General of the State of Texas. Weeks and then months passed. Finally, he got a letter from the Postmaster General saying, well, yes, the town of Goose Creek used to exist, but now it was called Baytown, Texas. "In fact," wrote the Postmaster, "I contacted your friend. He is a doctor and is Head of Staff at Baytown Memorial Hospital and waiting to hear from you".

Leonard Clarke had listed his address as Eureka, California. "He was a non-communicative kind of guy," smiles Lyle. "He never writes anybody, and as far as the war was concerned, he wanted to get lost. But I found it difficult to believe that he'd moved from Eureka." Lyle wrote and got no response. One time, when Lyle was at a Rotary Club Meeting, a visitor from Eureka, California was introduced. After the meeting, Lyle approached him and asked if he knew Leonard Clark. "No, but I just bought his brother's house," the speaker admitted. "Leonard Clarke still lives there." Lyle wrote a message for Leonard and the speaker took it back to Eureka with him.

Still, no word from Leonard.

Lyle chuckles. "When I first came to the compound (at Stalag Luft I), Leonard was lifting dumb-bells he'd made from bricks. I asked him what he was doing. 'I'm working out so I can escape,' Leonard soberly explained. He handed the weights to Lyle and asked him to try and lift them. Being new, I lifted them like they were feathers even though I was crippled," laughs Lyle. "It devastated the guy. He didn't give up, however, but he never had an opportunity to escape".

Lyle was not ready to give up on Leonard Clarke just yet.

Later, passing through Eureka, he found a phone and gave Leonard a call. "I got him out of the shower," Lyle explains. "When he came on, I said 'why the hell didn't you ever answer my letters?' I invited him to come meet me for a cup of coffee at a restaurant. He couldn't visualize what I'd look like forty years later. When he got to the restaurant, he was asking a bunch of really old men, men in their nineties, if any of them was Lyle Shafer. I introduced myself to him. 'Hell, you're a kid!' he said. We've been traveling together ever since".

Howard O. Brown was from Omaha, Nebraska, the last man to enter the camp after being shot down in March of 1945. Lyle wrote him a letter. It came back 'No house at this location'. He had a friend check out the graduating high school classes that reflected Brown's graduating date. The class representative told Lyle that Howard Brown lived in Iowa. He found Howard had moved to Iowa. Lyle called up the Howard Brown in Iowa. A lady answered the phone. Yes, her husband had been a POW, but he had died. Lyle asked a few brief questions about Howard. "This guy was six-three and in the infantry and Howard was five-six and in the Air Corps", remembers Lyle. He had tracked down the wrong man.

Two or three years later, he started over and tried again. He was living in Scottsdale, Arizona at the time he wrote another letter to Howard Brown, this time addressed to "Occupant" at the same address he'd used before instead of to Howard specifically. He got a letter from the man who lived next door, saying that the house had been razed, but that he'd answered the letter because he owned the property now. This man was able to tell Lyle that Howard was, indeed, alive and well. What's more, he now lived in Sun City, Arizona, only forty-five minutes away from where Lyle was living.

Jack S. Williams lived in Chicago. "There are probably five thousand Williamses in the Chicago phone book," admits Lyle. "And there were plenty of Jack S. Williamses, too. I started to run down the list randomly, calling seven or eight names every time I visited Chicago. But I didn't even know his full name for sure. Was it Jack or John or something else? Finally, I put an ad in *The Chicago Tribune*, saying I was looking for a Jack S. Williams who was a POW in World War II and giving specifics. A man answered the ad and said 'Jack Williams doesn't want to be found. He's running from the law. I'm his lawyer.' The lawyer offered to take Lyle to meet Jack for one hundred dollars. Lyle smelled a fish and said no.

Two years later, working on the knowledge that Jack had been in the 100th Bomb Group; Lyle called the 100th Bomb Group receptionist and asked about a Jack S. Williams. "Why, I just had a call from someone referring him as a prospective member in Maryland!" the representative told him. Lyle called the Postmaster in Maryland and tried to get the address for a Jack S. Williams. The Postmaster told him it was illegal for him to give out that information, but agreed to have a letter delivered to the address for Lyle. The postmaster asked the carrier to talk to Lyle. "Yeah, I see him outside all the time, mowing his grass," said the carrier. "But it can't possibly be him. He's too young!" However, the carrier delivered the letter to the young-looking lawn-mower, who called Lyle on the phone. Jack S. Williams was amused to find he had been on the run from the law. Lyle suggested Jack give the carrier a bonus because "he thinks you're a young man".

Eventually, Lyle was able to track down every one of his living Stalag Luft I roommates. There were twenty-two living members. He also found the families of the deceased three: Kenneth Frazee, Ed Slocum and Jack Wierman.

Lyle laughs as he finishes the story of tracking all the men down after so many years. "After I found all these guys, they all said basically the same thing. They said, 'Lyle, I don't know why you had such a hard time finding me—I've been right here all along!' Easy for them to say!"

"After I found all these guys, they started saying, 'Lyle, why don't you host a reunion?' Okay, I said, I'll do it, as long as it's in Dayton, Ohio". Lyle and his family had moved from Dayton, but he had spent his working career there. He set it up for the last four or five days of July, 1989. Seventeen of the survivors and their wives attended. They saw the Air Show, toured the Air Force Museum, and went to the Aviation Hall of Fame Enshrinement Dinner. Lyle had been on the National Aviation Hall of Fame Board of Trustees, and he arranged for the POW group to attend the prestigious black-tie event. During the gala ceremony, emceed by former astronaut and Senator John Glenn, Glenn introduced the group of older gentlemen seated together and asked them to stand to be recognized. The PBS affiliate in Dayton created a quality half-hour documentary about the group called "The Lucky Ones: A POW Reunion". One of the highlights of the tape is former POW Don Demmert singing "Ave Maria" in a rich, deep operatic voice, as he demonstrated how he sang for his fellow prisoners back at Stalag Luft I. There is hardly a dry eye in the studio when he finishes. Lyle hired his company photographer to shoot a group photo of the reunion mates.

Also at this reunion, Lyle finally collected on the roommates' pool for being the roommate closest to predicting the date of the war's end. He made $75 off his fellow kreigies.

The reunion was a smashing success, and Lyle was exhausted but exhilarated.

There would be additional reunions in the years to come. In 1993, Don Demmert hosted one in his home city of Williamsburg, Virginia. In 1995, Lauren Schwisow hosted in Olympia, Washington. In 1998, it was Rolland Olson's show in Chicago. Lyle agreed to host it again in 2000, on a guest ranch near his place in Wilson, Wyoming, only a short drive from the resort town of Jackson in the Grand Teton Mountains. It would be the 55th anniversary reunion of their liberation.

Age had begun to take its toll on the group. Each reunion brought fewer and fewer men, and successive photographs show men with whiter (or less) hair, more wrinkles, standing a little less erect. Lyle realized that, sad as it was to admit, time was running out for the bunkmates of Room 9 Barracks 9. Eventually, only a few would be able to make the trip to the roommate reunions. And then, one year, there would be no one left at all.

"The reunion in 2000 was kind of like the Last Hurrah," Lyle explained to me. "It was probably the last time many of us would be able to get together. I'm one of the youngsters in the group, and I'm seventy-seven." So he set about to make this the biggest and funnest reunion yet. Instead of just inviting the bunkmates, he also invited spouses, children and even grandchildren. "It took about two years to set this up," he says, "It took over a year just to make the reservations." The dates for the reunion were set for June

8-11, 2000. Lyle haggled with the owners of the Gros Ventre River Guest Ranch to get the cost down to where everybody could afford to attend. The owners balked at renting him the entire camp, saying they had a waiting list years long. In the end, Lyle and the Ranch agreed to hold the reunion during the four day period preceding the normal opening in order to avoid interfering with long standing reservations; a preseason discount; a discount for reserving the entire capacity of the Ranch; and a rate reduction for eliminating the daily use of horses, leaving individual guests the opportunity to reserve a horse when and if wanted.

He rented a private bus to take the attendees on an overnight trip to Yellowstone. He booked cabins at Mammoth in Yellowstone Park. It was a monumental undertaking. Lyle agonized that the weather would turn bad and ruin the reunion. He mailed out detailed itineraries to all the participants. And he arranged to hold a memorial service.

On the day of the reunion, the men of Barracks Nine and their wives, children and eleven grandchildren began to arrive, by plane, by car or by camper. Fifty-one people showed up altogether. Of the sixteen surviving kriegies, eleven attended the reunion. They ranged in age from 76 to 84. Four of the others were too ill to attend and one had a prior family commitment.

At each reunion, the kriegies hold a remembrance and memorial service for their deceased roommates and the deceased wives of roommates. This year the service was held at the Chapel of the Transfiguration, a seventy-five-year-old log structure at the foot of the majestic Teton Mountains in Teton National Park. And this year, it included their 44 crew members who did not survive when their planes were shot down. They also met to look at old photographs of their lives as flyers with the Air Corps, photos of smiling young men crouched in front of their B-17 and B-24 heavy bombers or, individually, in front of their fighter planes. There were also photos of life in Stalag Luft I, carefully arranged and labeled on rows of poster boards. There was an old Air Corps aviator's uniform, complete with crusher cap and medals, as well as other memorabilia from the war in the sky such as leather flight helmets,

a parachute harness, insulated flight clothes for the extreme cold
of high altitudes, pilot's wings, Distinguished Flying Crosses, flight
computers that look like old slide rules, and other flight equipment.
There was also a table covered with artifacts from the POW camp,
an empty Spam can, a can of Klim, desired as much for the can
and its many potential uses as for its contents. Lyle had wanted to
make a replica of the Klim can pan he'd made in the camp. He'd
called The Borden Company, the maker of Klim, and found that,
indeed, Borden still contracts to make the stuff for third world
countries. He finally tracked down some cans in Scotland, called
them and explained why he wanted some, and the company sent
him a shipment of Klim cans, which he still has sitting around
waiting to be made into kriegie replicas.

The group posed for a professional group photo near the end
of the reunion. In it, one can see the generations smiling back. It is
then that one realizes that it is only through extreme good fortune,
or the hand of God, that allowed any of these people to be standing
here at all. The eleven elderly men—husbands, fathers and
grandfathers—all managed to cheat death when their planes fell
from the sky. In fact, those very same planes had become the coffins
for forty-four of their crewmates and friends. They had managed
to survive in a prison camp on starvation rations, faced with lack of
sanitation and decent medical care, infested with lice and other
undesirable camp-dwelling hangers-on. They'd even survived the
drunken liberation by suspicious Russian soldiers. This was a
miracle gathering, each man alive and smiling and surrounded by
children and grandchildren. It makes one wonder about the men
who weren't so fortunate, who couldn't get out and instead spiraled
down in the wreckage of their planes, or whose parachutes snagged
on control surfaces, or who were killed after landing by angry
German civilians. The eleven men and their families truly are, in
the words of the PBS program about them, the lucky ones.

"There were twenty-five of us at the end of the war," says Lyle.
"In '89, seventeen showed up. In 2000, eleven showed up. Now,
ten have died, and four are victims of poor health. Still, we plan on

meeting again in a few years. This time we'll be meeting in Tucson in 2002. John Haney hopes to host it."

Lyle Shafer is now 79 years old. He was only eighteen years old when he went off to become a pilot for the U.S. Army Air Corps. He had his wings at nineteen. He was twenty when he was shot down. He had his twenty-first birthday as a POW. When asked why many Air Corps veterans still attend reunions fifty-seven years after the end of World War II, Lyle says it's the bonding, the sharing of an adverse situation. He says his experiences as a B-17 pilot and as a kriegie have made him a better person. He doesn't suffer from bad dreams, although he does dream occasionally that he is flying a B-17—all alone—and doesn't have the slightest idea how to land it. He's old enough to see "the same damn mistakes" being made over and over by people who refuse to learn from the past. He is content with his three kids, ages 40, 43, and 44. All of his kids are, like him, independent thinkers, proving, he says jokingly, that you have to be careful what you wish for. He has six grandkids: three boys and three girls. He is especially close to his youngest grandson, who recently turned three years of age and lives in Jackson with his mom. There is a special basket of toys in the Shafer living room ready for such visits-cars and more than a few planes as well.

Even now, Lyle Shafer is looking to the future, thinking about his kids and grandkids and how to make sure the grandchildren have the option of going to college someday. "You never get away from being a parent until you die," Lyle reflects.

And of course, Lyle is already looking forward to the next reunion.

Postscript: Since Lyle Shafer and I sat down and talked about the Reunion, time has taken another of the Stalag Luft I roommates. Elmer T. Lian, former pilot, and a roomate who attended the 2000 Reunion with his son Steven and his grandson Craig, was buried in Grand Forks, North Dakota on June 7, 2001. His funeral notice lists "The POW Roommates of Stalag Luft I" as honorary casketbearers. The Stalag Luft I roommates sent a floral bouquet for the funeral—flowers and ribbons of red, white and blue. Under a photo of a young Elmer Lian in his Army Air Corps uniform there is a short poem entitled "Goodbye My Friends".

Goodbye My Friends

As the curtain slowly lowers on the stage of
each life, soon all the "boys from Camp"
will have been stilled, all the
records have been blown away by the winds.

As one generation after another passes by
in years to come, many will be richer,
stronger, taller, wiser.

But remember also many men whose names
are now unknown, who have passed
this corner of life; their lasting
footsteps can be heard if you listen carefully . . .

By Elmer Lian

Notes

[1] All quotes come from extensive interviews with Lyle Shafer in 2001 and 2002, including a day in Wilson, Wyoming.

Photos

Fred Schoch as a B-17 Co-pilot, 34th Bomb Group, November 1944. Photo Courtesy Diane Schoch Russell.

Bob Hilliard, second from left, and E. Edward Herman, second from right, at the "Miracle at St. Ottilien" film premiere, October 2003. Author Photo.

A portion of the original program for "The Liberation Concert" at St. Ottilien, Germany, which Bob Hilliard attended on May 27, 1945. Courtesy of E. Edward Herman.

Dan Culler in gunnery school, Wendover, Utah, 1942. Courtesy of Dan Culler.

Commandant Beguin with prisoners at Wauwilermoos. Courtesy of
Dan Culler.

Memphis Belle Crew: Bassingbourn, England, May 17 1943
First to complete 25 Combat Missions

(L to R) Harold Loch, Top Turret Gunner; Cecil Scott, Ball Turret Gunner; Robert Hanson, Radio Operator; Jim Verinis, Copilot; Robert Morgan, Pilot;
Chuck Leighton, Navigator; John Quinlan, Tail Gunner; Tony Nastal, R Waist Gunner; Vince Evans, Bombardier; Bill winchell, L Waist Gunner.

Robert Morgan and the crew of "The Memphis Belle". Courtesy
Robert Morgan.

Irl Baldwin and the crew of Hell's Angels. Kiel Mission, May 15, 1943.

"Hell's Angels", first to complete 25 missions. This photo taken on October 10, 1943, after her 45th of 48 missions. Courtesy of Dr. Harry Gobrecht

Leonard Herman was a Jewish bombardier who served two tours over Europe during World War II, one with the 8th and one with the 9th. He is shown here as a cadet Stateside. Courtesy of Leonard Herman

The crew of "Ten Nights in a Bar Room./The Brass Rail", of the 95th Bomb Group. Photo taken just prior to fateful mission to Kiel, Germany. Bombardier Leonard Herman is kneeling, center, with chin on hand. Herman's beloved pilot, Johnny Johnson, is to Herman's left. The ace gunner of the 8th Air Force, tail gunner Bill Crossley, is standing at left rear. Johnson would be killed a few missions later. Courtesy of Leonard Herman

Ed Herzig, November, 1942, during flight training at Randolph Field, San Antonio, Texas. Herzig experienced the hardships of being a Jewish POW in Germany after his plane was shot down. Courtesy of Ed Herzig

Lee Kessler poses with the framed original of his Holocaust art, "The Hand", in Canton, Ohio, Summer 2003. Author Photo

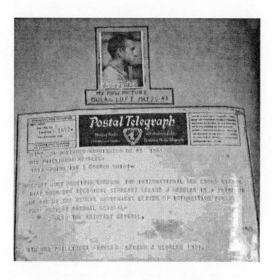

Lee Kessler's POW photo and the telegram received by his mother after he was shot down in May, 1943. Author Photo

John Carson, as a young Air Corps flight engineer and as a Lieutenant Colonel in Vietnam. Carson became a POW and was reunited at the end of the war with his twin, Gene. Courtesy of John Carson.

John and Wanda Carson in Spokane, Washington, 2001, with two of their ten motorcycles. They can be found traveling the highways of the United States with their pet sugar glider, Pockets. Author Photo

Gus Mencow, 390th Navigator, in the museum he created and oversees in Worcester, Massachusetts, 2002. Author Photo

Ball Turret Gunner Bob Capen receives his Distinguished Flying Cross, September 5, 1944, 95th Bomb Group. Courtesy of Bob Capen.

Frank Coleman, Ball Turret Gunner, with his Distinguished Flying Cross, 1944. Courtesy Frank Coleman.

Frank Coleman tries to squeeze into a ball turret forty years after World War II. "It was a tighter fit", he remembers. Courtesy Frank Coleman

A Sperry Ball Turret. Courtesy Frank Coleman

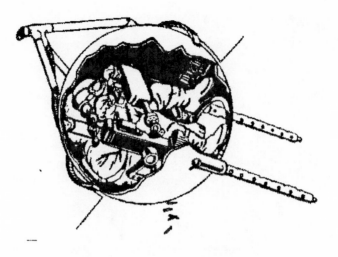

Schematic of a ball turret with ball turret gunner position. US Army Drawing

WERNER G. GOERING CREW - 358th BS
B-17G #43-37838 *Fearless Fosdick* (358BS) VK-A
(crew assigned 358BS: 07 Aug 1944)

(Back L-R) 1Lt William D. Sachau (B), 1Lt Jack P. Rencher (CP)(1),
2Lt Rex H. Markt (N), Capt Werner G. Goering (P)(2)

The Werner Goering/Jack Rencher Crew, 303rd Bomb Group, 358th Bomb Squadron. Goering was the nephew of German Reichsmarshall Herman Goering. 303rd BG Website

Sam Mastrogiacomo with his Distinguished Flying Cross, awarded over fifty years after the war and after his return from internment in Sweden. Courtesy of Sam Mastrogiacomo

Herb Alf, former B-17 pilot and POW, with the author and the author's wife in Oregon, Summer 2002. Alf wrote what he hoped to be a classic anti-war novel about the air war and was working on the screenplay at the time of his death. Author Photo

The stages of *Petals of Fire*, Herb Alf's lifelong work. He wrote the beginnings on whatever paper he could get as a German POW, including both sides of sheets of toilet paper. At right is his finished work. Author Photo

1. ROBERT DREW (D)
2. GLENNON SCHLUETER (D)
3. LAUREN SCHWISOW
4. DONALD DEMMERT
5. ORAH FULTON (D)
6. J. WILLIAM HANEY
7. JOHN WIERMAN (D)
8. ED SLOCUM (D)
9. ROBERT SILTAMAKI
10. LYLE SHAFER
11. HOWARD BROWN (D)
12. HAROLD SPECK (D)
13. ROBERT PEARCE (D)
14. JACK MURPHY
15. HOWARD RAY
16. JACK WALLACE
17. ROBERT McFALL (D)
18. AOLLAND OLSON
19. JOE BINGHAM (D)

ADDED BY COMPUTER FROM 1944 PHOTOGRAPHS.
20 KENNETH FRAZEE (D)
21 LEONARD CLARKE
22. JACK WILLIAMS
23. ELMER LIAN (D)
24. DUSTY RHOADES
25. W. T. JONES, JR.
26. COLEMAN JACOBSON

Using a 'liberated' camera, the POWs took this photo of their barracks mates shortly after liberation at Stalag Luft One. Lyle Shafer tracked down most of his comrades over thirty years later for a prisoner of war reunion. Courtesy of Lyle Shafer

Lyle Shafer as a young pilot, 390th Bomb Group. Courtesy of Lyle Shafer

POW photo of Lyle Shafer, badly wounded, after his bailout from his disintegrating plane and capture by the Germans. Courtesy of Lyle Shafer

Index

Lechfield, Germany, 218
Legge, Brig. Gen. Barnwell, 55, 74, 202, 206
Lehman, Herbert, 34
Lian, Elmer, 269-270
Linz, Austria, 104
'Little Chub', 214
Loka Brunn, 224
London, 159
Long, Robert, 55, 204, 208, 215, 220
Love, Nancy Harkness, 191
Lucerne, Switzerland, 57,68
'Luftgangster', 253
Luftwaffe, 108, 112, 152, 250
Lynch, Father TJB, 116

-M-

Madsen, 1st Lt. Parley, 90
Mahaddie, Group Capt. Hamish, 14
'Man's Search for Meaning' by Frankl, 231
MAPS Air Museum, 135
Marchuck, Yetta, 46
Mastrogiacomo, Sam, 224-230
Mauthausen, 122, 127
May, Donald, 155
McCarthy, Hugh, 154, 157, 162
McIntosh, Fred, 252
McKnight, Group Commander Dave, 102

Memphis, TN, 93
'Memphis Belle', 80-96
'Memphis Belle Association', 94
Mencow, Nathaniel 'Gus', 100, 103, 109, 152
Mencow, William, 163
Michalczyk, John, 44
'Mickey' Radar, 111
'Miracle at St. Ottilien' film, 44
Mitchell, Gen. Billy, 240
Molesworth, England, 84, 171, 178
Moosburg, Germany, 238
Morgan, Linda, 91
Morgan, Col. Robert, 24,81
Mormons, (Latter-day Saints), 167
Morris, Paul, 155
Mud Island, TN, 81
Munsingen, Swiss US Cemetery, 201
Munster, Germany, 21, 102, 103, 157-158
Muskau, Germany, 237

-N-

National Holocaust Museum, 123
Nebikon, Switzerland, 66-68
Nietzshe, Frederich, 244
Ninth Air Force, 29
Nuremberg, Germany, 237, 242, 253

BVG